THINGS WE FOUND IN THE GROUND

Eleanor Bruce & Lucilla Gray

Things We Found In The Grund

A Metal Detecting Journey through Britain

Harper North

HarperNorth
Windmill Green
24 Mount Street
Manchester M2 3NX

A division of
HarperCollins*Publishers*
1 London Bridge Street
London SE1 9GF

www.harpercollins.co.uk

HarperCollins*Publishers*
Macken House, 39/40 Mayor Street Upper
Dublin 1, D01 C9W8, Ireland

Published by HarperCollins*Publishers* Ltd 2026

1 3 5 7 9 10 8 6 4 2

Copyright © Eleanor Bruce and Lucilla Gray 2026

Photos and collages © RomanFound

Eleanor Bruce and Lucilla Gray assert the moral right to be identified
as the authors of this work

A catalogue record of this book is available from the British Library

HB ISBN 978-0-00-873760-3

Printed and bound in the UK using 100% renewable electricity
at CPI Group (UK) Ltd

All rights reserved. No part of this publication may be reproduced, stored in a retrieval system, or transmitted, in any form or by any means, electronic, mechanical, photocopying, recording or otherwise, without the prior written permission of the publishers.

Without limiting the exclusive rights of any author, contributor or the publisher of this publication, any unauthorised use of this publication to train generative artificial intelligence (AI) technologies is expressly prohibited. HarperCollins also exercise their rights under Article 4(3) of the Digital Single Market Directive 2019/790 and expressly reserve this publication from the text and data mining exception.

Ahakoa he iti, he pounamu
Although it is small, it is a treasure

To all the women who opened their farm gates, pantries and garden sheds, who, despite our muddy appearances, shared in the stories of those lost to the land, offering a warm brew and a homemade slice in return.

And lastly, to all the responsible metal detectorists, who have spent countless hours trudging up and down fields, adding to our history, filling our museums and fuelling our imaginations with treasures – made possible by their unwavering dedication to the hobby.

CONTENTS

Introduction	1
1. Empanda	18
2. Permission	32
3. Lead	49
4. Treasure	63
5. Lemon Drizzle Cake	75
6. Group Dig	91
7. Hammered	108
8. Death	126
9. Sheep	147
10. Winter	164
11. Women	180
12. Wartime	200
13. Ridge and Furrow	222
14. Rally Season	235

CONTENTS

15.	Beetroot and Feta Tart	256
	Epilogue	270
	Select Bibliography	277
	Acknowledgements	287

INTRODUCTION

2011, LINCOLNSHIRE, ENGLAND – ELLIE

Roman Britain first invaded my life on one of the many weekends spent with my grandparents, Mammette and Papa Allan, at their rural Lincolnshire farmhouse. Much like the actual Roman invasion of Britain in 43 CE, it wasn't a sudden obsession, it took a while to seep in – not quite the forty-five-odd years it took the Romans, but it spread its influence slowly, piece by piece.

A pair of slightly eccentric artists, neither of my grandparents are quite what you would expect when you think of a grandparent: they are more likely to be found collecting ridiculously heavy tables, laying concrete, and removing thick stone walls during the ongoing restoration of their second home – a medieval property in France – than sitting inside worrying about the vast progression of the internet from a threadbare armchair in front of the TV. They possess a stubborn productivity and activeness that's practically embedded in their gene code, and they always encourage us grandchildren to explore everything, whether erecting leaning wooden shelters in the village thickets or digging human-sized dirt traps in their garden (even after Papa Allan himself took a tumble down one in the dark). Needless to say, weekends spent with them are always an adventure.

The backdrop to these weekends – one of those typical, rural, Lincolnshire villages that's practically been frozen in time – is almost as eccentric as its occupants. Trailing ivy tumbles down the crumbling limestone walls of the quaint cottages lining the heavily potholed lanes, some of the residents seeming to have lived there – and not left the village – since the dawn of time itself; with the endless expanses of open fields surrounding this antiquated haven, watched over by the same family for over five centuries. Historically, Lincolnshire has always been a farming county; by the time of the Roman invasion, farming had already been around for at least 4,000 years, and much of the natural wild landscape tamed into cultivated fields and pastures. It's a vast, wide, flat patchwork of land that remains relatively unchanged today, and is utterly perfect for our weekend family tradition of an afternoon walk, topped off with a picnic diligently prepared by Mammette.

It's on one such picnic excursion that a new weekend tradition presents itself to me, sat as I am among the wispy long grasses and swaying wildflowers of a field margin, soaking in the country air and talking constantly (as I did at that age, and some say still do). Crustless ham sandwiches, wrapped tightly in clingfilm, yellow bananas, and a selection of chocolate biscuits are spread out on a thin blanket between Mammette and I; a rough brown landscape of tumbled plough before us – chunks of limestone, clay and leftover wheat stalks, churned into a busy mixture of texture and shapes. Mid-bite of a soft, buttery sandwich, I find myself frowning down at this soil beneath my feet – I've always had sharp eyes (Mammette often refers to me as her little magpie) – and just sat there, peeking out of the dirt, nestled between a white shard of limestone and a smooth pebble, is a small patch of grey – something that isn't quite in place.

'What's this?' I ask, grasping the curious object.

In response, Mammette clasps her hands together in excitement, immediately recognising the fragment clutched in my crumby hand – a shard, or sherd as they're technically known, of Roman grey ware; a type of pottery that, although not very high status at the time, was used by almost every household in Roman Britain and happens to make up 80 per cent of all the Roman pottery found on this isle.

'Oh, Ellie!' she delights, 'I think that's Roman!'

INTRODUCTION

Running my thumb over the prominent throw lines of this coarse and dusty body sherd in wonder, I can almost feel the ancient maker who crafted it. We rush back home, picnic forgotten, sherd clutched in one of my hands, the other grasped tightly by one very proud grandmother. The field becomes a haven to bond over, uncountable hours spent searching its ploughed soil – no matter the weather – building up an archive, piece by piece, which Papa Allan soon has to donate his garden shed for.

*

2004, TASMAN BAY, NEW ZEALAND – LUCIE

One morning I rise with the dream of finding an adze. There's something to be admired about an object made by the human hand, crafted from the Earth's raw materials – tamed and shaped. While discovering a golden nugget dislodged from the surrounding mountain ranges and deposited into the large tidal bay below my house would be exciting, here in *Aotearoa*, New Zealand it is these treasured artefacts we call *taonga*, skilfully carved from stone, wood and bone many centuries ago by Māori craftspeople, that hold the greatest stories. Perhaps the idea of finding a piece of history still lingers, but it is the only thing I can think about over breakfast.

Unable to dissolve the thought in my bowl of cereal, I make my way down the small, concealed track crudely dug into the cliffside inhabited by penguin burrows and cave wētā hiding at the bottom of the garden. Clinging to the path, much like the old beech trees that line it, the bay reappears through the undergrowth. To the east a prominent monolithic rock rises from the crashing waves – a guardian between the Tasman Sea and the vast shallow safety of the mudflats – and in the distance, a sandbar slowly shifts with the rushing water of a river mouth pouring in. To the west, a stretch of fine pale sand arrives at a sheltered beach where a corrugated iron bach, or beach house, built in the 1890s sits in solitude beside a small boat launch; an ideal place for building *waka*, timber canoes, and a natural playground to act out the fantasies of a child.

THINGS WE FOUND IN THE GROUND

My eyes are always observant, grazing the sandy canvas for *toki* – a stone adze used for cutting wood – imagining that one would actually appear, washed out from a crumbling bank with the eroding tide. Distracted from my daydreaming, a patch of beach stands out from my scan of the terrain, a small section, littered with driftwood, tangled strands of seaweed, and pipi and cockle shells, calling me over to dig.

Many of New Zealand's provincial towns in the South Island exist today as a result of digging; the gold rush of the 1860s commencing much exploration of the mountainous backcountry, prospectors following the old Māori trackways into the bush, carving out new pathways and building settlements in their search for gold. I spent my childhood summers with my sisters, perfecting this art of digging: building dams, diverting creeks, scooping sand, and, of course, looking for treasure. Digging generally involves a bit of luck and a good amount of intuition, but my connection to *whenua*, the land, runs deep. Reading it as my *tipuna*, ancestors, would have comes surprisingly naturally to me as *tangata whenua,* and through my Māori *whakapapa,* line of descent, the landscape imparts its sacred knowledge willingly.

Still digging, with a large pile of sand and a very deep hole to show for it, I commit to one last scrape, my fingers suddenly stopping mid-motion, interrupted by a cold mass among the damp leaf matter, the profile of an angular stone coming into focus through gritted sand, its edges purposeful and sharpened; the imaginings of an 11-year-old coming into realisation. The adze would be darkly polished, with tapered ends and streaked with ochre; made out of *pakohe*, a baked argillite that is best described as metasomatised mudstone – meaning the rock has been chemically altered by hydrothermal fluids. As New Zealand sits right on top of two active plates, the Indo-Australian and Pacific Plates, it certainly isn't short of these hydro and geothermals. *Pakohe* is found almost exclusively in the Dun Mountain Ophiolite Belt of Nelson's eastern ranges; possibly the most important convergence of these two plates and a location that has been the topic of interest for both Māori and European settlers for centuries.

INTRODUCTION

Brushing the sand from my knees, my daydream ungrasped, I make my way home, exhausted from digging, my mind still clutching onto the idea of *taonga*; refusing to give up, even though my body has, eyes scanning the sand restlessly. An iridescent glimmer flashes in the corner of my vision, a *pāua*, abalone shell, discarded among the rocks collected at the bottom of the cliffline by the last high tide. *Pāua* were harvested by Māori long before European settlers came to these islands – a valuable delicacy and material resource for the decoration of art and the creation of tools, the shimmering shells making attractive fishing lures – often traded between *iwi,* tribes. A *taonga* imparted from *Tangaroa*, the guardian of the ocean, and a *tohu*, sign, from my *tipuna*, a reminder to keep looking.

*

MARCH 2020, PLYMOUTH, ENGLAND – ELLIE

My aspirations of following in the footsteps of Andy Warhol, drinking wine at my art degree show and celebrating the successful application to the MA course of my dreams in London, were all shattered by a simple knock at the door, on the day after my twenty-first birthday – taking my planned course of life as an artist and throwing it into the back of my Fiat Panda.

Away from the expectations and pressures that governed my school days – never truly fitting in – I'd found a group of like-minded, wayward souls at art school in Plymouth, where it was celebrated to be a little odd and out there. The tight-knit family waiting at my uni house weren't afraid to embrace the parts of myself I hadn't dared to acknowledge, the parts I'd always kept hidden – especially when it came to my sexuality – reshaping my identity into what I had always wanted it to be, with no fear of the consequences, and no one, apart from my liver, to be held accountable to.

Then there was The Dirt Waders, a group from my art course, banded together over an obsession with old artefacts – and taking it to the tidal riverbanks and estuaries of Cornwall and Devon to hunt for the treasures lost in the mud. I was rediscovering the solace in searching from my childhood, disconnected by Mammette and Papa Allan's move away from the village, to spend more time in France than England. Before too long, The Dirt Waders became a common sight in the obscure Cornish pubs, squelching our way up to an assortment of bars, clutching one ditched and clanking carrier bag filled with the mostly broken – but sometimes complete – treasures (generally an assortment of tide-worn Victorian bottles) we'd just waded up to our necks in thick, smelly river mud to find. We might not have been the bartender's chosen customers, but sitting on a leaning beer-garden bench, sipping a cool, freshly pulled pint, and poring over the latest finds – I'd never felt more alive.

Only, the dirt wading, the booze, the poor life-decisions were all brought to an abrupt end on the morning of March the twenty-first, at around 8.30 a.m.

'Here's breakfast, we got you a McMuffin, Mum's going to help you pack your room.' University daydream over.

This was certainly the first I had heard of such extreme plans as my bedroom door opened, revealing a room still clouded in the thick, dense alcohol-fog of far too much fun the previous evening. Decorations still hung limply from the banister, they, too, feeling the effects of the night before. But with a national lockdown on the horizon, Mum and Dad weren't taking any chances and were unwavering in enforcing a rather rapid and unwarranted evacuation back to Lincolnshire.

*

MARCH 2020, LINCOLNSHIRE, ENGLAND – LUCIE

I've barely set foot on British soil when Lincolnshire calls, and it isn't a gentle beckoning to rediscover the countryside idyll of my early childhood:

'I think we're going into lockdown next week, you'd better get a train up here,' my mum's youngest brother Tom (four years my senior) cautions over text, plans for the extended family visit hurriedly brought forward – I wasn't expecting to stay for long.

INTRODUCTION

My flight to Europe had been an impulsive late-night purchase, one fuelled by a summer fling and false promises. I'd spent the last six months at my parents' Tasman Bay farm, tending to strawberry runners and picking boysenberries with crippling burnout; life as I knew it before, gathering dust in a storage unit. Its sorry contents: a fashion career and the belongings of a six-year-relationship that walked off into the night with only a duffel bag. I wanted nothing more than to pull up roots and escape – I needed a dopamine hit, and 'booking complete' gave me one.

The pandemic at this point was pre-global, and the first sign that things were about to get alarmingly global came while transiting through Changi Airport. I had left New Zealand, after twenty sheltered years, deciding it was very much in its own bubble, even before the pandemic. Geographically speaking, it is one of the most isolated countries in the world, making it the last landmass on Earth to be inhabited by people arriving over 700 years ago – remote really is an understatement. As I landed in Singapore, I caught a harsh first glimpse of the reality to come. COVID-19 came crashing into existence as everyone was body scanned and temperature checked at the end of the travelator, with large screens for all to see: we were given one final check, then herded onto the connecting flight.

Clinging onto what was left of my antipodean optimism, I boarded, putting thoughts of face masks and temperature checks behind. *She'll be right*, I told myself – the Kiwi version of Keep Calm and Carry On. I hoped so. It was too late to turn back, and New Zealand's safe but slow way of life was soon far away.

*

The family's home base in Lincoln has been a sanctuary since the 1960s. It's a large Victorian townhouse, set back from the road and enclosed on all sides by mature trees of beech and lime. Walking across the street, wheeling my suitcase, the old but familiar sight of red brick looms through the foliage, its façade hiding the many changes to its interior over the decades. Its current configuration is two houses – Grandad Papa Rob on one side and Uncle Tom on the other.

Having heaved my life up several flights of stairs, the top-floor landing welcomes me in again. I remember playing hide-and-seek up here during family gatherings, getting lost in its many rooms and throwing stones up at the windows with my cousins (maybe resulting in a broken window). I set up camp in my mum's teenage bedroom which overlooked the back garden, in what would become my new isolation. It's just Tom and me trapped in a bizarre reality on this half of the house – a reality that exists of *Outlander* and *The Bachelorette New Zealand* on repeat, as the days and subsequent months pass by.

With lockdown's length becoming an increasingly unknown entity, at what point do you get back on that plane and head home? With dual citizenship and refuge, I was in a position of privilege, I could essentially wait it out, but at what cost? I didn't feel homesick, I'd never felt a strong need to belong anywhere, preferring to be absorbed in my interests rather than the dynamics of a group. But nothing could have prepared me for the emotions I would experience from the abandonment of my own country: when the safety net was taken away a few weeks later, and the border closed to all travellers except returning citizens and residents. Only it wasn't as simple as booking a flight home, most airlines had stopped flying to New Zealand altogether, and the slim chance of securing a bed in a compulsory and scarcely available quarantine hotel upon arrival, was raffled off in an online lottery.

An estimated one million New Zealanders live overseas, so I wasn't alone in my displacement, experiencing intense bouts of rage and anxiety, followed by the immense wave of guilt, knowing other Kiwis were in far worse circumstances than I was, unable to see sick relatives or attend the funerals of loved ones – which often didn't count as compassionate grounds for entry. New Zealand became a lifeboat with no COVID-19 infections, those back home known as 'The team of five million', and us trapped beyond the border, left to tread water, far from the sanctuary of home. Well, unless you enter the raffle.

INTRODUCTION

AUGUST 2020, LINCOLNSHIRE, ENGLAND – ELLIE

Trapped in Lincoln, it seems like I will spend the rest of my life watching paint dry. Quite literally. That's the family business, you see, making wallpaper. As part of the manufacturing sector, we doggedly stay open throughout the pandemic, my parents utilising the family bubble to rope me and my brother into the workforce; the motley skeleton crew keeping the business afloat. My new job is hand painting every square inch of coloured background, and it's not the art career I had imagined. It's starting to feel like a life sentence – one I'm torturously serving, a metre at a time. As the weeks brush by, so do my aspirations, optimism and the identity I'd embraced back in Plymouth – I think I need a hobby.

'What about metal detecting? It's basically mudlarking on the land.' Mum is stretched to her limits at this point, making this desperate yet loving suggestion to improve my struggling mental health and boredom. She never quite approved of the mudlarking activities – finding the tales alarming, I think, especially that time I had to be rescued from a mudflat using a discarded car bonnet as a life raft – and only thought the worst of the deep, river mud. She probably wants to personally thank the Romans who canalled all of our waterways here in Lincolnshire, rendering mudlarking practically impossible (and she likely regrets this suggestion ever since it left her mouth), but she has always encouraged our strange and varied interests to a fault – at least I don't collect antique swords like my brother.

'Metal detecting?' Thinking back to the few episodes of *Detectorists* I was coaxed into watching with my dad – a big fan of Mackenzie Crook – all that comes to mind is camouflage, fishing vests and ring pulls: the Holy Trinity of detecting camaraderie. It was a hobby that intrigued me, though, and a show I secretly enjoyed, not wanting to give Dad too much confidence in his control over the TV remote – lest I end up subjected to more reruns of *Car S.O.S.*

'Maybe. I mean, how would I even do that?'

A week later, I've joined every public group on Facebook for metal detecting that I can find, and I've taken the first terrifying leap: pressing send, seeking advice about what metal detector to start with.

THINGS WE FOUND IN THE GROUND

Standing on the doorstep to Papa Rob's grand Victorian townhouse, just down the road from Mum and Dad's – and the current abode to most of the extended family and the largest and oldest garden I have access to – a freshly unboxed and assembled Minelab Vanquish 340 is clutched firmly in one hand, in the other, a Second World War military entrenchment tool, loaned to me by my brother (he doesn't just collect antique swords: specialised military digging equipment is apparently also included in his interests).

The initial plan to detect in the neatly maintained rear garden doesn't last very long; I am swiftly banished to the untamed front lawn after digging one hole and not finding anything for my troubles apart from a new dead patch in the grass. Undeterred, I start again in the front, fumbling with the buttons and settings on the metal detector, when my cousin Lucie pops her head round the corner, dressed in leopard-print slippers and grey pyjamas. She's been sheltering in the attic bedroom here since New Zealand closed its borders. Before this trip, I last saw her half a decade ago, on a family holiday to the 'Land of the Long White Cloud', meeting up for a meal in Wellington.

'What are you doing? Are you metal detecting?' she asks with a distinct Kiwi twang, curiously watching as I unearth a nail and battle through a thistle, another beep revealing a screw.

'Can I have a go?'

SEPTEMBER 2020, LINCOLNSHIRE, ENGLAND

Before we get into the digging, we need to set a few things straight about this odd little world we've found ourselves in. Just so you know what you're letting yourself in for.

Metal detecting is one of those hobbies that often graces the news headlines with shouts of incredible, life-changing discoveries. Yet it is almost confined to the same niche as fishing, a hobby exclusively, as it is stereotypically seen, for the middle-aged man escaping the clutches of his wife. But there's a lot more to it than that. There are actually thousands of women who pursue this hobby, and the escape it provides is about a lot more than just getting away from the missus.

INTRODUCTION

It's all about the search – some call us history hunters – out in the fields, praying to the gods we'll walk over something interesting. To onlookers, it looks very much like someone waving a pole over the ground, with an odd-looking television aerial attached to the end of it (and don't get us started on what the pinpointer, the mini handheld metal detector looks like). You'll observe this detectorist listening intently to the different beeps in their headphones and occasionally stopping to dig or sigh – both mutually inclusive – only to chuck something into the depths of one of their many pockets – and there are never enough pockets – before typically muttering about 'it' being in the next hole. 'It' being the proverbial treasure they are always looking for but never finding. That's the whole art to it, you see, the art of searching, though everything you find won't always be contained within the ground. We'll do our best to explain all things metal detecting as we go along, but don't worry, we aren't here for the technical jargon either, we find it boring, too. The digging and the adventure comes first.

*

Taking command of the bright red metal detector that, for a plastic tool, was quite the hit on Ellie's bank account, Lucie continues the amateur excavation unfolding in the front garden. She's swinging the machine back and forth, not really sure what might be hiding among the weeds, but enlivened by the prospect of something to do. Ellie, on the other hand, clutches her borrowed entrenchment tool and wonders why she spent so much money on something she isn't currently using.

'What do the numbers mean?' Lucie questions, as a multitude of them appear across the small display that adorns the plastic control box, followed loudly by an aggressive tone.

'Umm … I'm not exactly sure,' Ellie admits, having left the user manual in the box after a quick skim through – it was just a pamphlet anyway.

'Well, which ones should we dig?' Lucie presses.

THINGS WE FOUND IN THE GROUND

'All of them?' Ellie responds with a shrug.

As we pace a few more steps and Lucie gets to grips with finding a number, we find ourselves falling quite naturally into some very distinct roles – finder and excavator, playing to our strengths. Ellie is rather fondly known as 'Ellie Smash' in the family circle, after several instances of going in head-first with little regard for the consequences. Needless to say, patience in swinging a satellite dish over the ground and listening carefully to mindless tones is not her strong suit. She's already started to enjoy watching and digging, anyway, secretly not missing the arm ache of swinging the machine. Lucie, on the other hand, is discovering a calm in the task; the repetitive search offering a quieting distraction.

'Let's try this one!' A particularly shrill-sounding tone has captured her attention, and the attention of anyone within a few hundred yards, the Vanquish being a screamer. Unfolding the entrenchment tool, Ellie places the tip to the grass when Tom appears, skidding round the corner, looking more than slightly flustered.

'Not there!' He waves frantically over the middle section of the overgrown lawn, having just remembered the Virgin internet cable – a cable that, only a few inches below the surface, was mere minutes away from becoming the next victim of another 'Ellie Smash' incident – and warns us not to cut off the house's only connection to the modern world. Giving it a wide berth, we hunt down the next target.

Rather quickly, and with every new hole (that's not in the exclusion zone) we learn there is a little bit more to metal detecting than just finding a beep and digging. There's a whole new and unforeseen challenge that presents itself: actually finding the source of the beep in the hole.

'How are you meant to find anything?' Ellie grumbles, scrabbling about, soil flying in every direction.

'Keep searching!' Lucie peers on hopefully from above, convinced we can find something in this garden, grateful for the rest on her swinging arm, and very, very glad she isn't on her hands and knees searching through the dirt.

At this moment, we aren't entirely sure why we thought you could simply turn over the earth and a shiny gold coin would be looking up

INTRODUCTION

at you, just waiting to be found. It seems the world of digging holes isn't quite as easy as that. So, it's no surprise that the surface of the garden is soon looking like a plague of moles has suddenly set upon it – dotted with small piles of dirt containing nothing but frustration and the odd screw.

We can't really tell you how long we spent, or how many holes we dug on that first afternoon. It isn't even a relatively large patch of ground to spend one's time on, but time passes differently, governed only by the beeps, the holes and the growing patch of dirt smeared across Ellie's cheeks. Yet it must have been quite some time to the family onlookers, because we were eventually brought refreshments.

'Have you found anything?' calls Zoe, our aunty who, like Lucie, is stranded; back from her COVID-interrupted honeymoon in New Zealand and seeking shelter at the family residence. She wobbles around the corner of the house clutching a floral serving tray, balanced precariously with several options of biscuits and mismatched china cups of tea.

'Only screws and nails, but there'll be something here,' affirms Ellie, as she heartily accepts the offering of a steaming cup and grabs a chocolate digestive, brushing off some loose soil from her hands onto her jeans. We aren't quite sure if it is enthusiasm or stubbornness that is keeping us optimistic at this point, but one thing is for certain: we are going to find *something*.

Lucie is still waving the detector over every available patch of dirt as she, too, chooses her biscuit. The promise of finding something greater comes in the next signal, like in a gambler's next roll of the dice, meaning neither one of us has experienced an ounce of boredom.

'There's no problem in finding a signal, it's finding what's in the hole that's the issue,' Lucie offers into conversation as she scans over a semi-loud beep, voicing our greatest frustration.

'Oh! Wait there a second!' Zoe starts, and disappears to the sound of distant clattering at the back of the house. She emerges a few moments later, triumphantly clutching a slightly rusted and battered, wooden-framed soil sieve which looks like it's existed in the garage for decades. 'I use this for my gardening! It's perfect.'

THINGS WE FOUND IN THE GROUND

Equipped with this new piece of kit, we get a bit carried away, Lucie eagerly making piles of dirt ready for sieving as we engage in our own 'landscaping'. The garden looks less like a plague of moles has descended and more like no-man's-land as craters are now added to the dirt piles. Sieving away, Ellie tries not to think of the incident a few years back where the whole road had to be shut down after Papa Rob unearthed a grenade in the old spoil heap that now makes up the 'helipad' (a parking area fondly named after Papa Rob's piloting days in the Royal Navy) which we are digging into the side of – a heap moved several times with a mini digger before revealing its deadly secret.

In what is probably the fifteenth dirt pile of the day, Ellie stops dead in her circular sieving motion as the soil sieve starts rattling and a small round object emerges in the bottom.

'Lucie, quick, look, it's not a nail!'

'What is it?!' Lucie discards the Vanquish on the ground as she drops to her knees and peers into the bottom of the sieve with Ellie, both grinning ear to ear at the sight. In possibly one of the most unconventional ways of metal detecting (a soil sieve not being standard equipment), it appears we've sieved out a find.

There, lying in the palm of Ellie's dirt-streaked hand, is a button stamped unmistakably with a fouled anchor – the symbol first adopted by the Royal Navy in 1774 and introduced in the new uniform regulations (they've only been wearing uniforms since 1748!) – which is still in use on naval uniforms today. Distinctively entwined with its serpent-like cable, the fouled anchor is actually something best avoided at sea, so it does seem rather strange that it's the symbol of the Royal Navy.

We've sated our need for finding, at least for the moment, but now a new need has emerged; a deep kindled curiosity to know everything about this small artefact sat in Ellie's hand. To answer this call, we must delve back to 1588, to a great victory for England which first brought this symbol and the Navy together ...

1588, LONDON, ENGLAND

Lord Charles Howard of Effingham, the son of a great nobleman, who had recently experienced great success at the helm of military and naval

INTRODUCTION

command, is pacing down the flagstones towards the Royal Court, his heeled leather boots thudding with urgency. A great courtier, he knows the queen well, especially as his first wife, Catherine, was a close friend of Elizabeth's. He's just been summoned personally to her side as concerning news has broken, and the air is abuzz with chatter and worry over the 130 Spanish ships and galleons that have set sail from Lisbon – they have one target, and that's overthrowing the Queen of England.

Several tense weeks later, Lord Howard finds himself back at his home port of Plymouth, in charge of the English Fleet as the newly appointed Lord Admiral of England. A message has just passed through the harbour: a sighting of the Spanish Armada through the hazy mists off the Lizard – the most southerly peninsula of the British Isles. That evening, he and six of his finest ships set sail to defend their queen. Beacons lit around the country, as the last sight of them disappears from the horizon, a warning of the oncoming naval conflict about to commence in the English Channel.

A few days later, Sir Francis Walsingham, the principal secretary to the queen, receives a letter, marked with Lord Howard's personal seal – which includes a fouled anchor – bringing news of the Spanish Fleet and the cannonfire exchanged so far. Battles and attacks continue between the two great fleets for several more days, Lord Howard biding his time, playing to the strengths of the English ships; utilising their superior long-range gunnery to try and pick off the Spanish Armada from afar. Until the greatest opportunity presents itself: anchored just off the coast of Gravelines near Calais, the Armada awaiting reinforcements is vulnerable to a devastating strategic attack. Prompting eight English vessels, manned by skeleton crews, to sail quietly into the anchored fleet under the cover of midnight; the only warning of their imminent arrival, the gentle creaking of their main masts in the night breeze. Suddenly, the masts are set alight, forcing the Armada to cut anchor and flee, scattering the Spanish forces and driving them straight into the English guns.

As the last Spanish galleon retreats from English waters, Lord Howard has successfully led the English fleet to victory, accomplishing one of the greatest naval achievements of the era and establishing England as the new ruler over the waves. It's no surprise, then, that part of his personal seal, the fouled anchor, becomes the official symbol of the British Admiralty, and is introduced as the standard symbol for naval uniforms just a few centuries later.

*

'Do you think it's one of Dad's?' Zoe asks. Back in the garden, the family – their interest piqued by our infectious excitement – have clustered around to view our discovery.

'Surely not,' Lucie chuffs, not wanting the excitement taken away at our first and only find.

'It can't be!' Ellie interjects stubbornly, refusing to believe our treasured button was simply lost off the jacket of Papa Rob during his Navy days – it looks much older than that.

All digging – or we should say, sieving – is abandoned for the moment, as every focus is on this small button. Ellie's phone is gripped tightly between her muddy fingers as she scours every corner of the internet for a reference on its date. We know the history of its symbol, and now we simply must reveal its age. We can almost taste the history on our fingertips; we just need confirmation. Stumbling across a site reminiscent of the early internet era, we find a meticulous catalogue of British military buttons. Ellie carefully scrolls back in time, past varying styles of fouled anchor, until finally, she finds an almost exact match and some closure – 1774–1860. Much before Papa Rob's time.

'No way,' Lucie breathes, stunned. 'It's older than the house!'

Papa Rob is not the first naval officer to walk these grounds, an unexpected connection to the past that would have lain there forgotten for centuries without our discovery. Filled with an adrenaline rush, we look at one another and find the same glint in each other's eyes, knowing immediately, there's no going back. Craving our next fix, we pick up our tools and turn back into the garden, ready for the next target.

1.

EMPANDA

SEPTEMBER 2020, LINCOLNSHIRE, ENGLAND
'A keen metal detector fairly new to the sport.' Words that would have the more seasoned detectorist rolling their eyes in exasperation. Still, after several hesitant and subsequently deleted openers, the message is sent. It's been a few weeks since our diggings in Papa Rob's garden and scrounging around in the unkempt pieces of land entrusted to us by our foolish friends and family hasn't even come close to satiating our new cravings.

The shoebox kept on Ellie's chest of drawers has seen a handful of carefully tissue-wrapped treasures added to its bounty: A 1930s Art Deco make-up case, a 1990s token from Fantasy Island, Skegness, and a diecast Toyota Celica LB Turbo. And while these new additions contain the fascinating history of 'One of the best days out in Lincolnshire' and the only non-German car to compete in the top division of the German Series, DRM Championships, they are a far cry from the ancient history we *know* is on our doorstep.

*

The Romans have been consuming our every waking thought. There's something alluring about their empire, which began the day Octavian became Augustus – the sole leader of Rome in 27 BCE – and lasted for over 1,000 years. Maybe it's due to their eternal impact on how our world is shaped today; defining our languages, calendar, law, infrastructure and planets. The Roman Empire is not the largest empire to ever exist – it isn't even in the top five – yet, if we asked you to name any empire, we bet the Romans would spring to mind.

Almost 2,000 years later, they can still be found in the British landscape. Surviving in ruins such as the Newport Arch in Lincolnshire, the only Roman gateway in the country still used by modern traffic; Hadrian's Wall in Tyne and Wear, Northumberland, and Cumbria, the best-preserved frontier of the Roman Empire; and the Roman Baths in Somerset, one of the most renowned ancient baths and temple complexes in Northern Europe, attracting visitors to its thermal hot springs since foundation. Of all our ancient predecessors, the Romans are the ones we could probably tell you the most about. Here in Britain, they arrived twice before the successful conquest of 43 CE, and they didn't leave for another three and a half centuries. They built over 10,000 miles of road, twenty-two major towns, introduced a monetary economy, and, most importantly, wrote things down. The connection offered through their surviving transcripts, ruins and records makes them tangible, relatable and so easy to obsess over. 'How often do you think about the Roman Empire?' Well ... Ellie's never stopped.

Luckily for us, much of their history is still hidden in the ground and there's still a chance to add to our collective knowledge, lost in treasures waiting to be found. In 2010, detectorist, Dave Crisp, discovered Britain's largest coin hoard unearthed in a single container: the Frome Hoard, containing 52,503 Roman coins within a ceramic pot. Bringing to light more evidence that not all coin hoards were buried to be recovered, and rewriting our preconceptions and understanding of Roman coin hoarding in the late third century. With so many coins contained within one humongous, fragile vessel, the only way this hoard could have been recovered in antiquity would have been through its destruction – not something very handy when retrieving your valuables in a hurry. But it's believed this wasn't the point; located on high, boggy ground (the potential site of an ancient spring), instead it's a compelling example of a community coming together, adding to a group ritual deposit through separate smaller offerings over time.

We aren't asking to find the equivalent of the Frome Hoard, although that would be nice, but more Roman coin hoards have been found in Britain than in any other province in the entire Roman Empire – with many containing thousands of coins in one single location. So how, when we are based in one of the most important Roman cities in Britain, the Roman Fortress and Colonia of *Lindum Colonia*, aka Lincoln, are we unable to find a single coin?

*

Desperation has led Ellie to break down whatever social fears she had over sliding into a stranger's DMs on Facebook – and she has little to no experience of sliding into any DMs, for that matter. But as designated driver, provider of metal detector, and chief excavator, it's up to her to arrange the digs. Lucie just needs to be ready and dressed when she turns up.

There's one on this weekend, a group dig right next to a known local Roman settlement. Now, Ellie currently can't even set her dating profile to 'only women', fearing some unknown consequence, not realising the only real consequence is having to swipe left for hours on end to break through the endless sea of men on her phone screen. However, when it comes to driving to an undisclosed postcode in the Lincolnshire countryside – sent by a stranger on the internet the day before the dig … Well, that's no problem at all, not when the Romans are involved.

'The dig' is actually more than just digging, it's a whole organised weekend of camping on a rural farm a stone's throw from Horncastle. We won't be camping. That seems like a step too far, and we don't think a few hours spent fossicking around in the dirt is quite enough to remove all creature comforts and throw ourselves into a tent together for the weekend. Particularly when there's no toilet confirmed on site and the only tent on offer is a neglected pop-up one from the garage.

EMPANDA

The Facebook page for the dig is full of pictures from the metal-detecting group's previous visit, promises of Roman coins and brooches. It's our first toe-dip into the wider world of metal detecting, the first time we will step out beyond the gardens and into the fields. So we leave Lincoln early, earlier than we've both gotten up in a long time. We've learned we both aren't morning people, but today digging starts at 9 a.m. and we are far too eager to care about the early morning struggle. It's only a forty-minute drive, in a car filled with nervous trepidation, cautious excitement and the high hopes of finding a Roman coin. That, and the odd bump and clatter of Ellie's 2004 Fiat Panda Eleganza, European Car of the Year, and eighteenth birthday present from her parents.

The faded yellow, boxy machine complete with matching plastic interior reminiscent of a care home, wasn't quite the first car Ellie imagined driving, as hinted by the bold statement of its rear window sticker proclaiming, 'My other car's a Mustang'. And especially not when two weeks into ownership it left her stranded, half in, half off the Torpoint Ferry with only third gear remaining and the ferry staff refusing to help push – apparently that wasn't in their job description. An expensive tantrum from the Panda, which saw her cheered past her first-year uni accommodation in a tow truck and required a brand new clutch.

Yet somehow, since then, Ellie has become very fond of this ridiculous little car and now the trusty steed is responsible for delivering us to every dig. After all, it was originally named in 1980 after the Roman Goddess, Empanda, whose temple was always open to those in need – including weary travellers – so maybe her famous generosity will bring us some luck. You just have to look past the rattles, the colour, and the alarming sway of the rear end when you get over a certain number of miles per hour – it can only do a top speed of 96mph anyway, on a hope and a prayer.

Bouncing around in the boot is the Vanquish 340, a £12 spade, Aunty Zoe's trusty soil sieve and an old toffee tin Ellie's filled with foam in preparation for all the Roman coins coming home with us.

'You have reached your destination,' the satnav informs us in a helpful tone. There are plenty of fields in sight but not a single detectorist. We continue hesitantly up the single-track lane, dodging potholes, Lucie on the lookout, Ellie getting a bit fidgety, worried she's put the wrong postcode in, as we drive ever further away from civilisation.

'There!' Lucie shouts, pointing excitedly at some bright green teardrop flags, the outline of two metal detectors, crossed like swords, flapping in the wind as if they are an ancient coat of arms, marking the entrance to a farm lane. 'That's got to be it!'

Driving down the very off-road track for the poor Panda, the underside occasionally catching on a wayward clump of grass or loose stone – a blooming cloud of dust in tow – we find the stranger from Facebook waiting at the bottom, collecting the dosh. She's a lone woman clutching a ziplock bag of cash and a notebook, sporting a weathered baseball cap and a look that says she's had enough of answering stupid questions early in the morning. Twenty quid later, with our names and addresses handed over, we are pointed further down the ramshackle lane to find our 'parking' for the day – which, of course, is a field. Lurching into a spot, Ellie's beginning to wonder whether her parents should have got her the 4x4 Panda.

Trying not to feel underdressed, we grab our 'gear' from the car and make our way to the pre-arranged meeting place among a swarm of camouflage, hiking boots and wellies – for comparison, Ellie's in white Reebok trainers and Lucie a bright pink parka – we didn't realise we needed to come dressed for a skirmish. The 'meeting place' is a field entrance, opposite a cattle shed, identified by a huddle of fifty fellow enthusiasts, strapped up to the eyebrows in utility belts, military backpacks, and combat harnesses. We are both nervous but there's an infectious energy in the air, an animated chatter growing between the detectorists, and it's impossible not to get swept up in it. Only ten minutes until 9 a.m. now, and the adrenaline coursing through the gathering is the same as that felt on the starting line before a race.

This communal vigour has been stoked and fuelled by the close proximity to Horncastle, a town first recognised as a Roman settlement in the 1720s by Lincolnshire-born William Stukeley – an eighteenth-century antiquarian known today as one of the fathers of

British field archaeology. As a gifted artist, Stukeley left behind a valuable record of the ancient countryside recorded on his travels across Britain, including a plan of Horncastle in 1722, which identifies a previously unknown, walled Roman fort.

Horncastle's walls are the best preserved of the period in Lincolnshire, and our favourite glimpse of them can be found inside Jabberwock Books at 14 St Lawrence Street – where a piece of the Roman wall is hidden in the back room, nestled between the shelves of the history and archaeology section. Today we know the Roman occupation in Horncastle is split into two separate areas, the small Roman fort taking up only five acres and a much larger settlement to the south, which suggests occupation from the Iron Age to the Roman period. Only little is known about why a rather substantial Roman fort is based here. What required the presence of this military stronghold? One theory is that the fort was an extension of the Saxon Shore, a defensive chain of Roman forts built for protection against Anglo-Saxon sea-raiders who increased their attacks on Britain during the third and fourth centuries. Horncastle, during this time, would have been a lot closer to the sea than it is now, with a similar defensive advantage to the known forts on the South-East coast of Britain …

Our wistful daydreams of the Roman history, which could be hiding in this very field are abruptly cut short by the arrival of a man with a megaphone, swaggering to the front of the crowd – he's got to be the ringleader of this organisation. It's go-time. Silencing the attendees with a loud shout, he lays down the law in a stern tone: 'All holes must be filled in, all finds shown before leaving, and headphones must be worn at all times!' We look at each other in worry, dozens of detectors chirping and beeping into life around us, slowly quieting their din as headphones are found and connected. We don't have any bloody headphones …

Bickering between ourselves, we decided to switch the volume off – or at least turn it to its lowest setting.

'Everyone's wearing headphones!' Ellie despairs, the fear of being caught doing something wrong sending her into a spiral – she hates being singled out for anything.

'So, they won't hear our machine will they?' Lucie replies, more confident about bending the rules.

But that's the least of our worries. Digging has barely commenced and in the time it's taken to simply lower the volume of the Vanquish, the gaggle of detectorists has long dispersed, scattered across the fields at a rapid pace, and finding Roman coins for all we know.

'At least we have a soil sieve,' Ellie forces out a smile, trying to dispel the worry of being left behind.

The peaceful crunch of tumbled plough underfoot descends, interrupted now and then by the pitiful chirp of our gagged Vanquish and an odd electronic scream occasionally emerging from a crouched detectorist searching through a hole. We drop into our natural roles of finder and excavator, try to put doubt behind us and wait for a muted tone to catch our attention.

'This is impossible,' Ellie grumbles, as we soon discover a flaw in our prized soil sieve. You see, clay-based soils are perfect for retaining important nutrients for the farmer, but they are a nightmare for the fledgling, underprepared detectorist attempting to sieve a find out from what is undoubtedly a thick, dense, gluey, solid mass. An hour in and it's painfully clear, the soil sieve's days are numbered.

Watching the sorry affair, Lucie's realised she's picked the better job, or so she thought – searching for the signals offers a quiet escape from the world and the uncertainty she finds herself in – but not when you've been swinging away for hours with very little to show for it. Ellie, however, finds this solace in the finds, in the research and the history that comes after – when we find something, that is – and has little patience for the searching. Especially when this involves clawing fruitlessly at the clay trapped in the mesh of the soil sieve, while Lucie waits, slightly embarrassed at the sight, which was probably of high amusement to the other, seasoned, detectorists.

'What have you found? China?' The helpful input of said fellow detectorists comes from above, as Ellie, elbows deep in clay, is relying on touch and sight to spot any kind of metal artefact lurking beneath. She might as well be blindfolded. Looking up, she can see him chuckling to himself – our struggle to find the source of our signals has never been so dire.

'Hopefully it's Roman,' Ellie replies, ever the optimist. 'If we can find it ...'

Our new mocker-turned-friend takes pity on us, scanning his detector over our futile hole and teaching us to use the Vanquish to pinpoint and narrow down our search area – a technique that involves swinging the coil, (the satellite-dish-looking part of the detector), over the target and then turning and swinging over it again at an angle of ninety degrees, making an 'X' that hopefully contains a Roman coin bang in the centre – only, this Roman coin turns out to be a large nail, bringing out another chortle from our friend.

'A classic!' he says. 'You'll dig a dozen of these before you get the hang of it.'

Depressingly he knows what he's talking about, possessing something much more exciting in the deep utility pockets of his khaki fishing vest – a small, plastic screw-top tub filled with foam. Reaching his grubby fingers into the foam he pulls out a thin, flat coin. It's shiny ... and silver. We gaze upon it in awe, not daring to touch it. 'A hammered,' he gruffs, 'came from over there,' gesturing to the far end of the field ... 'beautiful signal,' he finishes nostalgically – lost in the memory of its discovery.

Several holes later – with a few shamefully abandoned and filled back in, after becoming craters that stubbornly remained empty – we have quite the collection of large nails. It's well into the afternoon now, the soil sieve has been abandoned back in the boot (subject to much muttering and cursing from Ellie) and we've had lunch, a Tesco meal deal sadly eaten in the confines of the Panda. Perhaps most people would have given up, but we've resigned ourselves to the fact that giving up simply isn't in our nature.

'One more hole'; 'The next signal' – phrases we use to keep each other going.

We are the youngest by a few decades among our fellow detecting peers; a group predominantly made up of very well-equipped, middle-aged men sporting various utility gilets and camouflage trousers. Every one of these numerous pockets is stuffed with a different tool: from trowels to miniature spray bottles, old toothbrushes, tubs for finds, and a curious device that looks rather like, well there isn't really a good way to describe this battery-powered device, so we will say a torch – that happens to vibrate. These 'torch' devices (available in a range of bright colours or black), are poked around into holes emitting a shrill, high-pitched sound every now and then, which increases in symphony to a grand crescendo of uninterrupted electronic screaming.

'Have you found anything?' calls a smiley-looking lady detectorist, swinging slowly towards us with a steady overlapping turn of the coil. She's casually dressed in a dark hoodie and leggings, a utility belt thrown across her shoulder, her blonde hair tied back beneath a cap. She comes to a stop next to Ellie, who's peering deep into our latest hole, Lucie watching on, expectantly hoping this is the one.

'Only nails so far,' Lucie replies glumly.

'It's our first group dig,' Ellie offers, pulling her nose out of the dirt and searching for any conversation to distract her from another frustrating search.

'Oh, you girls need one of these!' the lady exclaims after a brief chat about our struggles, holding aloft one of the black 'torch' devices. 'It's called a pinpointer, it makes a noise the closer you get to something metal,' she explains.

Suddenly, it all becomes clear; these torches are mini handheld metal detectors, designed specifically for searching and locating artefacts at close proximity. No more feeling around in the dark.

'Here, borrow mine for a bit and see what you've got.'

The pinpointer chirps into life in Ellie's hand pulsing to let her know it's ready to search. Cautiously, she moves it through the dirt in the hole, surprised when it vibrates and shouts louder towards the left-hand side. She claws some dirt away and pokes it around again. It's a constant scream now. There! Just poking out of the edge of the hole's dirt wall is a familiar shape. Yet another nail. Laughing, Ellie plucks it out and shows her two spectators. She likes this pinpointer. Before, it felt like she was drowning in clay and frustration, but now she's just taken her first few strokes, pulled her head above the surface and started to swim.

'You know they could be Roman nails,' Carol offers – we've got on a first-name basis with our new detecting bestie now. 'They did have nails and these look really old, look how crude and handmade they are.'

'Roman nails?' Lucie questions, but Ellie has a glint in her eye, Carol's words sparking a curiosity, and she places the nail carefully into her jeans pocket for safekeeping.

'We'd love to find a Roman coin,' Ellie says wistfully, 'have you had any?'

Carol reaches into her pocket and plucks out one of the plastic tubs everyone seems to have, inside are two Roman coins, the cheeky laurel-crowned busts of the Roman emperors almost smirking up at us as if to say 'Haha, find us if you dare.'

'Now you girls won't believe it, but I actually found these two in holes someone had dug and then covered over again, they clearly couldn't find them!' she laughs.

Ellie smiles along, trying desperately not to think about the holes we had abandoned after giving up on ever finding anything in them.

'So that's a good tip for you both!' Carol continues, 'even if it's a hole that's already been dug, if you are getting a good signal, trust your gut and dig it anyway.'

Carol stays with us for the next few holes, keeping us entertained between signals by showing us pictures of recent finds she's made, including a gold guinea she's had to split 50-50 with a farmer – paying half its face value to attain full ownership as per their detecting agreement, common practice between detectorist and landowner. It shines up at us from the phone screen, giving us a glimmer of hope that we might find something worthy enough to share.

'It really is the best hobby,' she says. 'And if you ever need any help, you'll find it at group digs like this, you couldn't meet a nicer bunch of people.' She's staying for the whole weekend and heads off to find her husband swinging away in the furthest field somewhere.

As she leaves, taking the pinpointer with her, Ellie watches longingly after – back to drowning. 'Roman Nails.' She can't get this comment out of her mind as she searches fruitlessly through the mud. Could they be? Surely, iron can't survive that long in the ground?

THINGS WE FOUND IN THE GROUND

AROUND 86 CE, JUST OVER TWENTY MILES WEST OF DUNDEE

The Roman legion, XX Valeria Victrix, are still building the legionary fortress of Inchtuthil, (pronounced, inch-tuth-ill), just as they have been since 83 CE. Under the orders of Agricola, the Roman Governor of Britannia, this fortress is set to be the heart of the campaign to control Caledonia, modern-day Scotland, and maybe even become the capital. Covering fifty-three acres, it's bigger than the legionary fortress at Eboracum (York) and consists of barracks, a temporary headquarters building, officer's houses, a huge workshop, a hospital, and six granaries – all of the buildings timber framed, much like the early beginnings of every legionary fortress. This is the furthest the Roman frontier has stretched into Caledonia, and it was all about to come to an end.

The fortress is abuzz with activity, only it isn't the sounds of construction filling the air. It's the opposite. News has arrived about the fate of the Legio II Adiutrix, reassigned to the lower Danube to fight in the Dacian Wars. Their previous posting, Deva (Chester), a Roman fortress of incredible importance to Britannia, lies empty awaiting the arrival of XX Valeria Victrix in replacement – but first they mustn't leave anything behind that could help their enemy, erasing the fortress they've spent just over three years building.

So destruction commences, a sweet rich smoke filling the atmosphere as buildings are dismantled and burnt. Over the noise of crackling wattle, a faint smashing can be heard, the sound of every single pot being taken out of the pottery store and shattered into pieces. Soldiers are walking through the fortress ferrying gravel into the sewers and drains, rendering them unusable. But there's one item they can't destroy, and they don't have the space to transport with them. The nearly one-million iron nails manufactured in their workshop, ready for the completion of this ill-fated fortress. At this time, the Caledonian tribes valued iron more than silver or gold, and to leave this many behind would have only equipped what was already a dangerous and volatile frontier with even more weapons.

So they don't. They dig instead. They dig twelve feet down into the corner of a storeroom and pour all of the nails deep into the earth. The pit is packed tight and the building burnt like a pyre, removing all traces of what they had done. The legion moves out.

EMPANDA

Almost 1,900 years later, in 1961, the pit was found. The top layer of nails had encrusted into a solid sheet protecting the 875,428 nails hiding underneath. They looked as fresh as the day they were hand-forged and weighing over seven tons. These are probably some of the most important Roman nails ever discovered – only, no one knew what to do with them. With almost one-million nails, there was enough to fill every museum in Britain, let alone Scotland. So they were sold off, you could buy a single nail for five shillings or a set of five for twenty-five shillings. And requests flooded in. The Birmingham Daily Post reported in 1963, 'Newsboys and bishops bought them, so did company directors and Japanese scholars. Publicans put them over bars, and hundreds of Americans wrote for sets.' The excavations at Inchtuthil needed funding and they got by with a little help from the fleeing Romans.

*

Whether our nails are Roman is quite unlikely, since all nails were hand-forged in the same way well into the 1700s, but they do have square tapered sections and large beaten heads, just like the Inchtuthil nails. We can dream, right? Besides, they are our oldest find yet and become treasured by Ellie who spends days obsessing. Soaking them carefully in a solution to remove the rust, much to her parents' delight, who banish her rusty potions to the conservatory after they start taking up too much of the kitchen counter.

*

Digging concludes at 5 p.m. We find ourselves back in the Panda, dirty, muddy and shattered. So shattered, that Ellie couldn't care less about the mud getting into the upholstery. In her pocket are twelve 'Roman nails' – our only meagre offerings from today's dig. Yet we've both had the best day. It's like the world of metal detecting has cracked wide open, all we can think about is the next dig. The next opportunity to fulfil our addiction. That and a pinpointer are the sole and main thought occupying Ellie's mind. Before she even places the key into the ignition, a bright orange pinpointer is in the online shopping basket and purchased, being delivered in the next couple of days, and there's no way she's heading out again without it.

The drive home is pretty silent, on Lucie's part, at least. She's become quiet after a full day of swinging and socialising. Ellie, however, fills the silence with mindless chatter, the odd tuneless hum to a melody playing through Bluetooth, and speculations about where to dig next. A loud PING interrupts our trains of thought, Ellie gesturing at Lucie to check her phone's notifications, which announce the presence of a new email.

'Quick, read it!' Ellie shouts – hoping it's the email she's been waiting for.

It is. It's from the estate manager of a field where we might actually find Romans, answering her many questions about gaining permission to detect.

'We're in!' Lucie grins, scanning the email's contents, all tiredness forgotten.

2.

PERMISSION

OCTOBER 2020, LINCOLNSHIRE, ENGLAND
The Panda lurches to a halt, slightly lopsided, as Ellie careens onto a muddy, narrow verge with little thought for its off-road capabilities. Pulling the handbrake up as far as she can – it's started to become less effective – she turns to Lucie with a wide grin. 'We're here!'

Sunlight casts through the windscreen, dappled by the overhanging branches of the copse alongside, twittering chirps and rustling undergrowth emanating from the wildlife hidden within its wooded depths. We've parked part way down a rural country lane, in an impromptu parking space next to a twisting mesh of hawthorn and hazel – which is almost clambering inside the Panda. The faint, dilapidated, leaning forms of the dens Ellie used to make with her brother are standing among the trunks; a mess of sticks and branches propped up against trees, thatched tight with clumps of moss and bracken. She remembers this place well, like an old childhood friend. In the thicket behind them is the 'swamp', the muddy patch that claimed many a wellie boot. Beyond that, the field where she slipped and fell head to toe in a cow pat, and in between the swamp and decaying dens, the vast oak tree bearing gifts of Victorian bottles trapped within its roots.

Through this thicket is where Ellie wants to take Lucie – up the hill to the corner of a field where she first picked up that sherd of Roman grey ware on a picnic with Mammette. Freshly signed and

PERMISSION

saved carefully into the files on her phone is the new contract, permitting them to dig unshackled in the very same field circled on the attached map; the blessed authority secured from the tenant farmer, land manager, estate managers and most importantly, the landowner – Lady H – a friend of Ellie's grandparents whose old Lincolnshire farmhouse stood within the bounds of her family's historic estate. She's a bit of an enigma, a grand matriarch whom this village seems to revolve around. We haven't had the pleasure of making her acquaintance yet, Ellie's only correspondence undertaken over email, relying on the good word of her grandparents, and Lady H's (hopefully fond) distant memory of a young, blonde, curly-haired girl running wild around the village.

Gaining a permission can be the most daunting part of the hobby for any detectorist. We are required by UK law to have the landowner's permission to detect any piece of land, be it public footpath, shrubland or riverbank – though there is the odd beach you can go on. There are various different routes the detectorist chooses when it comes to asking for this holy right, be it a handwritten letter returned to sender unopened, an ignored Facebook post that echoes into the void, a good-natured knock on the door only to have it slammed in your face, a cold call that results in a long tale of woe, or straight up grovelling on your hands and knees. Blindly relying on the goodwill of others certainly has its ups and downs, and you need a strong stomach for rejection, but don't let us put you off. By some miracle, we've managed to negotiate the *estate permission* (the most challenging of them all), fought through the red-tape barriers put up by the estate manager, persistently kept the email chain alive for months, and eventually signed our lives away on a six-page contract. Gaining a permission can be a large undertaking, but it's not impossible, you just need to be a stubborn extrovert to see it through – although turning up with a bottle of whisky often helps.

'Come on!' Ellie calls to Lucie over her shoulder, clambering over a fallen tree, slipping through a patch of nettles and ripping past some jagged brambles with little care for clothing, skin or dignity. All while holding the Vanquish aloft and using her spade to beat a path – the thicket being a lot more thickety than she last remembers. Lucie follows suit reluctantly, treading tentatively through the freshly battered undergrowth.

'You know we've got nettles that can kill you in New Zealand!' she shouts.

Ellie doesn't hear, she's stumbling over the last branch onto the soft pfffffttt of freshly turned soil, her white trainers sinking up to the laces. Her eyes are bright with excitement; this is the moment she's dreamt about since childhood – the chance to finally look deeper than the surface.

'Was this necessary?' Lucie curses, emerging from the thicket nursing a couple of bramble scratches on her arms. She looks up to the tumbled plough, suddenly forgetting all her grievances. 'This looks great!'

'This isn't the field,' Ellie replies, squinting up and continuing to trek to the top of a small incline.

'Oh,' she's beginning to wonder whether there was a more direct route to reaching this fabled Roman field; preferably one that didn't involve scrambling through the wilderness.

'This way!' Ellie calls, chattering away about her childhood walks in the village; it becoming increasingly clear this is one of them, it's just become a bit more overgrown in the decade since she was last here. 'We just need to get to the top of that rise,' she puffs, raising her hand to gesture to an opening in the hedgerow. 'Then we are literally right in the thick of it!'

There's a reason she's brought Lucie up this way; it leads directly to her pottery patch – a concentration of grey ware sherds covering the middle section of their destination. This field is larger than we've detected before and this seems like as good a place as any to start.

*

Reaching the end of Ellie's pilgrimage – the crest of a small hill – we breathe in the musty scent of wet stubble, taking in the vast expanse of ploughed field before us. The Romans have never felt closer.

PERMISSION

We can almost hear the thrumming of over 5,000 pairs of *caligae*, the military sandal, rhythmically hitting the ground, leaving hobnail imprints pockmarked into the dirt in their wake – maybe it's the march of the ill-fated IX Legion Hispana heading to the Northern frontier, their work here in Lincoln complete. They had first entered this region around 47 CE, setting up various marching camps, forts and the legionary fortress of *Lindum Colonia* – standard procedure at the time of the early conquest years – laying down the pathways and lookouts for the main Roman roads we today know so well (especially if you are a frequent flyer of the A15 between Lincoln and Hull, the modern day Ermine Street).

But at this imaginary moment in our heads, in the early 70s CE – heading north – the IX Legion was far from the might of the one that had arrived with Emperor Claudius; 35 per cent of their ranks decimated by Boudica, Queen of the Iron Age, Iceni tribe, during her revolt of 60–61 CE – the battle-worn survivors requiring an addition of 2,000 reinforcements from the continent. They march straight past this field, a diverse mix of soldiers, native Britons and Roman reserves. It is a noisy and awe-filled sight for the humble farmsteads around, not knowing this is the last they will see of the IX Legion, who vanish from the archaeological record entirely, just fifty years later – their last known location, somewhere north of York, battling the defiant Picts and Caledonians in 108 CE.

Opening our eyes back into the present, an empty field lies before us, the IX Legion dissolving into the soft whistle of wind racing through the valley, the quiet humming of a nearby tilling tractor and the odd bleat of a sheep caught in the breeze.

*

A nail is the first thing we find, eliciting a chuckle from Ellie who pockets it immediately – another 'Roman nail' for the collection. At around thirty-five acres, this field wouldn't make your local farmer bat an eyelid – apparently nothing more than 'average' – but looking down into the vast expanse of turned soil before us, we can't help but feel like a pair of ants. We are barely more than three metres in from the field margin and at a mere seven inches across and ten inches in length, the coil on the Vanquish has never looked so inadequate.

'How on Earth are we going to cover it all?' Lucie questions. 'Let alone find a Roman coin!' Ellie's already looked it up, on average they are twenty millimetres in diameter, we are literally searching for a needle in a haystack.

A harsh shout from the Vanquish cuts through our spiral, the sudden interruption of a *20* on the display, which to our rookie eyes and ears sounds great. Looking at each other in anticipation, Lucie swings the metal detector over the signal, practising the new ninety-degree pinpointing technique (swinging the coil side to side, then stepping clockwise, ninety degrees, and swinging again to locate the target in the centre of the crossing sweeps). It's the same kind of giddy rush we felt in the car on our way to Horncastle, we know this field is Roman – Ellie has the boxes of grey ware to prove it – could this be it?

The spade is in the soil almost immediately, Ellie on her hands and knees poring through the familiar mixture of straw, limestone and claggy earth streaked with clay, listening for the electronic screeches of her brand-new orange pinpointer – desperate for its baptism via Roman coin. Ellie's hand scrabbles against something hard, unable to quite make out its shape in the soil, but it's big enough to grasp in her fist. With a grunt and a bit of brute force it comes free, exiting its soil grave suddenly and with a shower of dirt. Ellie's left, one arm in the air, triumphantly clutching our prize. A horseshoe – one nearly as big as her head.

'Crikey!' Lucie exclaims. 'Look at the size of that!'

'How old do you think it is?' Ellie laughs, pretty happy with our find and already dreaming up the possibilities of a Roman horseshoe. It's a thick, heavy and solid form, encrusted in a reddish-orange rust, the odd handmade nail poking out from its curve. Definitely too big to fit in her pocket, it gets placed carefully in the wild grasses on the field margin, ready to be collected on the route back to the car (but probably forgotten).

PERMISSION

Lucie's already swinging away, searching for the next signal, before Ellie's even made it back to join her – emboldened by a find that isn't a nail for once. Ellie's brought them exactly to the imaginary rectangle she'd discovered in her childhood, the epicentre of the Roman pottery scatter, and Lucie isn't sure which she is more excited about: finding a Roman coin or finding a piece of Roman pottery. The thought of holding something so ancient, stretching further back in human history than she's ever found, filling her with the motivation she'd been struggling to grasp lately. She has no idea of the importance of this field and village to Ellie – nor any idea of exactly how fond of both she will become.

As Ellie grew older, venturing out alone and searching up and down the plough lines became her private sanctuary; an escape from the unpredictable environment cultivated at school, where she'd try her best to fly under the radar and not become more of a target than she already was – openly being a lesbian, in her opinion, would only add fuel to the fire lit by her exceptionally good grades. A social standing which was not helped by her extrovert tendencies to get involved in almost everything extracurricular that came her way: juggling jazz band, lifesaving at the local pool and the prom committee – the Holy Trinity for a hard time. Here in this field, though, there were no judgements – only her Romans.

'Here, Lucie, look!' Ellie triumphantly holds up a small grey artefact, that from Lucie's line of sight looks like a rock. Roman grey ware – a piece of vessel, last touched by human hands over 1,500 years ago, disturbed only by the plough in the washing-machine drum of cultivation.

'So …' Ellie says, placing the artefact into Lucie's eager hands, 'you feel how textured it is? It's gritty and there's a slight curve.' Lucie turns the piece over in her hands. 'Run your thumb on the inside,' Ellie insists eagerly, 'you feel the throw lines? That's a piece of Roman pottery – a body sherd.'

Absorbing every scrap of information imparted upon her by Ellie, master pottery-hunter – for the time being at least – Lucie memorises this delicate sherd. It's lighter than the stones she often picks up, always finding herself drawn to a possible worked tool or ambiguous pebble. Our unlikely duo finding a familiar ground in this big open field, plucking pieces of Roman grey ware from between the grassy fronds, clumps of soil and slowly decaying stubble. As opposed to the group digs and the one off fossicks we've experienced before, this feels permanent, like it's the start of something.

It helps that this is the nicest location of our own yet – somehow the ex-scrapyard-come-fly-tip field in between a roundabout and a McDonalds, filled almost entirely by a mega pylon that would send the Vanquish into a Morse code frenzy, didn't have quite the same escapism to it – although we did find that Skegness Token from Fantasy Island in there. Thinking about it, neither did the surrounding plot of a derelict windmill, so overgrown with brambles it was more like bushwhacking than detecting. And nor was the life-threatening visit to a paddock often used as an unofficial dirt track by local youths – the entrance to which was situated between two blind corners on a country lane and really tested the Panda's acceleration and Ellie's reaction time. Looking back, this was more like scavenging than detecting. Driven by desperation, we would detect anywhere we could get our hands on, no matter the waste land or slim prospects offered to us.

*

'ELLIE!' Lucie shouts.

'What have you got? Another signal?' Ellie looks up, about to pluck another grey ware sherd from the ground before the abrupt interruption.

'There's a man running at us!' Lucie replies in alarm.

'What?!' The grey ware sherd is abandoned.

'Over there, running across the field! I think he's wearing camo?'

And sure enough, dressed from head to toe in woodland camouflage, a large figure manoeuvres towards our hunting ground.

'Do you think he wants to speak with us?' Ellie questions, hoping for an innocent interaction.

Pausing our tasks to look around, the adjacent footpath sits quietly, empty of dog walkers – even the sheep quiet their bleating,

PERMISSION

as if scattered by the arrival of a new predator. We both clutch our tools a little tighter, not knowing if we might need to use them for purposes other than digging.

As the man arrives, he takes a moment to catch his breath. We glance at each other nervously, he'd been approaching for a while now – it was quite a distance – lumbering over the plough.

'Can I join you?' He finally exhales. He's a big, bearded bloke – more of a bear than a man – his question falling on deaf ears as we glance at each other again, still processing his arrival and utterly bewildered by the ambush.

'Umm …' Ellie offers uncertainly into the awkward silence.

'I spotted you from the road, I've got my detector in the car,' he continues, gesturing to the entrance of the field, where a black estate car is abandoned.

Ellie, normally the chattier of the two of us, is suddenly quiet, hoping the IX Legion will miraculously appear and save us from this bizarre situation. We had no idea this was a thing, load all your gear into the car and hit the road, taking your chances with the farmers – or the unassuming detectorist, it seems – by turning up at the right doorstep willing to let you in.

'Sorry mate, but you'd need permission,' Lucie replies, ending the growing silence between the three detectorists.

'Can I have the landowner's number?' he persists, undeterred by the answer offered and the not so subtle – well, at least we thought so – hint, that we would like to be left in peace to enjoy our afternoon; worried about the repercussions of breaking the unspoken bond of trust (that for us has only just begun) between detectorist and landowner by introducing a third.

'It-it took us six months to get this permission,' Ellie stutters into motion – having just come to terms with sharing her Roman spoils with Lucie, she certainly hadn't envisioned sharing it with a random bloke, quite literally off the street.

'No mate, sorry,' Lucie reinforces taking a stance, 'we had to sign a contract,' she adds, desperately hoping the hint is finally taken, and we will be left alone to continue digging in our new sanctuary.

He's hesitant to accept, but thoroughly put off at the thought of red tape over an easy win. Finally retreating, he turns away with a curt wave and a brisk, 'All right, then,' seemingly oblivious to the audacity of his actions approaching two women alone in a field without ever offering a name in greeting.

The threat over, the field springs back into life, a dog walker trots past and the painful silence disappears, the Vanquish chirping quietly in Lucie's headphones, reminding her of why we are both here and what we've just fought to defend.

'I didn't think he was going to leave,' Ellie mouths.

'Take the hint, mate,' Lucie agrees jokily, but underneath our humour, we are both a little bit shaken from his persistence to muscle his way onto our land.

'At least we know a better way out of the field,' observes Lucie trying to brush it off (still not forgiving Ellie for the bushwacking) and carefully watching him make the long walk back to his car.

'Maybe we need to start wearing camo? You know, blend in a little bit,' Ellie remarks, looking at Lucie's bright pink parka with a raised eyebrow.

'Never,' Lucie huffs.

Unashamedly we both felt protective over what would become our second home: a patch known by the name of Lincolnshire, renowned for being one of the flattest counties in England, the 'breadbasket of the nation', and the home of the yellowbelly. What you won't realise about Lincolnshire, however, is that ours is the second largest English county, has been the most important region in the country countless times throughout history, and *does* contain some hills – you just have to be in either the rolling Lincolnshire Wolds or the limestone escarpment of the Lincolnshire Edge to find them. But you'd be forgiven for thinking otherwise; since prehistoric times people have been more likely to merely pass through this farming county than to stop and look around, Lincolnshire known more for its wide array of cereals than its diversity.

For the Romans, though, Lincolnshire was an important gateway, trade route and thoroughfare, essential for expanding northwards into

Britain. At the time of invasion, this area fell under the administrative territory of the Iron Age, Corieltauvi tribe – one who put up very little resistance to the Roman legions – and possibly, one of the eleven who submitted to Claudius without any battle. It was an easy and accessible route north, so it's no wonder the fortress of *Lindum Colonia* became a terminal linking two major Roman roads – the Fosse Way and Ermine Street – into one great north road. Roman legions passing through, much like commuters do today, not giving a second thought to this vast agricultural plain.

For the native Britons already living here, life would have continued on relatively unchanged. Around them the legions metalled prehistoric tracks into straight roads, introduced canals connecting the Nene to the Witham, and the Witham to the Trent, and mined iron and quarried stone at Scunthorpe and Ancaster respectively. But the native farmsteads and homesteads would have carried on, maybe even welcoming the improvements to their trade network, gradually becoming more and more 'Romanised'; adopting Roman currency, brooches and a new Roman population. This might have been small, only in the tens of thousands rather than the hundreds, and restricted to agricultural labourers and retired veterans. But here in one of Lincolnshire's rural villages, it's nice to imagine life hasn't changed that much. The land worked and farmed today much like the labourers of the farmsteads built over 1,500 years ago, interrupted only by the soft rumble of the odd Roman legion marching past.

*

'Is that? …' 'Could it? …'

We are both crouched over the latest hole, heads almost touching as we peer at the object perched on Ellie's fingertips. It's small, round and looks old. Darkly rich in colour with flecks of green speckled through where the outer coating has flaked off.

'I can't see anything on it,' Ellie squints.

'Do you think it's Roman?' Lucie breathes – in disbelief we might have found something that wasn't either a nail or a horseshoe.

'I don't know …' Ellie says huffing frustratedly. 'I can't see a head or anything.'

Doubt and nervous excitement are clouding the air, but we don't have the confidence to confirm our suspicions without absolute certainty. So it gets tucked carefully into the toffee tin, the first time anything has been deemed more worthy than going into Ellie's pocket. Lucie, picking the Vanquish up from where it had been discarded in excitement, swings it around with a bit more vigour, her mind swimming with thoughts of the possible 'Roman'.

'It's got to be a Roman,' she decides later on the walk back to the car, after an unsurprisingly, distracted and uneventful end to the dig.

'Surely,' Ellie agrees. 'Like, what else is it going to be?' Although she still isn't certain, the lack of an obvious bust and any discernible detail only sowing doubt in her mind that their instinct is wrong. It's much more corroded than the ones Carol found at Horncastle, darker and covered in meaningless lumps and shadows.

*

For nearly a week, Ellie's been scrolling through Roman coins on the internet, glancing between the search results and the seemingly featureless disc we've found. It's probably the hundredth time she's squinted at it, turning it this way and that way, flipping it over, and repeat – when suddenly the light catches it at the right orientation. In a moment of clarity – like putting glasses on for the first time when you should have booked an optometrist appointment ages ago – laurels appear on the bottom left corner, hair is attached to those laurels, and an eye, a nose, then a whole face is glaring back at her. A Roman emperor.

For a while she can't do much else but stare at the stranger on the coin. She turns it over and nearly drops it in further excitement. What previously had been a foreign landscape of bumps and valleys is suddenly two Roman soldiers standing proud with a tall staff, made of circles and dashes between them, a Roman standard. She's seen this before, this image, she's just scrolled past it. It's like she's seeing with different eyes, she knows what she's looking for now. Scrolling back she finds the image and clicks on it.

'*Gloria Exercitvs,*' she mumbles, fumbling around the Latin words. 'Glory of the Army', the internet translates for her. Our daydream of the IX Legion Hispana hadn't been that far away after all …

The Roman Army was one of the most successful armies in the history of the world, and here in Britain we had the largest military presence of any other province in the Empire.

A highly organised, efficient machine, at its peak the Roman Army contained around half a million soldiers – a number that in itself would have been entirely uncontrollable if it wasn't for the ruthless organisation ensuring every ounce of fighting force was executed in a lethal strategy. Split into a series of legions, each containing around 5,000 soldiers, these were further divided into ten cohorts; each cohort contained six centurions controlling a group of eighty troops, known as a century – a decisive chain of command guaranteeing every soldier was commanded and accounted for.

But organisation wasn't the only ingredient required for an efficient army; having a belief system and a motivation to fight was just as important, and this is where the soldiers on our coin come in.

Known as 'standard bearers', the figures looking back at Ellie were arguably in command of one of the most important jobs in the Roman Army. You see, victory – for the Romans – was held within the standards: the tall staff on our coin. These were the emblems carried by each individual century and legion, and generally there were three main types: the *aquila* – or 'eagle' – identifying a whole legion, the *imago* bearing the portrait of the reigning emperor and an individual *signum* carried by each century. One Roman legion would contain one *aquila*, one *imago* and around sixty *signa*.

Naturally, the standards were used as important rallying points, signals and recognition in battle – as well as helping organise a camp. But the real reason for their great importance was the belief system surrounding them. Essentially, religious talismans, representing the pride and valour of the legion, they were treated with the greatest respect. Losing a standard in battle – especially the eagle – was an unimaginable disgrace and dishonour.

And it wasn't only in battle where the standards found themselves an important part of a soldier's religious life; if you were to visit a Roman fortress you would find its spiritual heart in the standard's storeroom – the legionary shrine – known as the *Aedes*. This room wouldn't be easy to miss, as the standard's importance was a crucial part of the architectural planning of the fortress; raised higher than the surrounding aisled rooms, always constructed of stone – even when the fortress itself was merely made of timber – and located in the *principia*, the main headquarters building. This religious room would have been left open to display the standards, and guarded day and night.

So it's no surprise the standard bearer – known to the Romans as a *signifer* – in charge of such important symbols of a legion's belief system, earned double the pay. However, while this may sound impressive and well-earned, when you consider the rest of a standard bearer's job (which wasn't just carrying the standards into battle) as the centuries' accountant and bank manager, it was meagre in comparison to the average centurion's fifteen times the pay. The signifer was a job requiring a great deal of courage and tenacity while holding an integral position in battle, as well as having literacy, numeracy and a sharp mind to take care of the finances – even if it seems the position was underpaid.

Sat there, laptop brimming with new tabs, the tiny coin in Ellie's hand is no longer featureless; instead, it's bursting with vibrant tales of Rome's mightiest soldiers. The standard bearers look back at her and she wonders what it would have meant to the humble Roman, the agricultural farm labourer living in this settlement. Maybe he was a native Briton on his path to Romanisation? Would he also glance down at this coin in his palm, and see an invading force his community stood no chance against, fearful of possible recruitment, or would he be in awe of the organised legions sweeping through his region, harbouring an aspiration to climb the ladder and emerge as an official Roman citizen?

*

PERMISSION

A consistent and solid tone reverberating through her box-fresh headphones has Lucie stopping dead in her tracks, a *14–16* target flashing across the small LCD display. Our field has been left fallow over the winter, ploughed after the latest crop and abandoned, gradually going to seed, a thick leafy grass taking root across its uneven surface – it's the perfect opportunity to dig in and hone our craft.

Digging has become a weekly occurrence for us now. As set out in our contract, Ellie is now a frequenter of land manager, Kieran's, email inbox, keeping him informed of our planned visits – to which he simply responds with a thumbs-up – and we've become a regular feature of the village landscape; the narrow verge by the thicket our unofficial designated parking space, the scramble through to the other side easier with each passing – Ellie's spade slowly wearing in a path. Our outings bring a much-needed routine to both of our lives, Lucie's even found herself reaching for something she thought was long buried in her youth – her antique DSLR camera, a Canon EOS 1000D, untouched in over a decade, and practically a fossil – this new hobby unwittingly on its way to becoming 'Roman Found' the creative outlet we both weren't aware we needed: originally starting as an Instagram account to document our finds, and cultivated from these early sessions in the field. Lucie did ask Aunty Zoe to lug the camera back from New Zealand, so she'd better use it.

This latest sound seems like a good one. Since acquiring some headphones, Lucie has found distinguishing the tones a lot easier, the padded earphones cutting out Ellie's constant chatter, the blustery winds and the crunch of soil underfoot – leaving only the beeps and the boops for company. Maybe there was method to the rules on the group dig, after all. It's a rather odd language the Vanquish speaks, but it isn't feeling too foreign anymore. Knowing just enough to get by, she could probably sit down at a restaurant and comfortably order a meal: a *12* could be a Roman coin, or *21* a halfpenny, but ultimately it's up to the shape, size and metal content of the artefact under the coil to determine its number identity and tone – although a *17* will always be a shotgun shell in our experience.

'Got a signal!' She calls to Ellie, who, unsurprisingly, is scouring for Roman grey ware behind her. It's our fifth visit to the field and we've fallen into a comfortable rhythm. 'Right here! It sounds good. Dig it!' she urges.

We've been out for a few hours now, each outing lasting slightly longer than the last, building up our stamina: Lucie in her swinging arm, Ellie in her knees. This is probably the fifteenth hole we've dug today, Ellie dropping to the ground and wasting no time in plunging the pinpointer into the hole, clawing some dirt out with her hands and sending a scatter of soil in Lucie's direction – much to her disapproval, she's become very comfortable not getting up close and personal with the dirt; dusty hands proving a sensory problem. Ellie bears no such qualms, unknowingly wiping a thick smear of clay across her cheek as she bends further into the hole, chasing the screams of the pinpointer.

'Lucie, Lucie look!' Ellie freezes in her excavation, pointing into the sidewall, a grin growing across her muddy face. 'Right there, can you see it?!'

Lucie finds herself crouched head to head with Ellie peering into the hole, making out the distinctive green edge of a small coin emerging from the dirt that has Ellie unable to contain her excitement.

'That's not a Roman!' Lucie exclaims.

'It's got to be!' Ellie dismisses her doubts, scraping gently to tease it free, unable to wait any longer. It tumbles out into her hand, eliciting a gasp and shouts of delight that could be heard in the next village over.

No longer caring about the dirt, Lucie joins Ellie on her hands and knees. 'Look at his face!' she says, almost unable to believe her own eyes.

Staring up at us is the cheekiest Roman emperor you've ever seen – there's no doubt that this is a Roman coin. It's a pale green, patinated with patches of brown, and struck in a high relief, the details so crisp you can see every strand of mid-length hair on his rounded, youthful head, every individual oval-shaped leaf on the laurel wreath

PERMISSION

encircling his crown, and the fragments of Latin letters clinging to its uneven outer edge. It's the *Roman* we've been waiting for. *Found* at last. Turning it over, two familiar friends, a pair of soldiers clutching spears and shields, stand vigilantly as they guard their sacred standard.

3.

LEAD

'That's a something, not a nothing,' Ellie claims, placing a small white blob into her new finds bag – with digging becoming a weekly occurrence, so has the postman with various new additions to our gear arsenal. She's also sporting a *Time Team* long-sleeve and matching navy beanie, wanting to look the part – yes, the hobby really is taking over our lives.

These words have unofficially become our new catchphrase, a way of keeping up spirits when we have no idea what we've found. The harsh reality being it's not all Roman coins lost in the dirt. The majority of what we are finding is disappointment and a stubborn desire to carry on and find *something* (even a horseshoe at this point) no matter the cost. We weren't warned getting into this hobby, we'd become addicts. But blindly wandering the landscape, finding nothing but these white blobs we believe to be lead, we can't shake this feeling we just need to wait for the next hole, the next signal, the next chance to roll the metal-detecting dice.

Unbeknownst to us then, lead is actually a very good sign for a field, not merely a traitorously 'good' signal bringing only dismay and obscure lumps into the finds bag. It might be something that goes against everything we have been taught about this poisonous metal – with lead poisoning in living memory, and leaded petrol still around until the year 2000 – but travel back a few hundred years and people were in oblivious bliss to the threat posed by this 'miracle' metal.

THINGS WE FOUND IN THE GROUND

It was found in copious amounts in the Earth's crust, was easy to work with due to its low melting point, available in excess, and relatively cheap. It can even be claimed that lead put Britain on the map for the Romans, and it is true, Britain was the main source of lead in the Roman Empire. The Romans, well, they loved their lead, and not just in their plumbing, either; this metal actually enhanced a fifth of over 400 recipes in the Roman cooking book by Apicius, and was seen as an essential ingredient for Roman winemakers – a complementary flavouring, in fact.

It shouldn't be of any surprise to us that things hadn't changed by the time of medieval England: lead finding itself fundamental in building, craft and general life. England was still one of the main sources of lead globally, and it's hard to find somewhere it wasn't used. From the roofs of buildings, to the creation of pottery glazes, the spinning of yarn, and even the extraction of silver. You make a hole in something – plug it with lead. You want to produce cheap souvenirs – make them out of lead. It was the answer to any problem. So when these odd white, indescribable lumps start appearing in your field, you shouldn't disregard them, they are telling a story, one of production and activity, maybe centuries or even a millennia ago.

Back in the field, Ellie is characteristically enthusiastic about these white lumps, and Lucie is starting to distrust the tones, less optimistic about this plague of 'trash'.

'That's a real pinger!' Lucie shouts, all of a sudden sweeping the Vanquish's coil back and forth over the same patch of promising dirt, each sweep sounding a ringing tone into her ears and flashing a solid *12* onto the small display.

'Dig it!' She shouts again, impatient, waiting for Ellie to run over from her Roman grey ware patch, only a few metres away, but not so fast with the weight of all the lead weighing her down.

'What have you got?' Ellie puffs, spade in the earth and dropping to her knees to begin the search.

'It's a twelve,' Lucie replies, 'but it's really loud, I can't describe it, it sounds good – it's different to the others.' It had been a long, long day of dull solid signals, but she hadn't heard anything like this yet.

LEAD

The pinpointer cuts off her train of thought screaming at the top of its electronic lungs as, furiously digging below Lucie's hopeful watch, one last brush of Ellie's fingers reveals the object sitting among the straw and grass tumbled into the soil. Silence falls as we both stare at what's been revealed.

'What is it?'

'I'm not actually sure.'

'It's not more lead?'

Sat there is a pale disc, of – you guessed it – more lead, much to Lucie's vexation. But this time it isn't a small meaningless blob, it's not perfectly round, but it's not crude either, it seems purposely made.

'Is it an artefact?' Lucie asks desperately. There's some kind of prong protruding from it and a raised symbol below.

'It's definitely a something, not a nothing,' Ellie chimes, carefully turning it over. Our collective gasp sends a startled pheasant scurrying out of the nearby stubble.

'Is that writing?' Lucie gulps, the air stolen from her lungs in excitement.

'It can't be,' Ellie mutters, astounded we've found a piece of lead that really is a *something*. It's hard to explain but we both know this wasn't lost in the last century, we don't know what it is, but we can tell it hasn't seen the surface in a very long time. Lucie joins Ellie in the dirt, the poor Vanquish discarded next to the spade, its job done for the day.

'What does it say?' she says impatiently trying not to pull it out of Ellie's hands to have a closer look herself.

'There's some symbol in the middle,' Ellie replies, turning it towards the dwindling light and squinting, 'but what's round the edge?' She smears the dirt on it with her thumb, feeling the bumps and valleys of the foreign squiggles engraved into the disc. 'It could be writing, but I can't read it, I've never seen anything like it.'

Sat over the shallow hole, the decaying stubble digging uncomfortably into our knees, we pass the object between us. This is our first taste of finding an artefact, and it's a very different experience to finding the Roman coins. Coins are merely transactional, lost change, but this feels personal. We all lose coins every day, down the side of the couch, slipping out of holes in pockets or spinning round and round the washing machine. But have you ever lost an artefact? A treasured necklace, or a ring, a childhood toy or maybe your phone? A coin you can get back, but an artefact feels like losing a part of yourself as well.

'It's got to be writing,' Lucie muses as Ellie packs the dirt back into the hole, with the light slowly dipping below the hedgeline and our fascination taken up solely by this mysterious lead disc. It's time to go home.

*

The post-dig wind down normally consists of collapsing in a heap, all of our energy left behind in the field. But this time Ellie is unable to put our little toffee tin come treasure chest down – Lucie's in a similar boat, and has already sent her three messages about the unidentified disc.

Usually the first step to identifying anything is cleaning off the excess mud, a seemingly mundane task which can prove disastrous for a rookie. Ellie's learned this the hard way, to her horror obliterating the face of an unsuspecting Queen Victoria with the harsh scrubbing of an old toothbrush in boiling water – never listen to the forums online. Now she'll only use a cotton bud, moistened with distilled water, in circular motions, and maybe the gentle scrape of a blunted, wooden toothpick, at a push, for those stubborn particles (disclaimer, anyone following this advice, or any other advice of ours for that matter, does so at their own risk). It's a rite of passage, destroying a find, never an easy one, but a life lesson never forgotten – Ellie's just thankful it happened to a Victorian penny and not a Roman coin, even if it took her a few days to admit her offence to Lucie.

Thankfully, the lead disc cleans with no qualms, and curled up in bed she opens the laptop, ready to uncover its identity. Uncertain about what to type into the search bar, she settles on the broad description of 'lead artefacts' to kick things off, hitting enter and heading straight onto images. She doesn't have to scroll far until

LEAD

another lead disc fills the small screen. It's a different design, with different squiggles, but it looks like the same object. *Click.* 'Seal matrix' Google informs, the medieval precursor to the signature.

'Tea's ready!' her mum calls up the stairs.

Quickly scanning the text, absorbing as much information as possible, she hurriedly closes the laptop. She knows if she isn't heard leaving her room in the next second, her mum's call will turn into a shout. It's lasagne on the menu tonight, her favourite, and much to her parents' delight the hot topic of tea-time discussion quickly becomes medieval England.

*

In 410 CE, the Romans withdrew from *Britannia*; growing problems in their wider empire saw all resources pulled from our far-flung island and sent to the barbarian frontline on the continent. The following centuries saw Britain fought over by the Anglo-Saxons and the Vikings, until a disagreement in the procession of the English crown saw William (soon-to-be) Conqueror turn up on the shores of East Sussex. The Normans had arrived.

Here in Lincoln, it's hard not to spot the influence of the Normans on the city – all 271 towering limestone feet of it. Lincoln Cathedral was built as a status symbol, watching over one of the most powerful cities of the time; strategically placed to control the North, and on its way to becoming the seat of England's largest diocese (religious districts controlled by a Bishop). The Normans were responsible for restructuring and reshaping much of medieval society, like reorganising the Church's power into dioceses. These seventeen religious districts dividing England were designed to exert the overarching power of the Catholic Church, which effectively controlled every part of people's daily lives.

In the subsequent building frenzy, castles, monasteries and churches sprung up across the country, and England's land was broken up and redistributed, seeing the emergence of a new ruling class. The power was now within the land, and William, the king, owned all of it. The peasants farmed for the nobility, the nobility provided money, knights and an army for the king, and in return the king chose who received the land – by the time he was finished barely 5 per cent of the country was left in the hands of its predecessors, the Anglo-Saxons, and was instead controlled by Norman barons, bishops and abbots.

Two hundred-odd years after its construction, Lincoln Cathedral became the tallest building in the world, casting a shadow over this new medieval society. Split into three distinct sections – those who fight, those who work and those who pray – the main industry of the time would have been agriculture; and with an abundance of land, Lincolnshire soon became one of the most populated counties in England. Life was changing, estates had passed hands, religion was at the forefront of people's lives, and here in the village, toiling the soil, a new age had begun.

*

'Medieval abbreviated Latin in reverse,' Ellie mutters under her breath, post-dinner and neck-deep into an article about seal matrices. 'Of course it bloody is.' She's managed to stumble upon a Finds Recording Guide specifically about them on the Portable Antiquities Scheme's website (the national database for the recording of archaeological finds made by the public, but more on that later), utter research gold dust.

In the thirteenth and fourteenth centuries there wasn't a great deal of literacy around; as low as 5 per cent in areas such as rural Lincolnshire. There was, however, and much to the contrary, quite the influx in keeping records – documents were kept in the courts, records were made for estates, bishops held registers, and wealthy merchants and churchwardens updated accounts.

So, there were quite a few legal documents trotting around in the Middle Ages, from wills, to property transactions, rolls and charters. But what do you do with this piece of vellum if you can't write your name? The answer was in this lead disc, an object which acted as a signature, engraved to leave an impression in the hot wax applied to a document – a form of medieval authenticity. There are three main types: the official seal matrix, carrying the name of an office instead of the individual; the anonymous, bearing generic slogans or mottos; and the personal, introducing you directly to a person.

There's just one problem, being designed to leave an impression, all seal matrices were engraved in mirror image. A tricky code to decipher … Oh, and to make it even harder, they were written in shorthand Latin to save space.

'It's fine, you can do this,' Ellie pep-talks to herself, mentally preparing for some problematic translating. She had once wanted to be an archaeologist, the reason for her revived obsession with *Time Team*, and a dream thoroughly crushed after a brutal A level in Russian History – seriously, who came up with a curriculum covering over a century of complex politics and revolutions in the largest country in the world – at least she got a trip to Moscow out of it. So it's no surprise she finds herself drawn to researching the origins of our finds, just as much as Lucie feels a pull to finding them.

However, several hours later, knee-deep in comparison pictures, scholarly articles and a medieval Latin dictionary, she is really starting to wish Latin had been an A level option instead.

Our seal matrix starts with an S' – that much is clear – and enough to reveal its identity as a personal seal matrix (S' standing for '*sigillum of*' – which in English simply means 'seal of'). Trapped somewhere between the dirt and this medieval code is the actual name of the person who lost our seal matrix, over 600 years ago. Yet, the name looks very different to what we would recognise today; firstly, because it's abbreviated in Latin and secondly, because medieval names and identities were written in the possessive.

You see, at the time, surnames weren't like yours or ours today; they were a recent introduction by the Normans, and very rarely were they hereditary. Instead, they revolved around identifying characteristics such as your father's first name, where you were born, your occupation, or even particular features in the location you lived – and they were dropped and changed at will. You could be Robert, Son of Thomas, Robert of Lincolnshire, Robert the Blacksmith or even Robert, Over the Hill; you would have simply adopted the most distinctive surname of the community you lived in.

Thankfully, personal seal matrices generally follow a set of rules, there's a formula to this code:

'SEAL OF FIRSTNAME OF SURNAME'

And one helping hint comes in the form of the 'OF' between firstname and surname, usually one of three options, and revealing which type of surname to decipher:

FIL'/F' meaning 'son or daughter of' for a parent-name surname, for example, Robert, Son of Thomas
DE'/D' for a place-name surname, for example, Robert of Lincolnshire
LE' to indicate an occupation-name surname, for example, Robert the Blacksmith

After almost a week of comparison, identifying the backwards and foreign letters into English, we have all the pieces of the legend, ready to piece together an identity:

S' ADE D' COTISHOV

The first name, ADE, is heavily abbreviated of course but there are lists and books out there translating them – usually men's names end in 'i' and women's names end in 'e' – and naturally, our name is one of the many exceptions to this rule. Why would it be so easy?

ADE turns out to be short for *Adamus* – Adam – and the 600-odd-year gap between him and now is suddenly within touching distance. His last name, COTISHOV, remains more ambiguous, however, until Ellie's GCSE in Italian actually comes in handy. Searching for 'COT', she's suspicious it's the root of some strange medieval-Latin plural or the like.

'Bingo.'

LEAD

Now we can't claim this is, by any means, an exact translation. British medieval Latin is a particular breed of language that has been influenced by a number of cultures – from the Celts, the Romans, the Anglo-Saxons, the Vikings and of course the Normans. It evolved over centuries and millennia, adopting local dialects and specific connotations, having no hope in hell of being translated by anyone other than those they were intended for. So without an intense, decade-long delve into local linguistics and specific etymology, we like to think Ellie's medieval-Latin trip down the rabbit hole is at least on the right track.

COT – IS – HOV

That's what we are working with here, three pieces left of the puzzle. 'COT' is where we start, the beginning of this mysterious, abbreviated Latin word. It's an inflected version of the thirteenth-century root word, '*cos*' (translating to '*whetstone*'), meaning 'IS' is an addition tacked on to express a tense, mood or gender; in this case denoting the word as masculine for Adam. What we are left with is 'HOV', likely the root word start of another word further describing the place name we are looking for. Ellie settles on '*Hovella*' – translating to '*Hut*' – a thirteenth-century word from the correct period of our seal matrix, and the most likely partner to 'Whetstone'.

S' ADE D' COTISHOV/The Seal of Adam of the Whetstone Hut.

It's a moment that has Ellie connecting the threads in her bedroom, somewhat dishevelled, open books sprawled across her bed, their pages stuffed with makeshift bookmarks to preserve the precious information, and air-dry clay impressions of the seal matrix drying out on her windowsill. Sending Lucie a series of fugue-state messages, Adam has become a new friend and no longer a mysterious stranger.

*

THINGS WE FOUND IN THE GROUND

Armed with our new Adam conspiracy, we are summoned to the village manor house, our first meeting with our permission's landowner, the fabled Lady H. We are both slightly nervous walking up the flint-gravel drive. Ellie white-knuckle clutching a vintage teabag tin large enough to contain all our treasured finds and adorned with the portrait of Queen Elizabeth II. Lucie soaking in the grand limestone house, formal gardens – and, is that a tennis court at the back?

'What's she like?' Lucie asks, curious about the Lady of the Manor, with over 500 years of family history backing up her powerful seat here in the village.

'Um ...' Ellie pauses, unsure quite how to describe Lady H; all she really knows is that she holds our fate in her hands, the yay or nay to our continued digging. 'I only know her from being a child,' she settles for, reaching forward to press the brass doorbell, and adding, 'she's old friends with Mammette and Papa Allan,' in an attempt to alleviate any lingering introductory nerves.

'Ah, girls!' Lady H greets us, recognising Ellie with a pleased smile, opening the thick wooden door fully and stepping backwards into a narrow hallway adorned with antique paintings, family portraits and heraldic engravings – the decades (perhaps centuries) old collection of a family firmly rooted into their surroundings. 'Do come in.'

We are ushered into the depths of the manor house, down the hallway, through the 1960s time capsule of a kitchen, and onto the polished hardwood floors of the formal dining room. It's hard not to let our eyes roam. A vast Rococo, gold-gilt mirror reflects our nervous faces back at us, a Great Dane-sized, antique, Indian elephant sits faithfully by our sides, two ancient-looking stone lions are in the corner. The light fixtures are sculpted cherubs, and the walls are crowded with centuries of family ancestors squinting down on us from their gilded frames. The Lady lives in a bona fide museum, and if ever asked about her remarkable setting, will simply reply, with a twinkle in her eye and a loud chuckle, that she is the 'oldest fossil in here'.

'Cup of tea?' – an icebreaker – eagerly accepted. Lady H disappears back into the kitchen, leaving us sitting, rather gingerly, on two mahogany chairs that don't quite seem like they should be for everyday

LEAD

use. Ellie is still clutching our vintage teabag tin, not daring to place it onto the high-polish of the table in front of us, Lucie scanning the room for some kind of coaster. A gentle rumbling interrupts our out-of-our-depth panic, as a mid-century tea trolley emerges from around the corner, pushed carefully over the uneven surface of Lady H's antique floors. It's laden with china teacups, a teapot complete with cosy, milk jug and – spied by Lucie – some biscuits. A pimpernel placemat painted with an antique still-life arrangement of fruit gets strategically placed in front of us, and Ellie sets the tin down at last.

'How have you girls got on, then?' Lady H asks, tea poured and sitting across from us. Her smile is warm and curious, much like her button-down cardigan, wide-collared shirt and blue and green tartan trousers, giving no hint of her grand status. She lives here, mostly alone, albeit from the odd interruption of her well-meaning land manager, Kieran, who is never too far away (currently mowing shapes round her garden orchard), and frequent visits from her beloved cleaner-come-internet-assistant and Waitrose-shopping companion.

As our treasures are placed out onto the table – Ellie's enthusiasm overtaking her nervousness with the emergence of each one – we forget where we are, forget our fears over a 'yay or nay' and instead find ourselves talking to a new friend, one who shares just as much passion for history as we do; her eyes lighting up at the image of a medieval peasant spinning yarn with our lead spindle whorl – one of the many artefacts that have suddenly started appearing among the blobs and lumps of lead.

Before we know it, we've been discussing the Roman coins for at least half an hour, a battered copy of an Ordnance Survey map takes over the table, find locations carefully marked in pencil, with a magnifying glass discarded un-coastered on the high-polish surface. But we've saved the best for last, revealing our pièce-de-rèsistance in what has turned into this grand show-and-tell – Adam's seal.

Lady H coos, 'Now, I think that's rather special.'

'Can you see the letters?' Ellie asks, no longer seated in her chair, taking on the role of 'main presenter', pointing out the script around the lead disc.

'I can, what does it say?' Lady H squints at the foreign squiggles through the magnifying glass, completely enthralled by what has become her favourite find.

'It's Latin,' Lucie interjects, 'and abbreviated ... in reverse ... but Ellie's managed to translate it!' She's still buzzing from the translation journey we've been on and has absolutely no idea how Ellie managed to figure it out.

'So ...' Ellie says triumphantly, still rather proud of her fugue-state translation. 'From what I've figured out, it is S'ADE D' COTISHOV –' she launches into a lengthy explanation of the translation, which we won't make you read about for the second time '– so it's The Seal of Adam of the Whetstone Hut,' she finishes, half expecting a round of applause.

'We think Adam might have been a local merchant,' Lucie adds, drawing Lady H's attention from where she had been watching Ellie with a mixture of amusement and fascination. 'Whetstones would have been used to sharpen tools so "Whetstone Hut" might mean he was the local metal worker.'

'And probably the only one in the village,' Ellie adds, 'for his hut to be the most important identifying feature of where he lived.'

Lady H has taken it all in intently, absorbing every drop of information we impart upon her, her hands moving between the seal matrix and the air-dry clay impressions Ellie has been obsessively making from it.

'Oh, and he might have been a Christian!' Ellie blurts, suddenly remembering more information, referencing the Cross Pattee symbol raised on the matrix's reverse – a classic Christian symbol referencing the resurrection of Christ.

'Hold on, hold on, let me get my book,' Lady H insists, keen to remember all of the many facts we've imparted. 'I need all this written down.'

Carefully inscribed into her notebook, Adam's identity is recorded, a stranger of the village's distant past – reacquainted. Lady H is delighted, excited and astounded by our in-detail research, explanation and clear passion – verging on unhealthy obsession – for these humble artefacts we've discovered. It seems that in finding Adam's

LEAD

seal, we have sealed our own fate. And in doing so, earned ourselves her blessing. We promise to keep her updated on more finds, and insist on leaving an air-dry clay impression as a memento, clearing up our discarded teacups as we make our exit. We've been here for several hours now, time flying with all the discussion about history.

'Now get back out there, I'd like you girls to find me a Sutton Hoo!'

Lady H's parting words follow us out of the door as we head off in the direction of the fields, fuelled by a new sense of purpose – an order, in fact – to discover archaeological treasure. And the good Lady doesn't seem like one who gets let down.

4.
TREASURE

NOVEMBER 2020, LINCOLNSHIRE, ENGLAND
One word comes up on these metal detecting Facebook groups more than any other: 'Treasure' – everyone seems to be finding it, everyone that is, apart from us. Maybe it's Lady H's order of Sutton Hoo that's got our brains turning to thoughts of pots overflowing with gold, chests of silver and intricate artefacts dripping in jewels, so we think it's about time we tick this digging rite-of-passage off – perhaps even share a post of our own. We've found Roman copper-alloy, we've had medieval lead, but where's anything remotely shiny? Are we simply digging in a village of peasants and paupers, or are we just not looking hard enough?

*

'Try again, that ten has to be here somewhere!'
    We've been at it for what feels like days now, having traipsed from entrance to furthest boundary, across crumbling plough and through the long damp grasses of a field left to seed. We stare down into the latest disappointing hole, it too, full of flaky signals and hunks of deep-crusted iron. Only resolute disappointment is filling the finds tin.
    At last, a shout from Lucie, a low promising number has finally appeared through the Vanquish's foggy all-weather screen cover. A *10* – a solid target – and Lucie is claiming it's a good one.

THINGS WE FOUND IN THE GROUND

Ten minutes later, nothing but the painful sound of whittling hard-packed earth and Ellie's frustration is arising from the ground. Lucie is hovering hopefully, watching and wincing as the edge of the cheap spade slowly chisels out a shallow hole.

'Are you sure?' Ellie puffs, as both spade and pinpointer are screaming to give up; one refusing to move more than a millimetre of dirt at a time and the other woefully silent. Needless to say, it's possibly the harshest spot to dig in the entire field. It's just two feet in front of the pedestrian swing gate that leads into the pasture field beyond, a challenging territory for the humble detectorist — perhaps we are now looking 'too hard'. Centuries of footfall by country travellers traversing between hamlets and villages has compacted and hardened the earth to an almost impenetrable state. Lucie, shooting a quick glance up towards the gate in the fear that at any moment eager ramblers could appear mid-excavation, offers some hurried words of encouragement.

'Keep digging! It's so clear!'

Ellie, on the other hand, is wishing Lucie had never heard anything here at all, and is already thinking long and hard about a hot cup of tea served on Lady H's mid-century tea trolley. It is mid-November, the beginning of a long English winter, and if you look on any weather app the words 'quite cold' tend to leap out at you. Of course, what 'quite cold' actually means is icily crisp, and certainly not the weather to be hunched over in an open field battered by arctic winds, stuck with the menial task of excavating a stubborn patch of ground. There is a reason we had to purchase the rather expensive all-weather screen cover for our Minelab Vanquish 340.

Ellie's ever hopeful and optimistic thoughts are cut short as a blip screeches out through the clear cool air. The pinpointer has remembered its purpose at last; screeching away, it joins Lucie in egging on the digging — sorry, the pitiful scraping.

Just a bit lower! it screeches out in its haunting electronic scream.

The latest scrape seems to have got it, and brings both of us hunched down, poring through the soil clutched in Ellie's dirt-streaked hand. More and more soil trickles through her fingers, her

TREASURE

grasp getting increasingly smaller as time and dirt quickly erodes. Finally …

'Is that it?'

61 CE, CAMULODUNUM, BRITANNIA

Life is simple, easy and calm, especially for those in Camulodunum. It's seventeen years after that first wooden vessel appeared, bobbing just off the South East coast – the Romans' third and final attempt at an invasion – and Camulodunum, previously the tribal centre of the South East, was now the provincial capital of Britannia. Coloniae (high-ranking Roman towns), fortresses and settlements have sprung up across the landscape, and uprisings by the native tribes are contained to the furthest reaches of Roman rule in Britannia – or so they thought.

The vast majority of this colonia have served their time in the Roman military, choosing to enjoy their lives building a family and showing their respects to Emperor Claudius (the slightly deaf and limping imperial reject who pulled off the successful invasion, turning himself into somewhat of a god) by attending his grand and monumental temple. The only problem: the sorely underestimated hatred and resentment simmering in the nearby, overlooked Iceni tribe – a hatred that's about to boil over. The Roman legions are away fighting the unrest in the North and the West, when the real threat is beginning right here in the heart of Britannia. Devotees gathered at the Temple of Claudius are interrupted in their worship, as taut and frightening word spreads through the colonia, the Iceni are out for blood, and Camulodonum is next in their warpath.

These doomed Roman citizens react, no doubt, in exactly the same way that we would today: through fear. Fight-or-flight kicks in, while all rational decisions go out the window. Those already in the Temple of Claudius find themselves with the greatest chance of survival, as retired legionnaires rally around the one defensible area of their town and bitterly hold out for a two-day siege. Those fated to be at home are soon surrounded by the flames and cries of the Iceni sweeping through the town, razing everything to the ground in their wake.

Most try to flee this wave of approaching death, but one couple – with smoke filling their lungs, their house set alight around them – desperately

THINGS WE FOUND IN THE GROUND

scrape a shallow hole into the dry dirt with their bare hands. A shallow hole into which they hastily throw their most valuable possessions: the family jewellery that has been passed down for generations. This small, lidded box containing gold and silver earrings, finger rings, armbands, bracelets and silver coins is frantically buried by a hurried scattering of dirt before the couple make their futile attempt to flee the deathly turmoil before them. Perhaps they thought that one day they might return to recover their precious artefacts.

After their hurried departure, a tribal warrior streaks through the burning building, a short, broad sword dripping with the blood of fallen civilians clutched in one fist. He is only looking for one thing, survivors, and fails to notice the freshly buried hole in the floor. Eventually, the timber and earth building succumbs to the flames engulfing it, and collapses into fiery pieces, further burying the small lidded box under smouldering debris.

For decades, centuries, and eventually millennia after its initial burial, it lies unnoticed in the soil. Civilisations collapse and new buildings develop around it; Camulodunum becoming Colchester. Concrete is eventually laid down, walls go up, shelves are installed, designer goods go onto these shelves and then thousands of shoppers wander across this very spot, perusing the various homewares, fashion, electricals, toys and furniture all on offer in the new Fenwick department store.

Until plans arise for a redevelopment and exploratory trenches are put in to test the archaeology of the foundations.

Ninety-four days into the excavations, and between a medieval lime pit, Roman foundation trenches and a modern-day sewage pipe, the small lidded box once again reveals itself to the light of day. A discovery that here in Britain we call treasure, the great prize we confine to curated glass cabinets for children and adults alike, to press their grubby noses against and dream of finding.

*

Kneeling on the hard, packed earth, hunched over a very small and shallow hole which probably has no right to even be called a hole, we

TREASURE

quickly see that our first ever treasure find is certainly not a Roman box full of gold and silver wonder buried in the middle of a tribal revolt.

'Is that it?' Lucie blinks, squinting towards the small metal fragment firmly pinched between Ellie's fingers. Those were the incredulous words uttered between us as we unearthed our first piece of official buried treasure. A treasure so great that an untimely gust of wind could taketh away. At three millimetres by four millimetres and barely visible to the naked eye, its presence was overwhelmingly underwhelming.

Before Lucie can flick it back into the dirt, or the wind take advantage of this precariously presented opportunity on Ellie's fingertip, the tiny shard of metal is quickly tucked away into the dark confinement and safety of the finds tin.

'That's a something,' Ellie mutters, before we uproot ourselves from the ground, on to the next target.

*

In the United Kingdom, there are over 1,000 reported treasure finds discovered every single year, and the majority of these cases are found through the hobby of metal detecting – 304 of these discoveries on average end up in museums. Of course, naturally, when you picture a treasure find, it is probably something more similar to the Roman treasures of *Camulodunum*, or maybe a medieval knight hiding his wages before a great battle, or even a king fleeing a rebellion clutching his crown jewels. We certainly did. What we certainly did not picture was a microscopic shard, a fragment – dust, if you will – of an artefact painstakingly sieved and sorted from the dry dirt to be ingloriously revealed.

Now, we aren't complaining, but we've all seen *Indiana Jones and the Raiders of the Lost Ark*, and a three millimetre-wide speck just doesn't seem anything like the treasure promised to us again and again by a popular culture that is obsessed with uncovering it. Indiana Jones isn't alone either, there's *Pirates of the Caribbean and the Curse of the Black Pearl*, *National Treasure* … Even tales like the Fenwick discovery weave a story of incredible buried bounty waiting to be found beneath a department store. We are all captivated by these stories, and that is because they aren't just stories: every single one of them bears a nugget of truth. Lost, buried treasure has tormented and bewitched the minds of all humanity for generations.

But don't worry, our own treasure legend doesn't end there, stuffed into the finds tin and forgotten about. No, Ellie has rather stubbornly decided that this thing, this 'speck', as we fondly start calling it, is a 'something'. Instead of being jammed into a poly bag, labelled with a big question mark and hidden in a box, it has been out and about. That might sound quite alarming for an artefact so small and so easily misplaced, but Ellie has had it under a newly acquired microscope, shown around at work and squinted at by a whole variety of people in a variety of ways. And they all come back with the same conclusion:

'What on Earth are we looking at?'

The answer, or rather the theory, doesn't surface until a Friday afternoon meeting with our Finds Liaison Officer (or, FLO for short), Laura. We are lucky in England and Wales to have a designated scheme – The Portable Antiquities Scheme, simply known as PAS – for the recording of archaeological finds made by the general public. So far over 1.4 million items have been recorded on the database, around 95 per cent of which have been found by metal detectorists and mudlarks. How it works is that each county has a designated archaeologist – a Finds Liaison Officer – who meets with finders to record their finds and report potential treasure cases (more on this later) to the coroner for inquest; keeping the database an ever-evolving resource of knowledge accessible by the general public, researchers and archaeologists.

We are relatively new to the recording process. It is actually our first ever meeting, having only been detecting a few months, and our boundless enthusiasm for practically every small piece of metal that we have unearthed from the ground is expressed from the moment we step through the door and take a seat on the black banquet chairs in the Lincolnshire County Council reception lobby – one rather battered, but deeply treasured shoebox clutched tightly in Ellie's arms, slightly bowed, weighted down with importance. Completing the look, and making it quite certain to all gathered in this vestibule why we are here, her heavy denim jacket bears dusty traces of our latest digging exploits from cuff to elbow.

Our names called out from behind reception, we are buzzed through an antique, dark-wood and glass room-partition to the depths of the old Georgian council building, Laura greeting us on the other side. She leads us down endless high-ceiling corridors, making light small talk along the way as we turn past a quadrangle courtyard, and enter through a myriad of locked double-swing doors, eventually reaching a nondescript room marked simply as 'Meeting Room 6'. Deep in the council warren, we place our box with reverence onto a twelve-person conference table, which seems rather oversized for a meeting of three individuals. Clutched almost protectively in front of Ellie with the lid pulled back, we reveal its precious poly-bagged contents, and the recording begins. Contrary to our nerves it's a relatively understated affair, Laura carefully perusing and examining all of our artefacts in a welcoming, calm and composed manner – never giving too much away – until, Ellie remembers the speck.

'Oh, and we've got this as well. It doesn't look like much, but I feel there's something on it.' Pulling a sandwich bag from the depths of this chaotic shoebox of artefacts, Ellie presents her offering for closer interrogation.

'Oh!' Laura's eyes light up as she, too, joins in on the squinting game. 'I think this is a piece of Anglo-Saxon silver!'

It's the first time we have seen Laura get excited as she squints closer than anyone has ever squinted at what we had deemed our underwhelming speck. Slightly flustered, Laura passes the speck back to us for more squinting and tries to point out the two eyes, triangular nose and harsh bushy eyebrows that have now emerged on the surface of our artefact.

Lucie is gobsmacked, Ellie triumphant that the speck is finally a 'something', and Laura is almost gushing about her speciality in the use of humanoid faces in Anglo-Saxon art. We might just have made her day.

Suddenly drawing an alarmingly official-looking piece of paper from her bag, Laura gets to work, writing in the details of our speck on the treasure receipt. Since the Treasure Act 1996 replaced the common law of treasure trove – which had been around since at least the time of Edward the Confessor (from 1024–1066) – all finds in England, Wales and Northern Ireland have to be determined to a specific set of guidelines on whether or not they constitute 'treasure'. Officially. And that, for the humble detectorist, is as good as finding the Holy Grail.

But, classing as treasure isn't easy: your find must either be an artefact or a group of two or more coins with at least 10 per cent precious metal content that's also over 300 years old, a group of two or more objects of prehistoric date from within the same find, or, finally, a find that is at least 200 years old and provides exceptional insight into national or regional history. And that's in brief. Now our speck might not claim to be the Ark of the Covenant, but it does claim to be one of the smallest treasure-finds to pass through the unwitting hands of the British Museum's treasure department, and a hard-earned chiselled digit to Lincolnshire's treasure tally.

*

The Anglo-Saxons are one of the most captivating civilisations to ever step foot onto our island, and that's largely because we know very little about them. Compared to the Romans who left such a rich and visual written legacy, the Anglo-Saxons have left mere breadcrumbs – astonishing when considering their 600-year-span of British history (from roughly 410–1066 CE) which far trumps the Romans' meagre 367 years. We learn the most about their world through the archaeological record, discovering tales of fantastical gold, intricately inlaid with garnets and enamels; through one-of-a-kind discoveries such as at Sutton Hoo where an entire twenty-seven-metre longship had been buried as a huge funerary monument for a mysterious Anglo-Saxon king; and the Staffordshire Hoard, the largest collection of Anglo-Saxon gold and silver ever discovered, comprising largely of weapons and weapon-fitting fragments, including a complete pectoral cross – an incredibly early Christian artefact. They were certainly far from a primitive society, but how did we get from the Romans to the Anglo-Saxons?

There are as many surviving accounts of the Anglo-Saxon conquest of England as you can count on one hand, and several are written decades, if not centuries, after the event – but surprisingly, they do all tend to corroborate the same, albeit frustratingly vague, story. Gildas, the sixth-century monk, holds the earliest account cheeringly titled, *De Excidio de Conquestu Britanniae* – or *On the Ruin and Conquest of Britain*. According to Gildas, Britain pretty much fell apart after the withdrawal of Roman forces; attacked from within (or should we say above) by the Picts and the Scots who suddenly found central Britain undefended. The Romans sent a couple of pity legions back to help fortify defences, but this was also to convey a message: the Britons needed to start defending themselves – the Roman Empire had far greater problems to contend with.

Only, instead of defending themselves, a prominent tyrant emerging among the Britons – suspected to be the warlord Vortigern – invited the Anglo-Saxons to come and do their dirty work for them, in exchange for some land to settle on, of course. Now the Anglo-Saxons had spent the best part of the last two centuries trying to invade and settle on Britain, being turned away by Roman forces. So they took this opportunity and ran with it, demanding more and more from the Britons until they just decided to mutiny and try and take it; ransacking the country in what became phase one of the Anglo-Saxon conquest, and requiring the leadership of ex-Roman, Ambrosius Aurelianus, to lead the Britons in war, and bring the Anglo-Saxons back under control. And that's about as far as the story goes. We know there was a period of peace afterwards, and then suddenly England was divided up into kingdoms. *The Gallic Chronicle of 452* claims in a 441 CE entry that, 'The Britains, which to this time had suffered from various disasters and misfortunes, are reduced to the power of the Saxons.' Phase two was clearly here.

Initially, the Anglo-Saxons weren't exactly a united people. In 600 CE there were no less than twelve kingdoms dividing England and they were all constantly warring with each other. It would take three centuries, but eventually, Anglo-Saxon Britain became more united, with the rise of Aethelstan, the first King of England, and the emergence of only four main kingdoms: Northumbria, Mercia, East Anglia and Wessex.

But what about your average villager? In this time of turbulence – seeing kingdoms fought over and absorbed, warlords fighting between themselves for chief dominance, and we aren't even going to mention the Viking problem – what would their lives have been like? Well, it seems that for the majority of people, life was relatively simple – agricultural – with the main hierarchy or division in society between free man and slave. There's much discussion that, in many respects, there would have been continuity between the Roman period and the Anglo-Saxons, with Britons once again finding themselves absorbed into another new culture, while around them, village life simply went on as usual – perhaps with the odd kingdom vs kingdom battle in the distance.

But the best way to get to know the Anglo-Saxons is through their artefacts, trapped between the layers of filigree gold and enamel, and woven into the intricate shapes and figures that aren't as meaningless as they first appear. During the period of our 'speck', the fifth and sixth centuries, and arguably the period of Anglo-Saxon history that remains a blur of vagueness and suggestion, the early Anglo-Saxon artistic movement that birthed our wee treasure (Style I) is often described as an 'animal salad' – and this is rather apt. Artefacts of this period tend to be a dense myriad of animal limbs and humanoid faces, woven together into one big Anglo-Saxon puzzle that to an Anglo-Saxon would have told tales of mythology and gods and fabled stories that have since been lost to the depths of time. Our 'speck' is just one tiny humanoid face, one fragment of a story, that once would have adorned, what Laura reckons, was a rather nice silver cruciform brooch – oh, what we wouldn't give to find the rest of it.

*

'Have you ever thought about becoming a self-recorder?' Laura broaches, peeling apart the treasure receipt and handing it over, revealing a bright yellow carbon copy underneath, which she tucks carefully into a new poly bag with our freshly labelled speck – sorry, Anglo-Saxon treasure.

'A self-recorder?' Ellie questions, oblivious to the screaming elephant in the room that is her huge, overflowing folder of research, which goes far beyond any depth required to record finds – an insight into the obsessive outlet she's discovered beyond the field, and a contained place, despite appearances, to direct her restless energy – she's never been great at switching off. With thousands of artefacts to record, and very little staff to do so, Laura knows exactly how to sniff out a new recruit.

'Why don't you come along next Friday, 2 p.m., bring your laptop, I can get you enrolled into PAS, and show you how to create online entries for your finds,' Laura seems coy, keen for Ellie to take the bait, but knowing ultimately that she will. 'That way you can record your own finds and I will just record the treasure.'

'Sure,' Ellie replies, nonchalantly, trying not to reveal how excited she is at the prospect of taking her role as researcher to the next level.

5.
LEMON DRIZZLE CAKE

MAY 2021, LINCOLNSHIRE, ENGLAND

It's the hottest recorded summer since 2018 – the ninth since records began – a blinding heatwave just in time for 'Step 4' of the Government's COVID-19 roadmap, seeing the majority of restrictions lifted. That, and the latest edition of our digging contract has landed in Ellie's inbox – all red tape removed courtesy of our new best friend Lady H – giving us access far beyond our favourite field.

Yet, it's only fitting that our all-singing, all-dancing pass to over 1,000 acres of prime detecting land comes at a time when the summer crop dominates the arable fields and the majority of our permission. The 'growing season' is one of the most frustrating times of the year for the metal detectorist, the farming calendar our greatest antagonist. It's all too easy to forget the fields have to be farmed, that they aren't *our* fields and instead are shared in joint custody between us and the spring wheat.

Of course, this doesn't put us off visiting the village, instead forcing us to become better acquainted with the estate's other cohabitants – the ones who make the backing track to our usual visits – and enter the domain of the farmyard creature. To our good fortune the permission contains a healthy scattering of grazing pasture (the Holy Grail for the detectorist who can't wait until harvest) but it comes with its own unique set of challenges.

Firstly, there's digging a three-sided plug. A field should always be left as you found it – what's that saying, take nothing but pictures, leave nothing but footprints? It's the same principle for metal detecting, apart from taking the finds of course. A three-sided plug is the best trick up a digger's sleeve, and it's pretty much exactly as it says on the tin. Imagine you're digging a square, with your spade cut 'three sides' leaving the fourth as a hinge, this allows you to flip the clod from the ground while it's still attached on one side, making it easy to replace the earth exactly as it was, and most importantly keeping the grass roots intact preventing any unsightly dead patches.

Then there's Adrian, the not so accommodating sheep farmer. Not only are we not allowed in the same vicinity as his precious flock, but we are also barred from entering any field they might graze – it's going to take us some time, if not an eternity, to win him over. The cows, though, they're friendly – too friendly, Lucie would like to add – just don't enter the field when there's calves, as they can be fiercely protective of their young. Not that Farmer Terry's offered us any warning.

*

'Did you bring any water?' Ellie asks, looking red in the face – not to be mistaken for embarrassment; she's sweating from wearing gardening gloves in the heat and wondering when her spade ever got this heavy. With temperatures clocking up to an all-time high for the UK, you would think she'd come more prepared.

'Here, that's all I've got,' Lucie tosses over one sad, plastic bottle, half empty. 'Why didn't you bring any water on the hottest day of the year?!'

Ellie swigs the already-warm water. Who knew it was going to be this hard to dig holes in the 30°C sun?

'I forgot.' Tossing back the now dirty water bottle – much to Lucie's delight. In all the excitement of exploring a new field today, provisions were the last thing on Ellie's mind packing the car this morning.

'Have you even put any sunscreen on?' Lucie scolds, still frazzled from the over-eager welcome of the twenty resident cows, who mobbed us the moment we touched the gate, thinking we were bringing them breakfast.

LEMON DRIZZLE CAKE

'I don't burn!' Ellie retorts.

An hour later we are sat next to the latest hole, a huge horseshoe discarded alongside, and Ellie starting to pant – the one water bottle between us, long run dry. The horseshoe is currently our 'find of the day'. It hasn't helped morale that the field we've picked seems barren of signals, and the cattle have taken a particular interest in the pinpointer, believing it to be a carrot. Lucie's found herself hiding from the herd in a hawthorn hedge on more than one occasion, and we've walked a lot, fruitlessly, the heat bearing down on us like lost, desert travellers.

Ellie shelters her eyes against the glare of the sun and squints into the distance, 'I think someone's waving at us,' she says, offering a tentative wave back to the distant mirage. A figure leaning over the low garden wall bordering our punishment ground shimmers. In the other fields, we were rarely bothered on our outings, a way out from any buildings, in the far reaches of expansive arable farmland. Our new pasture fields, however, bring us straight under the scrutiny of the village, bordering half a dozen gardens and today it seems our obvious struggle has attracted some attention.

'Have you found anything out there?' asks Janice – the inquisitive neighbour and an old friend of Ellie's grandparents. She's peering over her wall from an incredibly well-groomed garden, gloves and a small trowel discarded at her feet, a patch of Dahlias looking freshly manicured. Ellie brandishes our sizable horseshoe in response. 'It must be off a Shire horse!' She laughs. Janice is in her golden years, wearing a welcoming smile framed by wide crow's feet only earned by decades of happiness. She's fascinated by our adventures out in the fields, having watched Ellie grow up from her frequent visits to the village, her eyes growing wide at the pictures we produce of the Roman coins, and soon noticing our parched state, lack of supplies and neglected bottle of sunscreen.

'Oh, look at you both in this heat!' Springing into action, she rushes round to her garden gate, 'Here, come in and I'll get you something to drink.' Taking us in like her own grandchildren – saying no doesn't seem like an option.

Ten minutes later, we are both looking at each other across a small patio table outside Janice's kitchen door, where we have been forcibly seated as she clatters around inside the kitchen – she only went in for a glass of water, but it sounds like she's rustling up a luncheon. Taking in our surroundings, the carefully cultivated garden is even more impressive from this side of the wall. It's clearly one of Janice's proud accomplishments, its swooping borders overflowing with a flourishing mix of sweetly scented perennials, tulips and delicately woody lavender; the slightly sloping lawn a perfect blend of neatly trimmed and intentionally wild as it encircles a circular flower-bed centrepiece, merges seamlessly into a run of fruit trees and gathers under a weathered wooden bench down the far left side. Behind us is the farmhouse, a large seventeenth-century limestone building, one of the oldest houses in the village; it's all very idyllic, an oasis looking down onto the pasture field-come-desert that has been torturing us all morning.

Our new host soon emerges clutching a tray laden with goods – she wouldn't let us help her, no matter how hard we tried. 'Here we are,' she chimes, in her element and delighted to have guests, presenting to us a whole pitcher of iced water, three glasses and a china dinner plate each bearing a generous slice of what – we didn't know at the time – was her village-famous lemon drizzle cake.

'Crikey,' Lucie mutters, eyes wide at the delights on offer, suddenly very grateful at Ellie's eager insistence on introducing ourselves with the appearance of these frankly life-saving refreshments.

'Thank you so much, this looks amazing!' Ellie smiles at Janice, and with the pleasantries aside chugs half the iced pitcher, her body craving hydration and wasting no time before devouring her slice.

'Oh, it's nothing,' Janice replies with a warm smile, 'Just a few bits I had lying around.'

JUNE 2021, LINCOLNSHIRE, ENGLAND
'Bollocks.'

We are about five metres into our newest pasture field, one we've been dying to get into all week. It's on the opposite side of the village to our usual haunt, close to the village church, and drawing us in with the promise of a public footpath – one that's existed on the maps as far back as Ellie can find – and where there's footfall, there's finds.

Jutting off from the curve of the main street, a narrow, overgrown pathway slips between two stone cottages, guarded by a pack of enthusiastic dachshunds who snap at passers-by from behind their wire-fenced hedgerow, a route identified only by a lone green sign. Through the wooden posts at the end of this passage, an undulating swathe of pasture sweeps into view, often left to grow long for hay, the track continuing through and disappearing up an incline out of sight past the furthest boundary, the memory of previous journeys embedded into a sunken route across its plain.

A few steps onto this causeway and Lucie gets a cracking signal on the Vanquish – a solid *18* – but there's something missing; too busy babbling the whole way here about footpaths, coins and ancient travel, Ellie's gone to dig only to realise there's no spade in her hands.

'I've left it at home,' she breathes, the words hanging in the air between us in disbelief. The find tantalisingly below our feet and completely unable to be accessed, unless Ellie drops to her knees and claws at the dirt.

'You haven't?' Lucie scolds, praying this is some kind of joke.

'What are we going to do?' Ellie replies dejectedly. Yes, we could come back, but the dig would be shortened, rushed, Ellie can't possibly be late home for tea – her parents would likely evict her.

'Wait, what about Janice?' Lucie suggests.

*

'Oh!' Janice exclaims as she opens her door, delighted to see her two favourite detectorists back, and already planning which baked goods to pull from her larder. 'What a delight, what brings you two round?'

'It's a bit embarrassing, actually …' Ellie starts, 'but you wouldn't happen to have a spade we can borrow?' Lucie is lurking slightly round the corner, secretly alarmed at Ellie's extroverted confidence to just go knocking for supplies – even though she suggested it – only it turns out we barely have to ask twice.

THINGS WE FOUND IN THE GROUND

'Of course I do!' Janice claps her hands together in glee, delighted to be involved. 'Come with me,' she dips back inside to turn off her Aga, setting aside an antique-looking kettle mid-boil, and ushers us back down her garden path. Just off to the left, down a couple of flag-stone steps is a small wooden shed, Janice swings the door open with a triumphant swipe, revealing rows of beautifully organised garden tools – a sight to rival any respectable hardware store.

'You'll want to take this one,' she assures us, lifting a mighty-looking border spade off its hooks with surprising ease for a lady in her later retirement. It's green, with a strong wooden T section for a handle. 'It's my very best spade,' she promises, handing it over as if presenting us with a religious artefact.

Freshly armed with the pinnacle of Janice's gardening-tool fleet, she sends us back out into the fields immediately, with the promise of more lemon drizzle cake on our return … so long as we have something to show – no pressure for us, then, nor for Janice's prized spade.

*

'What a beast!' Ellie calls, Janice's spade sunk deep into the earth, that pesky *18* re-found and revealed at last. Compared to our usual trusty £12 spade, Janice's is a monster, at least twice the size, has some serious weight behind it and is wickedly sharp, cutting through the pasture like butter.

'Whoop!' Lucie cheers, 'Thank you, Janice!'

With a grunt from Ellie, the most beautifully cut, square dirt-clod that you've ever seen is flipped out of the hole, and Janice's spade is placed carefully down to the side, having successfully saved the day.

'Lucie! Lucie! Look!' Ellie's excitement is enough to get Lucie to drop to the ground immediately, peering at the object in the earth, an earthworm curling lazily round its edge, searching for its next meal of decaying plant matter to turn into nutrients among the dense jungle of grass roots.

'Is it a badge?!' Lucie asks joining her in the thrill.

LEMON DRIZZLE CAKE

Ellie picks it up and carefully brushes some of the airy soil off with the tip of her gardening-gloved finger. Hints of eroded enamel peek out, snatches of letters and a crest Ellie immediately recognises.

'It's Lincoln!' she delights.

'That's the Lincoln crest, here look—' Peering even closer, nose almost touching its surface, Ellie slowly reads out the letters encircling the crest.

'Lincoln ... cou ... n ... ty ... race ... club ... nineteen ... fif ... ty ... two!'

Slightly worse for wear and bearing a patina reminiscent of its time spent buried in the ground, the specks of faded green enamel, gold-coloured letters and red-and-white crest reveal a 1952, annual ladies' members club badge, for Lincoln County Race Club a blast from Lincoln's horse-racing past. Lincoln Racecourse was established in 1773, and for over a century and a half the famous Lincoln Handicap race (one where each horse would be allocated a weight to bring their abilities on to a level playing field) launched the entire flat racing season (in 1952, the title was claimed by the horse, Phariza, who belonged to a Mrs C Oliff-Lee). The track was closed permanently in 1964 after gradually declining crowds over the previous century saw funding pulled, but the Grade II listed 1897 grandstand can still be found on Saxilby Road, the racecourse now the West Common, a communal grazing ground for local horses.

The vintage toffee tin is triumphantly pulled from Ellie's yellow, cross-body camera bag she's repurposed as a finds bag, carefully placing in the first prize for Janice's spade. A trio of eighteenth and nineteenth-century buttons shortly follows, including one sporting the fine image of a horse; a long-lost piece of Victorian advertising for a 'Gresham, Newark'. The finds are flowing, spirits are high – Ellie, it seems, was right to be excited about the prospects of the public footpath – and the day that almost turned sour after the lack-of-spade incident had decidedly turned on its head. Lucie and our trusty Vanquish had never been happier, singing over the public footpath with no metal artefact safe from their search.

TWANG, CLUNK

THINGS WE FOUND IN THE GROUND

'Shit,' Lucie utters.

For a moment we both can't do much more than stare in horror. The Vanquish, our faithful companion, swinging loosely from Lucie's numb arm – decapitated. The plastic pin holding the coil (which is arguably the most important part of a metal detector) lying forlornly to one side – sheared clean in half, worn out by our overzealous enthusiasm.

'It's fine, it's fine,' Ellie reassures, turning the broken pin in her hands and leaping into 'fix it' mode, her brain running a million miles an hour to solve this problem. 'We just need a replacement – find something to jam in there.'

'Like what?!' Lucie asks incredulously.

Resembling a pair of picky spaniels, we hunt for the perfect stick. Just the right size to wedge firm, and strong enough to hold the weight of the coil in motion. After several rejects, a thick shaft of barley is tracked down from the adjacent field, and offered up to the task.

'There's no way that's gonna work.' Lucie raises an eyebrow as Ellie forces the slightly oversized barley stalk through the lugs of the coil – but somehow it does.

The next signal, however, has Ellie wishing she'd never come up with such a creative solution to keep the Vanquish limping on. She's at least two of Janice's spade lengths deep, the pinpointer happily chirping away, but the object remaining tantalisingly out of grasp.

She can feel Lucie's gaze bearing down into the back of her head, standing over the hole, phone clutched tight between her fingers, ready to film at the sight of anything remotely promising looking. Documenting our digs has become part of our method now, an extra step we've added into the act of finding – urged to record everything, and not just with Laura – building up our own online archive as Roman Found. There is an honour that comes with having this land, and, as the guardians of its artefacts, a duty in sharing their stories; connecting in the process with other finders of history, out in the fields and on the foreshore, doing the same.

'There!' Ellie shouts, the object coming within reach at last, prompting Lucie to drop to her knees, camera already rolling.

LEMON DRIZZLE CAKE

'What do you think it is?' she asks.

Emerging from the soil is a dark green, thin arch. Ellie carefully pokes and brushes away at the soil, feeling around, trying to work out the extent of the size of the object. It's big. Much bigger than anything we've found before (apart from the horseshoes of course).

'We've never found anything this deep,' she wonders aloud, working almost an entire arm's length below the surface, her mind running through the possibilities of what lies submerged. Ask any detectorist and they'll tell you: a dark green patina like this means you're touching something *old*.

We gasp as more of the object is revealed. The arch connects to another arch – a large peculiar-shaped nodule between them – both disappearing into the soil to an unknown depth. We have no idea what it is. Ellie slowly and gently wiggles underneath it with a finger tip, working it free – and it releases suddenly and with little warning.

'A buckle!' she shouts.

A passing dog walker gives us a curious look. She's probably never seen two people, crouched over a hole, excited by an old buckle before – but this isn't just any old buckle. Made of two loops joining at the centre with a narrowed bar, and possessing four, moulded acorn knops at north, east, south and west – their acorn hats (scientifically known as cupules) delicately engraved with cross-hatched decoration – this is a buckle that has lain here for around 400 years, and it even has the pin.

*

The word 'buckle' contains a big hint to its origin; coming from the Latin word, *buccula* – meaning 'little cheek' and referring to their use in the Roman military in holding together armour, most notably for the chin straps on their helmets. Buckles first came to Britain with the Roman invasion, but it would take over 1,000 years before advances in production techniques and changing attitudes in the thirteenth century saw them become widespread in fashion – and not solely reserved for the military and highest echelons of society.

By the time of our buckle, known as a 'spectacle buckle' and dating from 1550–1650, fashion had moved away from the utilitarian fastenings and bulky tunics of the thirteenth century and taken a step into the extravagant; embracing tight-fitting doublets, busty gowns and elaborate accessories. This was Elizabethan England after all – Elizabeth I, herself, owned over 2,000 gowns. Sumptuary laws are still in place, much like in the medieval period, determining the specific cloth and materials you were allowed to wear according to your social status. But Elizabeth held the reins over the fashion trends, specifically importing gowns from across the continent for her tailors to copy and borrow elements of – combining Dutch gowns with Spanish sleeves and French gowns with Dutch cloaks – creating outfits unlike anyone else. Elizabeth's influence didn't extend to only women's fashion, either. The simple act of having a woman on the throne meant that for the men, large codpieces and overblown shoulders were out; and as her silhouette became more exaggerated over time, so did that of her suitors; adopting tight corsets and stuffed bodices.

With all this opulence and decadence dripping from the fashion of the upper classes, it's no surprise this period sees the range of decorative buckles expand almost as rapidly as the general population did. The humble belt was worn by all levels of society – regardless of class, age or gender – providing an important opportunity to show off, and a fancy buckle was exactly the way to do it. A large buckle such as this one, could only have come from a waist or sword belt, an incredibly fashionable choice and a display of status, stemming from the medieval 'code of chivalry' that placed great value on swordsmanship.

Elizabeth I may have also had a hand in the choice of an acorn for its embellishment, with this ancient symbol often associated with fertility and new life, woven deeply into her story. Firstly, in the huge oak tree found in Greenwich Park (albeit rather horizontally now) known as Queen Elizabeth's Oak, which dates back to the twelfth century and was very significant to the House of Tudor – said to have been danced around by King Henry VIII and Anne Boleyn, and a particular favourite of Elizabeth I, who often sought refreshment in its shade. And secondly, in the oak at Hatfield House in Hertfordshire, which Elizabeth is claimed to have sat under when she was declared Queen in 1558, becoming a powerful symbol of her right to the crown.

Oaks and the Tudors seem to go hand in hand, so maybe this is the reason our mystery Elizabethan man chose the acorn to adorn his buckle; seeking a way to elevate his own status through a symbolic connection to the reigning royal family.

*

'Tudor?! My word!' Janice is absolutely delighted with our prosperous return to her doorstep, brandishing a now muddy spade and our buckle treasure. Insisting on a celebration, we are rushed inside before either of us has a chance to say otherwise, seated at a small, round, kitchen table, while Janice tends to a kettle already boiling on her pale-blue Aga, a fresh batch of lemon drizzle cake produced from the larder.

Janice's kitchen, much like Lady H's, hasn't changed since the 1960s and Ellie wonders if all of the houses in the village find themselves similarly trapped in time. It's the epitome of country-farmhouse chic, has the dream Aga, (likely to be the envy of every housewife in the village), a flagstone floor and linen tea towels of mid-century floral heaven. Chatting away as she pulls out some retro teacups from the cupboard, Janice reveals that the Aga has been here just as long as she has, kept in top form by the careful care of her mechanic husband, Errol, who is about somewhere tinkering in a shed.

Clasping her cup, Janice joins us round the table, steamy wisps of tea drifting past her gaze, we have her undivided attention, eager to hear all about her spade's incredible find. And Janice's buckle is quite the story to tell, a grand statement of affluence and class, yet Tudor Lincolnshire was going through one of the roughest periods of its history.

THINGS WE FOUND IN THE GROUND

1485–1603, LINCOLNSHIRE, ENGLAND

It's quite a slap in the face to Lincolnshire's residents, who have spent the last few centuries as one of the richest regions in England, but the great 'wool rush' of the thirteenth and fourteenth centuries is over. And that's not all, the ill-advised decision by the Bishop of Lincoln in 1179 to build a bridge across the River Trent at Newark, came back around to bite them in the arse; the resulting diversion of the main North road, only exacerbating Lincolnshire's naturally isolating frontiers – the Humber, the Trent and the Fens – and with no wool trade to visit for, Lincolnshire soon found itself bypassed.

Falling from one of the most heavily populated counties in England, to one of the most isolated, Lincolnshire pretty much drops off the map. Instead of wool and prosperity, it became known for uprisings and wild fen folk, causing many to believe the county too dangerous to visit. This lack of good press wasn't helped by Henry VIII's scathing remark that Lincolnshire had become, 'the most brute and beastly of the whole realm'. But in his defence, the 1536 Lincolnshire Rising – the violent retaliation to the dissolution of the monasteries and the 'Ten Articles' that attempted to redefine the Church of England and the twelve short days that mark Lincolnshire's one entry into the history books for the entire Tudor period – had significantly challenged his reign, spreading the seeds of discontent and ultimately leading to the largest rebellion faced by a Tudor monarch: the Pilgrimage of Grace.

Henry wasn't alone in his bashing of Lincolnshire, joined by early antiquarian, John Leland, who described its towns as 'much decay'd'. And while we might not have as fine a selection of Tudor buildings as some counties, we do have Doddington Hall and Grimsthorpe Castle – which are worth a visit. But sadly, it is true that Lincolnshire suffered during this period: behind in the fashions, taking centuries to trickle up from London and lacking in timber, causing many poor cottagers to resort to building homes out of mud and clay walls.

Quite the fall from grace for a county that only a century earlier contained the third most important city in the realm. Now typecast as dangerous, backwards and decaying; at least there is some of the richest agricultural land in the country to cling to – even if it will take centuries

LEMON DRIZZLE CAKE

to drain. But somehow, we don't think the draining of the fens is top priority for the isolated people of Tudor Lincolnshire, it will take several centuries to recover from this – if we even have.

*

With night drawing in, bellies full and the teapot empty, we depart Janice's for the Panda. We know this won't be the last time we'll visit the farmhouse – and not just because Janice has earned herself the title of our official DIY store, lending out tools and welcome baked goods to the poorly prepared diggers in the field. No, it will be to visit our friend who, despite the over half a century age-gap, joins us in our childlike glee at the act of finding old things in the dirt.

Our discovery of the Tudor buckle doesn't go unnoticed in the village either. As it appears someone can be quite the gossip at Sunday service, especially when it was their spade that made such an infamous discovery. On our return the following week, we had become celebrities overnight, and the entire village was holding its breath just waiting to see what we were going to find next …

*

Not daring to breathe, Ellie carefully extracts the orb from the ground. Lucie is silent next to her, both of us not wanting to voice our suspicions. Lucie's convinced a bronze Roman votive offering is going to emerge from the soil, Ellie is slightly terrified it's going to turn out to be a grenade. With a gentle tug, it comes free from its loamy resting place.

Ellie holds it aloft, almost reverently. Silence still grips us as our brains struggle to place its familiarity. It's tennis-ball sized, bronze with a hollow, short neck – not unlike the collar of a small pot or jug.

'Wait,' Lucie snorts, suddenly placing it and stifling a bout of laughter. Ellie looks back at her with wide eyes, the object still cradled in front of her in two hands as if making a silent offering to the metal-detecting gods.

'It's a doorknob!' Lucie screams, unable to keep her mirth in any longer, collapsing to the side in hysterics. 'I was convinced it was a Roman offering,' she cries.

'A fucking doorknob.' Ellie can't breathe, nearly falling into the hole.

'We've got to tell Janice about this one.'

Janice absolutely loves it – so will the attendees of next Sunday's service – and we are still chuckling about our 'Roman offering' when Ellie pulls onto Lucie's front lawn – which has long since recovered from our first foray with the Vanquish.

'Same time next week?' She turns to Lucie.

'Yeah, sounds good,' Lucie replies without question, eager to better today's humiliation – even if it is a moment that will go down in history.

'You doing anything this weekend?' Ellie asks, toying with the idea of squeezing in a cheeky out-of-hours dig.

'I might go on a date, actually,' Lucie responds vaguely.

'Oh, I've been talking to this guy!' Ellie blurts out, suddenly wanting to confide in Lucie – the holy doorknob incident, still opening doors, even emotional ones.

'You have?' Lucie sounds a little too surprised.

'It doesn't seem to be going anywhere.' A pause. 'I've also been talking to this girl …' Ellie's instantly relieved at her tentative information dump, successfully breaking the ground into previously off-limit topics – aka not metal-detecting related – and lifting an anxious weight she'd been holding onto unnecessarily.

'Tell me more,' Lucie's long-held suspicions are confirmed instantly, and she can't deny she's a little relieved the conversation has switched its spotlight onto Ellie's love life over her own; dating proving more isolating with every failed attempt to connect, a task not helped by the restrictions of lockdown, her anxiety around trusting someone again, and, of course, the unfamiliarities created by not growing up in this country.

Out in the field, conversation rarely shifts beyond the broken body sherds and faceless coins, the task at hand, all too good at shutting out

LEMON DRIZZLE CAKE

the struggles back home – they don't exist among the dirt. Metal detecting requires you to be present between the stubble stalks, grass fronds and uneven plough; focused only on the sweeps of the coil over the terrain and the adrenaline rush accompanying every stuttered tone and dusty artefact reclaimed from the earth. Reality often only breaks through long after the fact; once you've re-emerged from the soil, the high has eventually worn off and the troubles you thought you'd left behind come tumbling back – but only until the next dig.

6.
GROUP DIG

NOVEMBER 2020, LINCOLNSHIRE, ENGLAND
'Can you see anyone coming?' Lucie frets, the methodical swinging of her metal detector halting suddenly as a particularly loud beep catches her attention. She's on the final stretch of a heavily trampled grass footpath, a narrow strip that runs down the margin of our fondly named 'Roman field'. Now, many, many digs down the line, there isn't much of this field we haven't already dug up – apart from this short stretch of pathway.

'Not at the moment,' Ellie replies, currently on ramble-watch – we'd been sheepishly dissolving into the field at the sight of any oncoming pedestrians, lest we inconvenience their passage.

'Okay, quick, let's dig this one, I don't think it's very deep, you know.' The signal sounded bright and worthy of investigation – and to Lucie's ears, our most promising mark yet. We had already spent the morning plucking a handful of toasted (a classic metal-detecting colloquialism for a coin whose details are eroded far beyond recognition) seventeenth-century half pennies from the busy thoroughfare, and with every step down the muddied track, we move closer towards the end of its generosity – this might be our last signal of the day.

The pinpointer screams the minute Ellie places it to the ground, desperate to reveal the location of our target. Scratching through the compacted surface mud with her fingertips, she stops dead as a glint appears through the dirt – just a few centimetres below the passage.

'Lucie ... Is that?!' We both look at each other with wide eyes, surely that can't be what we think it is. Shaking, Ellie carefully peels a thin silver disc from the footpath, cradling it in her palm and staring in enamoured silence.

'It's a hammered,' she whispers.

'Hammered' is another one of those nerdy metal-detecting/numismatic terms that you will likely never come across unless one's staring you straight in the face. But essentially, a 'hammered' is a silver coin, produced by striking a blank disc of silver (the flan) between two engraved coin dies – quite literally with a hammer. All coins were made this way up until 1662, but only the coins from the Anglo-Saxons onwards are known in the metal-detecting trade as a hammered – we have other nicknames for the ancients.

'There's a hole in it,' Ellie marvels, holding the worn piece of silver up towards the sun, as if making an offering; close to the outer edge of the flan, a small circle of light flickers through a muddy perforation, dancing a shadow across her mud-streaked face. 'We'll have to show this one to Laura,' she adds.

Silver coins deliberately pierced like this can be classified as treasure, transformed from coin to object – for example, a coin being turned into a brooch by the addition of a pin – and, therefore, must be reported within fourteen days of discovery. But the possibility of this being our second ever treasure find is dwarfed by the momentous occasion, the detecting rite of passage that is finding your first hammered coin, ours, a very worn Charles I half groat, dating from 1625–1649.

JULY 2021, YORKSHIRE, ENGLAND

This seems to be our very first and very last taste of hammered silver. It has been months and months of searching now (eight long months, in fact), either the fields are unwilling to reveal their treasures, or we're just shit at detecting? Probably the latter, but we need to find another hammered soon, there's no question about it, *Coins of England* (the bible) has arrived through Ellie's postbox and it's full of them – these are a type of coin minted for over 1,000 years after all – and every single one is winking up at us from the pages, daring us to find them.

GROUP DIG

So Ellie, rather rashly, has proposed a solution to our dried-up prospects, another group dig. We've just about recovered all dignity from our last one, our very public appearance with the soil sieve, so why not put our names down for a whole weekend away detecting? And, you know what, to punish ourselves even further, let's camp!

*

'Christ, I think we're here,' Ellie confirms, turning the Panda through the field entrance and double checking the satnav after a last-minute location change – it's been at least a two-hour drive already, these group digs scattered far and wide across the country.

'Did you know we'd be camping on stubble?' Lucie asks in disbelief, looking around in horror at what lay before us. And this wasn't any old stubble we were faced with either, this was gnarly, rapeseed stubble, with the thickest, most unforgiving stalks you've ever seen – a detectorist's worst nightmare. You wouldn't dare to drive a car through it, let alone plan to sleep on top of it for two (what are looking to be quite miserable) nights – it's a good thing Ellie's packed the gin.

'Don't mind the stubble girls!' a familiar voice rings out as we lurch to the end of the muddy farm track. Ellie winds down the window to greet Barry – event organiser, come parking warden and cash collector – reluctantly handing over some freshly creased notes from her wallet, and wishing she hadn't received the Facebook message with this new location of hell.

'Park yourselves up over there,' Barry gruffs, pointing towards the middle of the knee-high rapeseed field where a scattering of camper vans and tents have already precariously pitched, before grabbing a stalk with his bare hands and yanking it with all his might. 'Just give it a good pull!' he says with a straight face and the confidence of a wheeler-dealer. His parting words, a desperate and failed attempt to alleviate the concern plastered across both our faces.

Ellie closes the window, ready to contain the inevitable onslaught of swearing – time to commit. Swinging the car into the field, she floors it. WHACK, 'FUCK', WHACK, 'FUCKKK', stalks violently scrape and snap against the undercarriage, Lucie's head hits the barely cushioned grey roof headliner and Ellie clings onto the wheel for dear life, as we bounce across the ridges and plough through the stalks. Slotting abruptly into the nearest gap in the line of fellow camping victims, we decide this is far enough into the field – getting stuck and becoming stranded is a genuine fear.

'Okay, then,' Ellie claps, turning off the engine and putting on a brave face for Lucie, 'let's camp!'

'Fucking hell,' Ellie mutters, bent double with both hands clutching at a stalk, it takes all her body strength, but the bastard comes free, sending up a shower of soil and Ellie staggering backwards from the effort.

'That's one done!' she calls, waving it cheerily at Lucie who is watching on sceptically before attempting the task herself. Several grunts, swears and unhappy mutterings later we've cleared a sizable patch of stubble, Lucie's thoughts turning to our accommodation.

'What tent have you got?' she asks, peering into the Panda's backseat which is rammed full of a myriad of mismatched camping equipment.

'It's Mum and Dad's,' Ellie replies. 'I nicked it from the garage; it's that big round orange thing.'

'Three-man pop-up tent,' Lucie reads on the label, her thoughts confirmed as Ellie throws it up onto our stubble-free patch – more than enough space for two. In the boot is her hiking tent – a one-man coffin – and looking around at the already dire conditions, she quickly decides she doesn't need to subject herself to being zipped into claustrophobia overnight.

'Shall we share?'

Tent pitched, and sat comfortably on our camping chairs – also 'acquired' by Ellie from her parent's garage – she whips out a small blue camping stove that resembles a secondary-school Bunsen burner. Despite the situation, our spirits are surprisingly high, we can almost taste the hammered silver – we've also cracked open the bottle of gin, so that's helped. Setting a couple of halloumi burgers to fizzle on the stove, this camping business doesn't seem too bad after all.

GROUP DIG

'Did you say there was a bathroom here?' Lucie asks.

'Oh, yeah, there should be one according to the Facebook …' Ellie trails off as she spots the toilet situation for the weekend – a lone Portaloo plonked unceremoniously at the edge of the campsite – and looks around at the fifty-plus vehicles and tents around us. That's a lot of faith to place on a single Portaloo for three days. And as if our situation couldn't get any worse, the heavens choose this exact moment to open up.

Scrambling to protect the halloumi burgers, Ellie throws open the back passenger door of the Panda and dives in, sending an assortment of camping goods scattering, emerging triumphant, clutching a tarpaulin and two bungee cords.

In a hasty, improvised moment, we hoist the tarpaulin between the Panda's roof rails and our three-man tent, creating just enough space to squeeze two camping chairs and the Bunsen burner underneath. In a matter of mere minutes, we've gone from civilised camp to makeshift shanty town. God knows how we were going to survive the weekend.

What started as a rapid deluge, quickly transforms into an overnight hurricane. Halloumi burgers scranned, we desperately seek shelter among our painfully thin camping mats, and second-hand sleeping bags inside the pop-up tent – at least Lucie has a silk pillowcase.

Prisoners inside our nylon shelter, any hopeful thoughts Ellie had about sharing a can with a fellow detectorist over a roaring campfire are shattered – our only entertainment trapped inside this one-litre bottle of Gordon's gin, which in itself already carries a tale of struggle between Ellie and a particular cashier in Asda who woke up and chose to abuse their power, the morning of our pre-camp supply run. The crucial element we are missing – Lucie's passport – one she thought best to leave at home. According to this cashier, Lucie (elder to Ellie by a good six years) looked like a minor, Ellie getting barred from Asda after sending Lucie to the car park after the first failed attempt to purchase, with an alert sent out over the radio to say she was a criminal supplying a minor. Needless to say, we had to take our commerce elsewhere.

By the third flagon of gin – Lucie not used to this level of drinking – we make up our own entertainment for the evening: our tragic love lives, and more importantly our dating profiles. With Lucie in a new country and Ellie, well … Ellie doesn't really have any excuse, but anyway, we are both starting over – from scratch. And it is apparent that love, much like in metal detecting, is something that in this day and age needs to be searched for. And that unfortunately means putting yourself at the mercy of whichever cruel dating app promises the best match.

'Nope, this won't do – here – I know exactly the right thing!' Upon hearing Ellie's chats aren't progressing beyond the app, Lucie decides to put her over-qualifications in the dating department to good use …

Lucie doesn't know how to do things in halves – unless she finds something boring – she approaches things with her whole being and unfortunately that includes dating (which is far from boring). Dating is all-consuming and intoxicating, and the consequences often dire. If she isn't suffering in the emotional turmoil of the inevitable crash, it is the unhinged scenarios she often finds herself in; catching spontaneous flights halfway round the world only to be stood up, having the future of a new love-interest hinge on her ability to keep a moss ball alive, or going on dates (accidentally) with a patched gang member, who while sat on a moonlight beach, confesses to a stabbing – nothing says romance quite like the unsolicited details of a drug-related kidnapping. Maybe men will be her undoing, but she's survived the dumpster fire that has been her love life so far.

'I think I'm just misunderstood,' she explains to Ellie. Lucie longs to be understood, that someone will gently scrape back the earth, slowly brush away the loose soil, and reveal the parts of herself she always has to bury.

Yet despite her misfortunes, she is hopeful love exists and is more than happy to offer some guidance – whether or not Ellie should follow it remaining up for debate. With some quick flicks, she deftly edits the latest 'digging queen' picture of Ellie – featuring her triumphantly

GROUP DIG

muddy in her iconic *Time Team* long-sleeve, clutching our first ever seventeenth-century crotal bell fragment (a warning signal for oncoming animals and horse-drawn vehicles at the time) – and uploads it straight to picture number one on the app. Who wouldn't want to match with such archaeological chic?

'There! Get swiping!' Lucie hands back the phone, satisfied she's overhauled the photo offering.

'What radius are you set to?' she questions, as we settle into a swipe-athon, the dating apps working like a GPS homing system to only show you worthy – and unworthy – singles in your desired area.

'Oh, I dunno, like twenty miles,' Ellie replies.

'Twenty miles! Are you mad? Double that right now,' Lucie's aghast. No wonder Ellie's been having trouble, trapped within the meagre dating pool of Lincoln. She's had to up hers to 100 miles, just to cut through the belt of RAF boys – at least Ellie doesn't have that problem.

But as the gin whittles down, so do the potential matches, leaving us both to face the daunting next steps with the fruits of our swiping session.

'God, I never know what to say,' Ellie complains, battling with anxiety over acting on any of her matches. She had a dilemma, make the first move or risk losing the match – the person on the other end could have exactly the same nervousness as her.

'It's easy!' Lucie reassures, 'Look where we are, there's so much conversation you could make.' Just to punctuate her point a particularly strong gust of wind threatens to send us airborne. Lucie swipes through the profile Ellie's been deliberating over. 'Katie,' she reads aloud, 'she looks lovely, why don't you ask if she's on any adventures this weekend?'

It turns out, Katie is. She's just got home from hiking up Mam Tor in the Peak District, and Ellie quickly finds herself swept up into her first match with real dating potential, plans set to meet up the following week to debrief on their extreme weekend adventures – maybe coming away on this dig wasn't a mistake after all.

*

THINGS WE FOUND IN THE GROUND

Clattering utensils and the whooshing of the Bunsen burner serve as Lucie's unwelcome wake-up call – her head slightly sore from the inordinate amount of gin the night before as she reluctantly rises from the tent.

'Breakfast?' Ellie calls out – surprisingly chirpy – tossing over a ham and cheese croissant, loosely wrapped in tin foil. Our shanty town, and ourselves, have survived the night.

The campsite is already humming with activity as we quickly wash down our toasted croissants with hot – and much needed – instant coffee. It is an abusively early start – digging always commences at 9 a.m. at these events and we really aren't morning people. It's a miracle Ellie has risen early enough to whip up some morning sustenance.

As we grudgingly get ourselves ready for the day, Ellie optimistically entertaining thoughts about hammered silver and treasure (or maybe even both); a cacophony of machines chirp to life, tent zippers are pulled closed, and the grunts and slaps of outdoor boots pulled on fill the air. A congregation of eager detectorists has already gathered by the Portaloo and we just about make it in time for the morning briefing. Barry's up front and centre, as usual, clutching an air horn, ready to deliver his detecting sermon for the day.

'Right!' he calls, quieting all excited chatter humming between the detectorists, 'Today we've got this field,' he gestures to where we are all stood among the stubble, 'and those two fields just yonder. But tomorrow, folks … that's when we'll open up the exciting stuff down the road.' He then descends into tantalising promises of 'medieval villages' and 'ancient trackways'.

We both look at each other in glum resignation – any tentative hope we had about escaping the camping hell early after a good dig today, shattered – we are definitely going to have to stay another night, there's no way we are missing out on new fields. Barry finishes his address and sounds the air horn – the dig is open.

*

We thought sleeping on the stubble was pretty bad, but that's nothing compared to swinging through it. It's less swinging, really, more like

GROUP DIG

weaving and jabbing through the gaps, the stubble resistant to any kind of give or generosity to move out of the way. Finding even a hint of a signal in this maze feels like a minor miracle, but to our delight it isn't long before we turn up a Second World War-era RAF Tunic Button – it might not be ancient silver, but it's something to get excited over. We find a second and we're on a roll, then a third turns up, and a fourth and a fifth. By the sixth it's resembling a plague.

'Have you had anything?' comes the cheery greeting of a passing detectorist, he's in his fifties, clad in desert camo – from head to toe – we almost didn't see him coming amid the throngs of the stubble.

'Buttons,' Ellie replies 'loads of them!'

'Same here.' He grins, opening his finds tin to reveal at least a dozen, and every single one identical to ours. 'That's shoddy for you,' he chuckles – and, thankfully, it turned out he wasn't referencing our metal-detecting skills. Saving Ellie a deep dive into the local military history of the area, Peter, our new desert-camo-clad friend, enlightens us to the strange phenomenon of shoddy – an obscure form of fertiliser used by farmers on the fields.

*

In the early twentieth century, Napoleon's blockade of the English Channel during the Napoleonic War prevented the import of wool into the country. This caused huge problems for the British wool industry, mainly based in Yorkshire, as they couldn't get enough raw materials to produce the cloth required by the clothmakers. So what did they do? They recycled.

The shoddy industry was born in Batley around 1813, under Benjamin Law, who worked to develop rag-grinding machines (nicknamed 'devils') to mulch down and recycle old cloth and leftover fabric clippings into usable fibres; these could be blended with the short supply of wool to create a greater volume of 'new' cloth – essentially diluting the stock. This method of collecting, sorting, grinding and respinning old fibres into shoddy cloth transformed the clothing industry. It was ultimately up to the clothing manufacturers how much shoddy cloth they could use to dilute their products – a fine balancing act between low price and quality – but naturally the overuse and exploitation of shoddy cloth to produce inferior clothing (much like the soldier's uniforms which had to be created rapidly for the American Civil War) led to the negative connotations and associations we have today with the word 'shoddy'.

But not every piece of old cloth could be ground up into shoddy, the fibres produced might not be long enough, or the cloth could contain buttons which couldn't be ground down. So it ended up on the fields, sold to farmers as a cheap fertiliser. After the Second World War, shoddy was losing its reputation; and public opinion, having just experienced rationing, valued quality goods over price – ironically at a time that saw an abundance of old forces uniforms flood the recycling market. All this discarded wool had to go somewhere, and once again agricultural fertiliser became the solution for this waste product. So next time you find an old button in a field – just think of shoddy.

*

Lucie is delighted to discover the quirky fashion history behind our influx of buttons, Ellie on the other hand – upon learning their loss wasn't quite as romantic as falling from an officer's coat, during the hasty turnaround of a Spitfire – feels the magic is gone.

'This is trauma,' she complains, adding the fourteenth button to our tin, many hours later.

'I wonder what this chap's found …' Lucie replies, much more interested in the bloke digging nearby who has started suspiciously taking pictures next to a hole.

'Let's ask him!' Ellie delights, striding over, much to Lucie's horror. Knackered after the stubble bashing, she's not quite sharing the apparently endless depths to Ellie's social battery.

'Anything good?' Ellie calls out, relishing the chance to use this classic metal-detectorist's greeting.

GROUP DIG

The chap, a young mid-thirties lad who has opted for classic khaki, tactical gear over camo, turns to Ellie with a beaming grin.

'Here, what do you make of this?' he replies, handing over a small Roman disc brooch, beautifully detailed with a lobed star design, retaining its original red-and-blue coloured enamel inlaid into the pattern.

'Stuff's in here,' he beams, 'you just gotta find it.'

*

Returning to camp with our 'shoddy' buttons, we walk past the Portaloo in horror. Barry's in there battling for his life, clutching a spade, ramming it down the now backed-up loo like a plunger.

'I think it's time for more gin,' Ellie deflects, firmly of the opinion some things are best left ignored. 'I'll start dinner, shall I?'

On the menu this evening is meatball pasta: farfalle coated in Asda's finest – extra-special chilli and tomato sauce – but immediately any notion of dinner is a non-starter, quite literally. We can't find the matches and the Bunsen burner has run out of gas.

'No problem,' Ellie says cheerily – still ever the optimist. 'I'll just change the canister.' Reaching into the depths of the Panda's backseat, which still resembles the interior of a camping store, a fresh canister is produced.

'When was the last time your parents used this thing?' Lucie questions, slightly alarmed at the old-school and frankly retro gas canister Ellie's brought forth.

'Dunno,' Ellie replies, 'I've never seen it before in my life.' Her response doesn't fill Lucie with much hope, more like dread, as Ellie proceeds to squint at the minuscule instructions printed onto the side of the butane canister.

'Click and twist,' Ellie mutters to herself.

'Do you know what you're doing?' Lucie panics.

'How hard can it be?' Ellie replies, brashly twisting off the old canister and going straight for the new one. How these butane canisters work is: as they are screwed onto the single-ring hob attachment, the top of the canister is pierced and sealed into the mechanism, and controlled by a valve on the side – in theory it's meant to be easy.

'FUCK.'

A menacing hissing fills our small shanty town as gas leaks rapidly from the poorly installed gas canister, the thread is stiff from decades of disuse, Ellie struggling to screw it tight enough to seal.

'IT'S LEAKING!' Lucie shouts, having visions of us, the Panda and our shanty town igniting in one big bang.

'I KNOW!' Ellie shouts back, standing up frantically, looking around for any assistance, and spotting one of our neighbours – a middle-aged camo-clad chap frying up a storm of sausages on his much more substantial looking double-ring burner. She darts over, leaking gas held outstretched.

'Blimey!' he starts, taking the canister from Ellie and grunting as he twists it closed. 'There we go,' he smiles, handing it back, 'they can be real bastards sometimes these things.'

'Thank you,' Lucie breathes in relief, 'I thought we were all going up!'

He chuckles and we all laugh at our expense, sharing a few grumbles about the stubble and buttons.

Thankfully, no hurricane threatens to wash away our camp this evening, and we are treated to an act of God; as the sun begins to wane, a passing ice-cream van ambitiously pulls into the field, through the stubble, and right up to camp – are we hallucinating from gas exposure? We're not. We sprint over, practically whooping in delight. Anyone would have thought we had been camping for weeks, let alone two days, discovering a vital solace within a chocolate-sprinkle covered whippy cone with a flake – no expense spared from the small change we've frantically scavenged from the finds tin and the floor of Ellie's Panda – desperate times. We sleep a little easier that night, worn out from all the stubble bashing, shoddy buttons, and the narrow avoidance of a dinner explosion, yet somehow still clinging to hope for the next day ahead.

*

Sunday morning, and the Portaloo is a humanitarian crisis, propped open permanently to air by a sacrificial spade. Barry's announced the fabled opening of the 'right alongside a medieval village' fields. Swinging

GROUP DIG

through the rapeseed stubble is thankfully behind us and the digging is going decidedly better. We've even bumped into an old friend, Carol, who we met in Horncastle – her husband's found a silver hammered, the lucky bastard. But mostly we've been observing, taking time to watch how other people detect, seeing them slow down and stay in one place – others are racing off with itchy feet – those with finds are all around us, pottering. These things we are all looking for have been lost for centuries; some, thousands of years, even. They aren't going anywhere fast, and they certainly aren't in a hurry to give up their secrets.

'You had any luck?' Ellie calls to an old boy – a silver-haired digging veteran in a navy fishing vest and zip-off trousers – she's been thriving making small talk in the fields while Lucie hunts down the signals.

'I've had a cracking one!' he calls back, placing his spade into the ground as a detector rest and pulling his headphones from his ears, beckoning her over to see his spoils.

'Whoa ...' Ellie coos, seeing a thin gold posy ring occupying his plastic finds box.

'Can I listen to it? Lucie asks, having wandered over to see what all the fuss is about, and intrigued to know what gold sounds like through her headphones. 'We've never found a ring before.'

'Sure thing,' he replies, delighted to help. 'The best way to learn is through listening.' He finds a clear patch among the loose earth and pops it down for a test swing, encouraging Lucie to swing over it from every angle, even part-burying it on a slant for a real test. Lucie commits the tones to memory; every type of metal, shape of artefact, angle of burial bears a different note among the Vanquish's three tones (low-, mid- and high-pitched). The gold ring sings a bouncy mid-toned symphony, one she would be sure to recognise again.

'What a legend,' Ellie smiles to Lucie after his departure, lifted by the interaction of a seasoned detectorist with an epic find – an aspiration.

So we stick it out all day, check out every field, even the furthest one that's a real trek. We still find a few buttons, but they are of the eighteenth-century shiny, tombac variety, followed by a bright green George V penny, a battered George I 'dump' halfpenny (so named for being smaller and thicker than the previous halfpennies) and a lead hem weight – used to make drapes of fabric hang straight and prevent them from billowing in the wind – a nice variety to fill the finds tin.

'How have you girls got on today?'

We stop as a shout catches our attention on the walk back to our motley camp – digging coming to a close for the day. It's a group of ladies situated in the camp in the row across from us, rather sensibly in a caravan which has its own toilet.

'Much better than yesterday,' Ellie calls back with a warm smile.

'Let's see!' They wave us over encouragingly.

The ladies turn out to be a riot, experienced detectorists and avid digging-weekend goers. We chat for ages about how we started detecting, revealing our latest quest for a hammered coin, the short, spiky, silver-haired ringleader of the group, Jane, producing a folio full of them in response – a collection built up over a lifetime of detecting. She's also wearing a medieval ring, silver, another one of her finds – iconic.

'We really hoped we'd find a hammered here,' Ellie says opening our finds tin and revealing our myriad of buttons, coins and the lead hem weight.

'Well you have!' One of the ladies, Sally, beams – a bumbling, blonde-haired woman in her mid-fifties – plucking out a thin, very battered, coin-like artefact with a reddish patina, one we had been deliberating over.

'This is a jetton!' she proudly states.

'A jetton?' Lucie questions, having never heard of such a thing.

*

Struck out of copper, it's not quite the silver we were after, but these numismatic curiosities known as jettons, are actually 'hammered' – and many even bear similar designs to the silver coins of the day, the first early English jettons of the thirteenth century actually using the same punches for the bust of the king as was used in the production of official coinage.

In a world governed by Roman numerals, as opposed to the Arabic numerals we use today, arithmetic was incredibly difficult. By the medieval period, the rise of trade and commerce was starting to become restricted by the complexity of the calculations that had to be undertaken – they needed to simplify – so as visual learners they introduced jettons and exchequer boards (which were actually checkered cloths). This was essentially a chess set, but for counting. The jettons were used as counters, set in distinct rows that distinguished between different values – such as pounds, shillings and pence – making sums and accounting much more accessible. It's contemporarily described as more of a chessboard than a draughts board, as in its main use in the Royal Exchequer, 'battles' would commence on this checkered surface between the accounts of the treasurer and the sheriff.

As the use of chequer boards became more widespread with merchants and tradespeople, jettons became in high demand and huge quantities were imported in from the main manufacturers, France and Germany, in the fifteenth and sixteenth centuries. Ours has most likely come from Nuremberg, their jetton-making families and guilds dominating the English jetton-import market by the middle of the sixteenth century. However, a secondary usage for these coin-like counters was also starting to emerge. You see, Tudor England wasn't very good at producing small change, our coinage was only either gold or silver, and with monarchs (cough, Henry VIII, aka 'Ol Copper Nose') heavily debasing the coinage, very few small denominations, such as farthings or halfpennies, were actually minted – why would they – for a moneyer, minting a larger denomination coin was much more worthwhile than a farthing that required such little silver it could be blown away like a grain of sand in the wind.

This was all well and good for upper society, but what about your everyday people who wanted to buy a single pint of beer or a loaf of bread? Their answer was to turn to unofficial alternatives, minting their own trade tokens (a business that exploded in popularity in the sixteenth and seventeenth centuries), and substituting jettons for the small change they so desperately needed. Maybe that's how ours was lost here? Tumbling out of a drawstring purse; a jetton cuckoo among a handful of official small change.

THINGS WE FOUND IN THE GROUND

*

'What on Earth are you two doing here?' Jane questions.

After the jetton revelation, conversation has moved onto our permission, and the ladies seem gobsmacked – maybe we were too quick to doubt our permission. Medieval village, ancient trackway, all the promises that got everyone raring to go here in Yorkshire, we have all of that back home. Metal detecting is about patience and perseverance, after all. To quote the mantra of our Roman disc brooch friend in the rapeseed stubble: 'Stuff's in here, you just gotta find it.'

Our minds and bodies might be traumatised by this truly feral digging weekender, but we experience what can only be described as a 'come to Jesus' moment. Why have we left our village? Our sanctuary? It's become so obvious now, our silver hammered is waiting for us there – we simply need to look for it.

Leaving our lovely ladies to head back to our shanty town, Lucie voices both of our thoughts – or maybe it was just fears about having to use the Portaloo again.

'Can we go now, I can't stay another night.'

7.

HAMMERED

AUGUST 2021, LINCOLNSHIRE, ENGLAND

If anything can drag Lucie out of bed, it is Ellie banging on the front door, eager to get out digging. Ellie is used to finding Lucie in various states of readiness (even after giving her a half-hour head start), sometimes appearing at the door wrapped in a towel, trouserless, or without her wellie boots. Today, she seems to be ready, surprising considering the weekend we've just had.

'Mornin—' Ellie starts.

'Could you fill up my drink bottle?' Lucie interrupts, thrusting an empty bottle towards her – which usually means she needs to find some extra time by keeping Ellie busy.

'I just need to brush my teeth ...' she adds, before disappearing into the bathroom upstairs. Ellie knows Lucie doesn't always have the best sleep, often plagued by night terrors, anxiety, and her own unwillingness to go to bed at a decent time – regardless of important plans for the following day.

'Have you got everything?' Ellie asks as Lucie re-emerges from the bathroom, ready to get this show on the road and anxious to return to the permission.

'Yes, wait, no ... I can't find my dig bag,' she sighs, running back upstairs and flitting around her bedroom, emptying a suitcase out onto the floor and tearing through the latest accumulation of stuff on her bed in a frenzy – seeming to live in a room-sized version of a 'doom drawer'.

HAMMERED

'I've already put it in the car!' Ellie shouts up after her, highly amused she's somehow become the 'organised' one – our digging duo a helpless situation of the blind leading the blind.

*

As we approach the final turning into the village, our nerves are tinged with guilt, we can't help but feel like we've cheated on our permission – sliding into Barry's DMs for a one-night stand via postcode – now making our return as dirty stop outs.

It's far too easy to get swept up in the temptation that a change of location will bring more luck. Our permission had presented us with treasure – if you count the speck and perhaps the pierced half groat? But in return we chose to stray to greener (or not so greener) pastures, without becoming properly acquainted with what's already right in front of us.

How dare we doubt these hallowed lands? Let's hope the gods aren't too upset with our misdemeanours among the rapeseed stubble – we've come crawling back with a tin full of buttons and a phobia of Portaloos, surely that's penance enough.

A field freshly freed from the clutches of crop starts things off with a blessing, containing delicate, short, wheat stubble – much to our relief. Just beyond our Tudor-buckle field, the permission opens up into a patchwork of arable, surrounding the continuation of the public footpath; this broad, rectangular field harbouring a short and highly promising stretch before it gets lost into a vast sea of swaying wheat.

'Bloody hell!' Ellie exasperates as her spade crunches solid ground, a mere few centimetres below the surface (to think we'd been let off the hook so easily). It's the beginning of another heatwave and we've got Janice on standby. But even the prospects of a blistering day and a field baked to smithereens can't extinguish our excitement to be back in the village.

'It'll be fine,' Ellie grunts, wiping perspiration from her brow with the back of her thin black, polyurethane work glove (kindly donated from her Dad's garage), adding a smear of dusty clay to the sweat gathering on her forehead. 'I'll just have to whittle.'

There was no way we were going to give up, if the weekend had taught us anything, it was that those who persevere, prosper. Even if we have to chip away at every damn signal in this godforsaken dust bowl, so be it. The hunt for a hammered is back on.

It's hard to describe this constant hunger we have for finding a hammered coin. What is it that makes these small discs of beaten silver so attractive? Maybe it's the appreciation for their beautifully engraved details: the abstract crescents and pellets forming the stylised kings of the early short crosses, the lombardic fonts that encircle them or the incredibly realistic heraldic coats of arms and imagery of the Tudor coinage? Perhaps it's the fact they are struck out of precious metal, emerging from the ground in near immaculate condition despite the passage of centuries. Or is it the opportunity they present to connect us to the people of medieval and Tudor England through the change that quite literally passed through their hands?

To be honest with you, we think it's a combination of all of the above. But, ultimately, finding another hammered is our chance to prove it wasn't just a one-off, to cement our position as real detectorists and creep ever closer to the seasoned veterans of the weekend past.

*

'Okay, it's in this,' Ellie calls to Lucie, we've been in the field about an hour and depressingly this is only hole number three – and not for lack of signals – the levering, whittling, chiselling of chunks out of their concretion, are taking an inordinate amount of time and effort. Ellie's about done-in, caked in dust and sweat, rolling the latest cannonball-sized lump in front of her, the pinpointer screaming at dead centre.

'Here we go,' she grunts, waving a hand back at Lucie, who wordlessly passes over her most recent Amazon purchase – the comedy trowel. This comically small tool is the result of Lucie's recent quest for the perfect 'cute' trowel to flick out pieces of pottery without getting her hands dusty, and a tool more useful for pointing delicate plasterwork than any kind of digging – much to Ellie's endless amusement and relentless teasing.

Gripping the flimsy handle of the inadequate tool, Ellie embodies the techniques of a stonemason, carefully applying pressure down to crack open this solid ball like an egg. It splits in two, slightly off-centre. Grudgingly, she does have to admit the comedy trowel has its uses. Checking again with the pinpointer, the larger half gets discarded, Ellie studying the split for any hint of an artefact. A sliver of metal catches her eye.

'Lucie!' she shouts.

'What …' Lucie replies from her expectant hover above.

'Get in here,' Ellie beckons, 'I think we've got something.'

'What is it?!'

'I'm not gonna jinx it … but it's good,' she teases.

Lucie settles into position above, phone ready to record the moment. Ellie grips the remaining lump between her hands, carefully squeezing and pulling apart the clod.

Lucie sucks in the breath she wasn't aware she was holding.

'It's a hammeeeeeerrrrreeeeedddd!'

The dense mud peels apart, beautifully, revealing a stamped silver reverse proudly beaming up at us both. It's perfect, crisp, and approximately circular with the characteristic thin and uneven edges of a hand-struck coin.

'I knew it,' Ellie can't keep the smile off her face, plucking the coin from its perch in awe. 'Who needs a digging weekender?'

1558, LONDON, ENGLAND

The last Tudor Monarch, the second ever Queen of England, and the first unmarried queen ascends to the English Throne. From birth, she's always been a disappointment, not the strong male heir desired by her father, and born into a country that couldn't imagine being ruled by a woman – ironically, this was also a country that would soon embrace this female ruler as a symbol of a 'Golden Age' of English history, that would even be named after her.

THINGS WE FOUND IN THE GROUND

We are, of course, talking about Elizabeth I, one of the most revered monarchs to ever rule over England, and a portrait we recognise instinctively from her iconic ruff, as Ellie carefully turns our new hammered between her fingertips.

As the last of Henry VIII's children to ascend to the throne – her sibling and half-sibling lasting a mere six and five years, respectively – Elizabeth could have accepted the pre-established gender roles of an inherently patriarchal society, ones reinforced by her own father's provisions to ensure she should lose her right to rule should she take a husband, but she didn't, she turned the tables on them and used her own gender as a weapon in her political arsenal.

In international and home politics, reputation has always been important, but never more so than for a single female ruler. Elizabeth navigated the misogynistic waters of royal politics with a careful strategy, likely harnessed through her love of chess and card games, keeping her fingerprints off the most explosive political choices of her reign as a result of her womanhood; much like her initial refusal to sign Mary, Queen of Scots' death warrant, claiming, 'my sex doth not permit it' (even if she did eventually change her mind and condemn poor ol' Mary). But her most ingenious move was to harness her reputation as the 'Virgin Queen' simultaneously symbolising her devotion to crown and people – strengthening the idea of her divine right to rule – and sticking a massive two fingers up to the patriarchy and her father.

But deep-rooted patriarchy wouldn't be the only toxic legacy left behind by Henry VIII, which threatened Elizabeth's reputation. England was also £227,000 in debt following Henry's expensive campaigns in France and Scotland, and its coinage still hadn't recovered from one of the largest debasements in English history. This, coupled with rising inflation as a result of a growing population, only spelt disaster for the new queen; especially with foreign traders refusing to accept the watered-down English currency, dealing only in gold.

Subsequently, with a gold shortage on her hands, and the reputation of the English monarchy at stake, Elizabeth had no choice but to issue a recoinage; on the precipice of an era of trade and expansion for the English empire – public confidence in English money was imperative. So, the year 1560 sees the sterling restored back into England's silver currency – and the new issues that followed were of a level of quality and power that had been missing from English currency for decades – as well as reinforcing Elizabeth's own reputation as a monarch here to lead her people into greatness.

Therefore, this threepence from 1573 is far more than lost change. It's a legacy of strength, stability and prosperity ushered in during Elizabeth's forty-five-year reign, and a symbol of a tenacious female ruler England has never forgotten.

*

Lucie's next weekly video call with her parents back home in New Zealand is filled with talks of fine ruffs, hammered silver and a very successful day out in the fields – a welcome change from the increasing COVID-19 restrictions of New Zealand's first national lockdown in over a year, after a single case was detected in the community, amid its ongoing self-isolation from the rest of the world.

'The finds tin was full!' This was no exaggeration on Lucie's part – Ellie could barely close the tin at the end of the dig – it was full with not only an Elizabeth I threepence, but a medieval belt mount, an eighteenth-century Dandy button, a George V halfpenny, a musket ball and a George III shilling forgery – not to mention the plethora of toasted seventeenth and eighteenth-century coinage.

'How come you found so much?' Karen asks, both of her parents enraptured by their daughter's discoveries. Her father, Paul, is reminded of his own vintage metal detector – a Geo-Electronics, Type C440 – bought after visiting the British Museum's *Treasures of Tutankhamun* exhibition of 1972, now gathering dust on top of a bookcase, in a country whose metal history doesn't stretch back much further than the nineteenth century.

'You've got to go back!' Paul encourages, reminiscing on days in his youth spent plucking hammered coins from the family farm in Lincolnshire, and enjoying the new shared experience, not of a global pandemic, but of finding history out in the fields.

*

Tentatively, we name this new field, The Field of Dreams, and the passage of the week before our next visit has never felt longer, broken up only by the delivery of a small eight-inch coil for the Vanquish – the best 'stubble basher' in the business – and an edge digger – a comedy trowel upgrade for Ellie. Nothing can stop us now. Well, apart from Ellie's consistently poor fashion choices when it comes to dressing suitably for the field.

'Why are you in shorts?' Lucie is speechless as Ellie turns up on her driveway for our next dig in a pair of retro, green and navy swimming trunks.

'It's like thirty degrees outside!' Ellie replies, exaggerating as usual – it's actually twenty-three degrees.

'Your legs are gonna get destroyed,' Lucie shudders, imagining nothing worse than scratched legs in the itchy stubble.

'It's hardly going to kill me,' Ellie laughs, willing to put her legs on the line for another chance in The Field of Dreams.

Our overspilling excitement to return to this now legendary field is revealed the moment Ellie jerks the handbrake on, before the Panda's even come to a complete stop. She's out the door and clattering through the boot, spade and detector lobbed onto the verge in her sheer eagerness. Throwing her yellow camera/dig bag around her neck, she grabs the spade and is halfway up the footpath before Lucie can say 'hammered coin'.

'It's been ploughed!' Ellie whoops, delighted, as our expectant field comes into view.

'What?!' Lucie shouts jogging up the path in glee.

A ploughed field to a detectorist is the same as a firm green to a golfer – the perfect playground. The farmer's plough is both friend and foe. Sometimes, all you need is a good plough in your favourite field and the abundance of signals will be like you've never dug there before. But reward doesn't come without risk. Every time the plough blade churns through the earth, the chance of it clipping an artefact, shearing a Roman brooch or tearing a hammered coin grows ever greater.

'C'mon!' Ellie beckons and we sprint.

HAMMERED

'She just keeps on giving,' Lucie shouts triumphantly as Ellie plucks a dark green 1900s Queen Victoria penny from just below the surface, merely a few steps into the dig.

'Field of dreams.' Ellie smirks. But is it the field? Or have we become far better detectorists? Better at understanding the Vanquish's bizarre little chirps and, more importantly, better at listening to the landscape and digesting the information presented to us through its dips and rises. This is an old public footpath, so of course we are going to find coins here, it's likely been used for centuries as a route of passage, but it's taken us months and months to earn the patience, perseverance and listening required to actually find them. In the beginning, we couldn't go for more than four hours, but now we won't stop digging until we've found something we are ecstatic to be leaving the field with. It might be a bit premature to say it (we have only had the one hammered out of here) but we think we've turned over a new leaf.

The next hole turns out to be the discarded lid from a tin of curried mackerel — giving Ellie visions of a diabolical farmer's snack mid-plough — so maybe we aren't quite experts yet.

'Pass us the batteries' Lucie beckons, the Vanquish requiring a steady supply of AAs to keep the search going, and using up its last beep on the mackerel tin.

'Aren't they in your backpack?' Ellie replies, alarm rising as Lucie empties its contents onto the hard earth — not a single AA battery in sight among the camera gear and crisp packets. We both look at each other in resolute silence.

'You better hope Janice has some.' Lucie fixes Ellie with a blank stare, thoroughly washing her hands of any AA responsibility — both knowing that the gear technician (aka Ellie) has let the team down.

Thankfully, Janice's battery supply turns out to be as bountiful as her tool selection, the Vanquish up and running in no time, after a brief rummage through her pantry — Ellie slightly puffed out from the jog there and back.

*

'Jesus.' Lucie grimaces, her ears nearly blown off by the high-pitched ringing of a strong *13–14* on the VDI, the new batteries adding some grunt to its demanding tones. Thankfully, a perk of our new tiny coil is that its smaller surface area is much better at pinpointing, so she only needs to swing over and deafen herself a few more times before confidently uttering our digging mantra. 'Dig here,' accompanied by a point of the foot.

Ellie drops to her knees very eagerly for someone braving the stubble in shorts. Lucie might have been right, her legs are ruined, but she'd never admit that, ignoring the raised scratches, pockmarks and dents that are creating a rather alarming looking stubble-rash across her exposed flesh – you can't say she isn't dedicated.

Much like Lucie's tiny coil, the digging team, too, is very happy with its recent upgrade, the new edge digger and pinpointer working in tandem, one chiselling out, the other discarding lumps of consolidated clay until … bingo … the latest chunk relinquished hits the jackpot.

'There's an edge!' Ellie calls, patiently waiting for Lucie to perch herself comfortably among the stubble to get that perfect angle for recording on her phone, pointing out the tantalising sliver of a thin, round looking artefact peeking out of the soil.

'Do you think it's …' Lucie trails off as she hits record.

'Don't jinx it!' Ellie grins, carefully peeling clumps of dry earth to reveal the artefact.

It emerges out of the soil, round, flat, and silver-looking, a fine crust of dirt obscuring its features.

'Is it a hammered? It's a hammered!' Ellie whispers, not daring to believe it, recently shamed by the trickery of a button and let's not mention the ring-pull (any detectorist will know our pain).

'What is it?' Lucie hushes, quiet, too, both of us too scared to voice our suspicions in case we somehow scare it off. She's desperate to take a closer look, confirm for herself, but too invested in her video to move from her spot.

Ellie turns it over. We each hold our breath, just waiting for the shank of a button to appear on the back and dash all of our hopes and dreams.

HAMMERED

'FUCK OFF,' Ellie draws in all the air her lungs can handle.

'WHHHHAAAAOOOOOOOORRR,' Lucie joins in, the solid cross and pellets on the reverse unmistakable – a design of English coinage absolutely iconic of the Middle Ages.

*

In the Middle Ages, for the first time since the Romans left Britain, the economy was on the up. It's hard to say explicitly that it had returned to the period of intensive growth experienced under Roman rule, but one thing was for certain – the monetary economy was making a comeback.

However, this unprecedented scale of trade in the thirteenth century that was transforming society – driving out the barter and trade economy and greasing the palms of merchants and traders with shiny silver pennies – was far from perfect. While the widespread circulation of precious metal created flourishing markets and developed industry, it also provided ample opportunity for unscrupulous individuals to make a quick buck. Known as 'coin clipping' (the act of shaving or snipping, small amounts of silver from the edges of coins to be melted down into ingots or reminted into new coins; leaving the original coin lightweight and undervalued) this criminal offence plagued English currency for centuries, prompting recoinage after recoinage in an attempt to keep the quality of circulating coins at an acceptable level.

This new discovery, our first-ever medieval hammered, brings us crashing into this world that saw the development and expansion of the English nation. A world of coin clippers, conquest, and a great recoinage, establishing a new pattern for the design and production of English coins that was to last for more than 200 years, and through eleven reigns.

*

'Is there a piece missing?' Ellie questions.

'What?!' Lucie replies.

And sure enough, upon closer inspection, what appeared to be a perfectly imperfect, handmade disc of silver, did indeed have a missing piece. Far too deliberately placed to be nicked by the plough, a quarter of the legend has been carefully snipped out, with great care taken to cut around the inner beading and ends of the solid cross.

'Do you think that's normal?' Ellie muses.

*

Edward I could be described as a highly militaristic king. He spent his early life fighting and winning battles for his father (Henry III) in the Second Baron's War and out on Crusade in the Holy Land. By the time of his coronation in 1274, he was a highly respected military victor determined to reinforce England's standing as a powerful nation.

But there were several obstacles standing in his way, and a large proportion of them revolved around the English currency. Much like the problems Elizabeth I faced centuries later, the quality of the circulating English currency was a mess. His father's previous recoinage had failed to thwart the coin clippers, and this prevalence of clipping was driving people to hoard the better quality coins in circulation, leaving only the worst coins passing hands. This simply wasn't acceptable, a low-grade currency only led to higher inflation and the deterrence of foreign trade; to be a strong nation, Edward needed a currency that could be relied on.

Plus, Edward needed money. His early reign was entirely absorbed by his conquest of Wales – which was still governed by a series of princedoms and did not recognise England's king as sovereign – and his extensive programme of castle building and infrastructure, to consolidate his victories, was racking up quite the debt. To Edward, a recoinage had never seemed more attractive, not only would this elevate English currency to a level necessary to further its developing trade, but it would also generate a handsome profit from the fee Edward charged for re-minting the currency – much-needed funding for his conquest aspirations.

HAMMERED

So commenced the Great Recoinage of 1279. But, unlike his predecessors, Edward took his recoinage one step further, overhauling the entire English currency system. Die production was changed, introducing more complex punches which elevated coin art; the naming of the individual moneyer within the legend, a practice dating back to Anglo-Saxon times, was removed; and three new denominations were introduced: the farthing, halfpenny and groat.

The new coins were stronger and better suited to a rapidly developing European nation, plus the variety of denominations available removed the need for pennies to be cut into halves and quarters to create small change; prompting the introduction of the solid long cross on the reverse, instead of the voided cross that had adorned the pennies of the previous century. In theory, this created fewer opportunities for the coin clippers, but how effective this was remained to be seen – we will remind you of the clear, clipping evidence present on our coin.

Regardless, this was one of the most noteworthy recoinages of the medieval period, remaining largely unchanged for the remainder of the Middle Ages, but it came at a cost. Edward's drive to squeeze maximum profit from the recoinage led to one of the most horrific acts to taint his reign. In one targeted operation, Edward had all those accused of coinage offences rounded up and persecuted, reaping a profit from the fines imposed upon them and the confiscation of their property. The main group to come under fire – at the time associated with being the primary moneylenders – were Jews. Edward had already prohibited the act of moneylending, which had recently crippled their industry, and now he set to further damage the Jewish population, disproportionately accusing them of coin crimes and executing those he deemed responsible – all while enjoying a profit of £36,000 from his 'great' recoinage.

So was the clipping present on our coin 'normal'? Prior to 1279, it could even have been described as commonplace, a grievance expressed by almost all of the medieval chronicles. But to be present here on a coin after Edward's Great Recoinage it bears a much deeper context, one that brings into question the effectiveness of his currency reforms and the murky reasonings behind the persecution of a minority.

*

Riding on a hammered high, the next find, less than a metre from our Edward I penny, turns out to be an 1862 Victorian 'bun head' penny, but the triumphant whoops and cheers as Ellie excavates the large green disc from the earth could have any onlookers fooled into thinking we've just found gold.

A run of halfpennies follows, a George III, William III and George V. 'Coin shooting' as Lucie calls it, swinging with purpose over our patch – the Vanquish simply an extension of her arm at this point – more in tune with both the land and machine than she's ever felt before. We've slipped into an easy rhythm, the finder and the excavator, working in tandem as one unit. Relieved of the pressure we felt on the group dig to find something, *anything*, of note, the mood was light, easy and utterly exhilarating. So naturally this makes way for some conversation.

'How's Katie?' Lucie inquires with a teasing grin, invested in the fruits of her dating-profile photo overhaul.

'Oh, um great!' Ellie replies never really one to excel at talking about her feelings, especially when the talking stage is heading into new territory, with plans made, beyond the app. 'We're actually going on a date this weekend.'

'Really! Where are you meeting up?'

Thankfully, before she can assemble her cluttered, nervous thoughts into any form of an eloquent reply, a buzzing in Ellie's pocket provides her with a welcome excuse to escape the interrogation into her new love life. Spying the caller ID she answers immediately.

'Hello! ... Yes ... of course ... see you soon.' Hanging up she turns to Lucie with a smile, 'Lady H wants to see us.'

It seems the village rumour mill (aka Janice) has been working overtime and our recent success in the fields has prompted a summons. It's been a satisfying dig, the finds tin bursting at the seams, and the afternoon sun has long been casting lengthy shadows against the ground. Time to see the good Lady.

This summons marks our second visit to the manor house, an honour likely fuelled by our long nerdy chats about history on our previous appointment. Straight from field to manor house, we plod up Lady H's drive, flint gravel crunching underfoot; this is the first time we've dropped in post-dig, unknowingly setting a precedent that will re-shape our future visits to the village.

Pausing halfway stretched to press the doorbell, Ellie catches sight of a small, white-green-and-pink painted wooden sign hanging from the door handle. 'I'm in the Walled Garden' it reads.

Lucie breathes a silent sigh of relief, thankful we don't have to enter the manor house in our wellies and risk scratching the mahogany dining table with the finds tin – well, Lucie has wellies, Ellie's still sporting a pair of rather trashed (no longer white) Reebok trainers.

Lady H is indeed pottering in her walled garden, her carefully curated haven of shaped box-topiary and formal flowerbeds – Ellie's personal favourite: the hedge clipped meticulously into the shape of a prancing unicorn. We find Lady H deadheading the roses, preening an immaculate border of full colour and fragrance, a simple pleasure for the Lady of the Manor.

The entire village seems to revolve around the centre of gravity that is her gentle aura; entranced into a firm respect and immeasurable fondness – none more so than Kieran, her land manager, faithfully going above and beyond the call of duty; often found making endless phone calls to BT as the latest phone-line disaster strikes, forever on the ride-on mower maintaining the grounds, and generally dropping everything for her call. He's a bit of a gentle giant of the village, his warm nature disguised by his bearded and tattooed appearance. In reality, he's just as loyal as his big, slobbery, labradoodle and bouncy cockapoo – a trio we often bump into on their daily walks round our Roman field.

'Girls, come with me!'

Just like last time, our conversation with Lady H branches off into a variety of intersecting tangents. Now committed into the latest, we find ourselves escorted through a small outbuilding and into a much wilder, informal, section of the garden, nestled between the village church and a tennis court.

'This is my very special path,' Lady H informs us, as we weave up a winding passage carefully mowed through the wildflowers and grasses that stretch almost waist high towards the dwindling sun – the upkeep of which is one of the many small projects she has entrusted to Kieran.

'Here we are,' she welcomes, waving her walking stick as a pointer as a small, ruinous, stable tucked away into the furthest corner of the garden emerges into sight – hidden by the gentle overhang of a large oak tree sprouting from the grounds of the churchyard. 'This is my favourite place to sit.'

We conclude our walk tucked snugly together on a leaning bench, unusually crafted from a fallen tree by a certain land manager, and positioned perfectly in front of the stable ruin to catch the last rays of the afternoon sun. A rather unlikely trio, the countryside unfolding before us.

'I'd quite like you both to have a go in there,' Lady H starts, swiftly descending into a long story of her curiosity in the presence of the peculiar landscaping in the field just beyond her garden fence. You could describe it as a sort of terracing – not too dissimilar to that you would find in a small Mediterranean vineyard. 'I've always wanted to get an archaeologist in,' she finishes off, giving the field a particular hard stare, as if its enigma has been personally impeding her.

'Well, we can certainly give it a go,' Ellie replies, never one to say no. 'We'd just have to get Adrian's permission first … He doesn't like us going near his sheep,' she explains at the quizzical turn of Lady H's head.

'His sheep?' she muses, entertained that such creatures are standing in the way of what happens on *her* land. She's particularly fond of the sheep, less so of their stubborn tenant farmer, but there's been sheep in the village, on these very fields, for centuries, and it's a sight she's grown used to out of her window.

'Maybe I can have a word …'

HAMMERED

Conversation finally comes back on track – not that we weren't enjoying any of the tangents – Ellie producing our finds tin, the hammered silver winking in the ebbing light.

'Oh, I say,' Lady H sparkles at the sight. 'I do like silver.' She winks. 'And who, may I ask –' peering into the face on our coin '– is this fine chap?'

'It's Edward I!' Ellie delights, and descends into a 'brief' splurge of his history.

'Is this … treasure?' Lady H hushes in a mock conspiratorial whisper, thrilled by all and every aspect following our 'speck' of a treasure find through the official channels (Ellie had to print out the treasure report for her archives), and all too excited for the prospect of more.

'Sadly not,' Lucie laughs, 'unless there's more hiding out there!'

'Well, say no more,' Lady H throws her hands in the air theatrically. 'I expect a dozen more next time – the 'village' hoard, I quite like the sound of that!'

Looking at each other as we chuckle, we easily see ourselves being added on to the list of people willing to do anything for Lady H. After all, metal-detecting the permission is as much for her as it is for us.

*

A week later – visit number three. Spurred on by Lady H's challenge, we are looking to make it a hat-trick. Surely, we can't be classed as rookies anymore? Not with two hammered coins under our belt? We decided it would probably be best to stake our claim with a third …

'WAIT!' Ellie calls, bending over, her nose close to the ground as if in prayer. 'It's there!' Parting the stubble stalks, a glint of silver reveals itself placed delicately on the surface by the last turn of the plough… another hammered.

'It's a hammmmyyyy!' Lucie sing-songs, doing a little triumphant jig.

The small coin is held reverently up to the light, our third hammered, a bent one this time, but a sign none the less – rookies who?

'Who do you think it is?' Lucie questions, bracing her phone against her knees to get a stable close-up of our new coin – the perfect moment for Roman Found to share later, introducing the encouraging, online detecting community to our recent silver success, finally getting the hang of this digging business and our social media presence.

'Hmm ...' Ellie ponders. 'It's hard to say.'

Medieval numismatics is a tricky world for the amateur. Coins, as one of the more widely distributed objects to bear images, made them the perfect vessel for propaganda, and at a time like the Middle Ages, where society struggled through famines, plagues, wars and even the instability of the monarchy; conveying stability and longevity was often the chosen message. Unfortunately, this meant the designs of medieval coins varied very little, the busts of the kings often looked the same – abstract and stylised, masking the flaws and problems behind the real monarchs.

'They're nearly all called Edward and they've all got the same choppy bob,' she concludes, pulling a snort out of Lucie who runs her hand through her own tousled bob.

8.

DEATH

SEPTEMBER 2021, LINCOLNSHIRE, ENGLAND
One thing you need to know about this hamlet that has become our second home, is that, like many other rural Lincolnshire villages, it was badly affected by the plague – not COVID-19 – the Black Death.

You could be easily fooled walking around the façade of crumbling limestone walls and ivy-clad houses, absorbing the notes of the morning chorus – a melodic symphony interrupted by the throaty clucks of the resident chickens – and losing yourself in the sweet and tangy aromas emerging from Janice's Aga. But this idyllic country village possesses a sombre undercurrent. What you see before you is a reincarnation, the harrowing rebuild of life itself. Beyond this charming appearance, are the scars of an earlier village, burnt into the landscape – all that remains of a desperate attempt to purge the community of a pestilence so dire, there were fears it would end humanity itself.

But not every community had the chance to rebuild. Here in our village, the settlement was large (and some would say, lucky) enough to endure the wrath of the Black Death. Out in the fields, however, on the far edge of our permission, existed a much smaller hamlet, which was not so lucky ...

1348, JUST NORTH OF OUR VILLAGE
A thick, woody, white smoke curls lazily from a small opening in the thatched roof of a cob-walled house, the sign of a simple broth left bubbling

DEATH

over the open fire. This timber, clay and straw home is the residence of a married couple in their late twenties – not too bad an age – and so far, a relatively typical day in the Middle Ages. Beatrice, the wife, is idly spinning yarn with her distaff, stirring the broth every now and then; her husband, Thomas, is out working the strip (his allocated piece of land). It's late July and the small hamlet they live in is slowly awakening with a flutter of activity, increasing steadily in fervour alongside the ripening ears of wheat, and approaching harvest.

No more than a dozen houses make up this agrarian community, a handful of families, couples, cattle and sheep, living life on the open field. It's an honest and ordinary existence, guided only by the solemn sermons and religious counsel offered by the portly, red-faced priest, often seen bumbling around their village church. Richard is his name, a man who has it easy tending to his small and devoted flock – after all, the biggest impropriety this community has ever faced has been the instance of a jilted marriage in the next village over. That is, until now.

Richard is muttering and distressed, his face redder than usual, his hands instinctively crossing over his chest, seeking comfort within his faith, a hastily sealed, parchment letter fallen from his grasp onto the flagstones below, its damning words forever burned into his mind.

For weeks, alarming stories have been rifling through the small spring line settlements clustered along this arable plain, spread by the merchants and traders attending the fairs and markets scattered across the county – the burgeoning English wool trade turning Lincolnshire into a hub of international commerce. These merchants, however, brought more than just silver for Lincoln cloth, sharing tales of a great 'pestilence' that had emerged abroad.

Today we know this 'pestilence' as Yersinia Pestis (Y. pestis): a deadly bacteria manifesting first as a continuous acute fever, or the emergence of a hard, black boil, known as a bubo, under the armpits or in the groin. The afflicted often fell into a stupor, coughing and spitting blood relentlessly until taking their final rattling breath, in some cases this could be the very same day as falling ill, others persisting on for a further three to five wretched days.

This scourge spread like wildfire through the sea lanes from its emergence in the vast grasslands and deserts of the Central Asiatic Plateau (specifically that of present-day Mongolia), decimating a claimed 90 per cent of the population of Constantinople, ravishing Turkey, Syria, Greece, Iraq and Iran, and entering an unsuspecting Europe with a ferocity, akin only to unpredictable doomsday events like Pompeii's eruption – Sicily, Genoa, Venice, and Pisa never stood a chance. And then it became landborne, spreading along the trade routes to take central Italy in less than half a year. France fell next, and while the rate of spread had slowed, the mortality rates were still unthinkable – in Avignon alone, one out of every two people died.

The news of this sickness circulated only as idle gossip in England, wrapped up in a false certainty that this was Europe's problem – it was never going to happen here – and quickly forgotten about as the latest tale of Robert's adultery in the village beyond was brought to the table. However, the looping, inked words, seared into Richard's mind revealed a different truth. This damning piece of parchment was a letter from the Bishop of Lincoln, John Gynewell, one of the many notices which had been received by every priest and every parish church in the diocese.

Confirming the imminent threat of this pestilence, John urged his priests to practise the power of prayer, to save the souls of their flocks through confession, and stave off the coming wrath of God by repenting all sins. Processions, sermons and special anti-plague prayers were to be held regularly, including a call to faith and confession dictated within this very letter, which was to be read out in plain, simple English to all. The end was coming, and the church was going to lead the way to salvation.

The bishop of Lincoln was one of the first to mount a religious response to the threat, an initiative quickly followed by the office of the Archbishop of Canterbury, on the order of Edward III – shortly after the plague takes its first steps onto English shores – issuing a widespread letter remembered notably for its very first opening word: Terribilis.

> 'Confess your sins to one another and pray for one another so that you may be healed'
>
> – James 5:16

Unsurprisingly, Richard's deliverance brings a dark shroud over the village, especially when accompanied by the onslaught of miserable

DEATH

rain that would quickly characterise the remainder of summer. For the following months, the church has never been busier, service after service, packed with attendees desperate to confess their sins.

Preachers also travel the countryside, delivering sermons and repentance, but they are the very few who do, most choosing to isolate within their communities in fear. Panic muddies what little information is available, it's hard to know where the infection has spread and if there are any survivors?

Entering the new year is a grim state of affairs, the plague has been running rampant since the first Gasconian ship docked into the port of Melcombe on the Dorset coast of August the year before. Edward III has lost his 15-year-old daughter, and the surrounding fields are being converted into cemeteries to contain the overspilling deaths in London.

Here in the village, harvest is only a few months away, the wheat is growing strong and despite the gripping fear, the community is looking forward to the hard work ahead, providing a much-needed boost of additional income. Yet, one of the strips in the open field – Thomas's – hasn't been tended to for a couple of days. He hasn't been seen around the village, and neither has his wife, Beatrice, their house quiet, offering only the occasional rattling cough and gasping splutter into the country air.

There wouldn't be a harvest season in the year of 1349, instead the crops rotted in the fields, left without a community to gather the wheat.

*

The busiest and most fleeting time of the year begins around September – for both farmers and detectorists alike. Marked by the constant humming of combine harvesters and trundling tractors holding up the traffic on the country lanes, harvest season sees the farms spring into life, working on tight windows and narrow margins to reap the very best productivity rates. Sadly, this means a field can be on a swift rotation, harvested, ploughed and drilled within a mere few weeks, making way for the waiting winter crop.

This is the predicament we find ourselves in; it seems the whole estate has been harvested overnight by Stan and his farmhands, we're suddenly spoilt for choice, and it's a very short window of opportunity.

There's one piece of land which has caught our eye, a vast arable plain to the north of the village – one of the biggest expanses of uninterrupted field on our whole known permission. Its swaying heads of wheat have been jeering at us for weeks from the Field of Dreams, and it's also the subject of village myth, a fabled land muttered about in passing by Kieran in the manor house kitchen and whispered between pews at Sunday service. All fields are hiding history, and if the tales are to be believed, this one just happens to be hiding the remains of a deserted medieval village – unscheduled, of course – and for the first time since we've started detecting in the village, it was sans wheat.

But before we dare to venture any further and step foot in these acclaimed fields, it's important to mention we aren't breaking any laws. There are over 3,000 deserted medieval villages in the English countryside, many still unknown. The most significant ones are scheduled, protected by law to prevent members of the public disturbing the archaeology (and publicly searchable on the National Heritage List for England). But a vast number are small, poorly documented or already muddied by later land uses – such as ploughing. This is what we have here, an 'insignificant' village, ploughed out each year, with every subsequent pass breaking the archaeology down even further and de-stratifying the context. In these instances, metal detecting is one of the only ways to salvage the stories lost to the soil, gathering information spread thinner with each pass.

Luckily for us, harvest has arrived at the perfect time. Ellie's got a week off work and you can bet every minute of it will be spent in the fields.

*

'Crikey.' Lucie whistles, the sheer scale of the field only hitting us as we reach the crest of the sloping public footpath leading up to it. 'She's HUGE.'

'Fucking hell, where are we going to start?' Ellie groans, a few paces behind, weighed down by all our gear in the blazing sun. Looking

DEATH

across the swathe of freshly cultivated land, a heat mirage dances across the horizon, her vision becoming hazier the further she squints into the distance, trying, and failing, to spot the furthest boundary of this vast endless expanse.

We hadn't quite realised, packing the Panda, just how open this field was. It's essentially a desert, devoid of any stand-out features and seemingly life itself. Maybe we should have thrown in some extra bottles of water. Ellie's half expecting a tumbleweed to roll by.

'Well, you gotta start somewhere.' Lucie shrugs, stepping detector first into the nearest patch of cleared dirt.

Immediately, she's deafened by a signal. A mere fraction away from the field margin, and millimetres from being stepped on.

'There you go!' she announces, rather pleased. What are the chances?

'Unbelievable,' Ellie chortles, kneeling down to discover that the spade she's dragged up the public footpath is useless – the field proving desert-like in body as well as spirit – the soil resembling the consistency and texture of fine sand or dry biscuit crumb. Digging has been replaced with sifting; she'd have been better off bringing the soil sieve out of retirement.

'Whatever it is, it's not very deep,' Ellie rats around in the dirt, clawing through the soil/sand, pinpointer screaming, prompting Lucie to stoop over in anticipation.

A roughly rectangular fragment, pale green in colour emerges from the earth, broken on several edges, with the remnants of a small junction protruding out at a right angle, making a sort of 'L' shape. It's plain on one side, the other outlined by a variety of dot and circle markings.

'What the bloody hell's that?' Lucie exclaims.

'I want to say … Saxon? …' Ellie speculates, the markings stirring thoughts of recognition, 'but *what* it is … I have absolutely no idea.' She shrugs.

*

Thankfully, the following week, Laura provides the answer to Lucie's question. Ellie's become the latest recruit to her weekly

THINGS WE FOUND IN THE GROUND

Friday afternoon self-recording sessions held in the Lincolnshire County Council's 1960s office block – which is round the corner and decidedly less grand than the ex-Georgian mansion of our first visit. It's everything you would expect from a mid-century office – open-plan, hot desks, large windows – even with its clinical, white-washed modernisation. On the approved visitors list (confirmed via email each week), Ellie gets buzzed through reception, following a narrow passageway through the office-space marked by filing cabinets and desk partitions to 'Meeting Room 2' in the left-hand corner – the council workers, used to the diversity of visitors Laura attracts, unfazed by her appearance.

'Anything exciting this week?' Ellie wiggles her eyebrows, her standard opening line upon entering through the glass door and taking a seat at the oversized conference table – early for once. She knows full well Laura can't really tell her if there is anything mind-blowing to share, but cheekily pushes the boundaries anyway, in the hopes of a display of nice Roman brooches or gilded, Anglo-Saxon, hooked tags to ogle over.

'Maybe ...' Laura replies cryptically, amused with their archaeology banter, but firmly keeping her secrets under her hat as always. 'Have you had anything?' she counters.

'Some bits ...' Ellie replies, pulling our strange fragment out of her bag, 'What do you make of this?'

Laura's eyes light up as they always do when something Anglo-Saxon is brought to the table – her special interest, and professional field of study. 'It's a girdle-hanger fragment,' she replies instantly, turning it carefully over and peering under her glasses, 'Anglo-Saxon,' she confirms, 'where did you find this?'

Her eyes betray her excitement at our discovery, and even more so when Ellie brings a map up on her phone, likely knowing more than a few archaeological secrets about the area.

You've probably never heard of a 'girdle-hanger' before – we certainly hadn't – and that's not surprising considering they are a very specific type of grave good (personal possessions and artefacts intentionally buried with the dead) that only appear in up to 5 per cent of Anglo-Saxon female graves from the fifth to sixth centuries, and are, therefore, cripplingly under-researched. The complete artefact takes the form of a decorated, ancient key; a flat pendant thought to imitate a type known as a 'T-Key', dating back to the Iron Age. Yet, often only around two millimetres thick, made out of copper alloy, and with embellishing prongs and decorated lobes, these objects are far from functional.

As a result, it is believed that girdle-hangers transcended the need for function, and instead are a visual signifier of a specific role or person within a community – their main occurrence in female graves pointing us towards being used in a predominantly feminine role (although it's also important to note the likelihood of flexibility within Anglo-Saxon gender identities). They would have hung from the wearer's belt or girdle (hence the name), at the left hip, as an important piece of their identity, which saw the girdle-hanger restored instead of replaced in any instance of damage. This shows the value placed on the individual girdle-hanger, not simply the object as a whole, but the *specific* one possessed by the wearer – so significant they even took it to the grave.

We might never know the exact role these girdle-hanger wearers held within their early Anglo-Saxon communities, appearing in both high status and common burials. But it has been suggested they were worn by those possessing medical knowledge, perhaps even those dealing with birth and death – symbolically wearing the keys that controlled the gateway between this realm and the next. The girdle-hanger is just one of the many mysteries left beneath the soil – a world of artefacts and curiosities which history didn't bother to record – and it's not always possible to understand their purpose, take the Roman Dodecahedron, a twelve-sided, hollow polyhedron, cast from copper-alloy to contain different-sized circular holes and a variety of protruding knobs, which remains a much debated enigma. But in many ways this air of mystery only adds to the allure of these objects, and drums up a primal intrigue deep within us, intoxicating in a world where we can learn almost anything with a few quick strokes on Google.

'Will you let me know if anything else like this comes up?' Laura asks. It's not unheard of for a detectorist to stumble across a burial site, the location of so many ancient cemeteries and graves have been lost across time. Normally, it's only the odd horse's tooth and sheep's bone that gets churned up by the plough, but it's important to know what to look out for, to recognise which artefacts appear as grave goods and ensure they get recorded so these sites are re-found – even if it takes a substantial amount of time to gather enough evidence. And, of course, to stop immediately if anything appears under the shovel which suggests you've accidentally uncovered a grave – be it a cremation urn or a suspicious piece of bone.

*

With our first find safely nestled in the finds tin, we make the mistake of looking back up from our position crouched in the dirt, engulfed instantly by the arid chasm of virgin land, and trying desperately not to be overwhelmed by the huge task in front of us – one about thirty football pitches huge.

'If that's Saxon ...' Lucie trails off.

'There's gotta be more here,' Ellie finishes, her eyes already scanning around this patch of land, trying to pull as much information as possible from what little features lie before us. Reading the landscape often reveals crucial clues to its use and the type of historic activity that could have been enacted across its surface. A roughly straight, grassy farm track bisects the field into two, following the undulations of the land and disappearing off into the hedgeline in the far distance. An uncultivated, wild grass scrubland and manure heap stands at the highest crest – midway down the field – providing a good strategic vantage point and likely the best location for any kind of settlement. This dissects the left half of the field into two distinct portions: the small flat, slightly sloping rectangle we are currently standing on, and a much larger section we can't entirely make out from our position – obscured by the scrub and slightly steaming manure – we've essentially taken on three fields in one.

By some act of blind luck or divine intervention, Lucie's brash step into the smallest section of the three has mercifully given us an area to

DEATH

start – a place to settle into our new surroundings – a promising Anglo-Saxon fragment already distilling some of our unsettled anxiety. Time to get to work.

'What about a seven?' Lucie calls, unable to leave this tiny target which has captured her attention.

'A seven …' Ellie scoffs, forever bemused by Lucie's innate ability to find the smallest of targets – often leaving her with the task of searching for a proverbial needle in a haystack.

'Yeah, I think we should look for it,' Lucie announces – the royal 'we' meaning Ellie should get onto her hands and knees and look for it, while Lucie watches.

Huffing, Ellie lies down yet again, getting up close and personal with the dust, unhappy with the signal she's been sent to look for, but never able to say no – the curiosity too great, what if this time it actually is treasure and not just a minuscule fragment of foil leftover from a rambler's lunch stop.

The pinpointer immediately screams to attention, whatever it is, it's here sculling a mere few centimetres below the surface, just waiting to be found. Poking around with her fingertips, Ellie moves the dirt and straw around with an almost scientific precision. Much to Lucie's satisfaction, like a dinosaur fossil being brushed from the loose earth, a silvery grey coin no bigger than a button emerges through the dry, sandy soil, eliciting a resounding gasp from both of us.

'No fucking way,' Ellie breathes, Lucie's intuition being proved right yet again.

Sitting at the base of the well Ellie's formed in the surface of the field, not unlike that made by bakers into flour, the image of a tiny, yet cleanly struck, prehistoric bird is frozen as if mid-flight. Its claws hanging, grasping at something just off the edge of the flan, long plumes of feathers springing from a row of dots on its back like the spikes of a porcupine, its long curved, stork-like beak encircling an annulet.

We daren't touch it. Not for a long moment.

'That's *old*.' Ellie exhales, gingerly lifting it from its perch with trembling fingers.

THINGS WE FOUND IN THE GROUND

'I've never seen anything like it,' Lucie gushes, poring over the coin sitting in Ellie's dusty hands.

Flipping it over, we see that the reverse resembles the abstract face of a dice, five annulets, infilled by a pattern of pellets and enclosed within a square border of closely linked dots. The two sides so distinctly different, yet connected through the language of mark making.

We have to know what it is immediately, turning to Google to reveal its identity, pushing our flaky mobile-data reception to its limits.

'A sceat!' Lucie shouts, landing on a page filled with mythical beasts, strange geometric symbols and abstract runes. Our coin isn't as prehistoric as it had us believe, instead emerging from the muddled years of early Anglo-Saxon Britain.

'This might be my favourite find yet.' Lucie looks to the sceat in awe – a newfound obsession unlocked.

*

Sceattas – as they are formally known – represent an odd and relatively unknown numismatic period in Anglo-Saxon history; the return of the monetary economy in the late-seventh to mid-eighth centuries after its collapse following the withdrawal of Roman rule.

Prior to this, the Anglo-Saxons had only dabbled with the development of coins, producing a limited gold coinage that stylistically borrowed from Roman coinage to embed a sense of smooth succession and play into the 'Romanitas' (the spirit and fond memory of Rome) still circulating among the Britons – and Romans – left behind. Economically, there wasn't much need to produce a coinage, as communities were surviving through barter and trade, and any foreign money brought into Britain largely ended up being used as bullion or transformed into jewellery.

But the year 680 CE saw a pivotal shift for Britain as new silver coinage flooded in through the south and eastern parts of the country – the sceattas – minted both here in England and by our North Sea trading partner, the Netherlands, as a way to trade and exchange silver bullion. This simultaneously replenished Britain's depleted silver resources while also signifying the prolific importance of Anglo-Netherlands trade at this time. Our type in particular – a series E 'plumed bird' continental issue – was minted in the Netherlands.

Today, they appear in burials, urban and rural settlements, and seemingly isolated losses in the open country – a clear indicator that this coinage had great commercial uses. Yet no one knows what value it carried or even the true meaning behind its iconography; but religion is believed to have been a key political factor behind the development of the currency, following the wave brought in by the conversion to Christianity – begun in 595 CE, after St Augustine arrived on a Christian mission from Pope Gregory I. The wide range of images they were minted in – the birds, the four-legged beasts, the writhing serpents, spiky-haired busts, god-like human figures, horned death masks, votive standards, and the myriad of crosses – combine imagery from Christian sources with Roman, Frankish, Byzantine, and pagan roots, quite the unconventional blend. But perhaps this was the entire point? – a way of reinforcing the Christian message, while also suggesting an element of continuity from the old ways.

These sceats didn't stick around for too long, lasting around a century, their types diluting over the years to become more and more abstracted, eventually reformed into the silver penny which would remain the main coin type in England for half a millennia. They are a unique and often overlooked ancestor of English coinage, and an ongoing mystery, with only a limited number on record – added to occasionally by the odd detectorist stumbling across one in the field.

*

'That's Saxon find number two' Ellie sounds, voicing the weight of our discoveries. We thought we'd be discovering the story of the Middle Ages in these fields, but instead we've stumbled across the tale of a thriving community, one which occupied these lands since at least

THINGS WE FOUND IN THE GROUND

Anglo-Saxon times – a village evolved over countless years, nurturing dozens of lives, until a deadly bacteria emerging over 4,000 miles away erased these centuries of existence from this arable plain.

It's a story more complex than we ever imagined and we can't help but get entangled in its web. We've barely even covered a tenth of this field, fossicking around on the outskirts of the deserted village, pulling up a small scattering of grotty, indistinguishable Romans for the rest of the day – hinting even further at the depth of habitation which existed on this site.

One day, as expected, proves to barely scrape the field margins, nightfall driving us home reluctantly, gone 9 p.m. – long past any notion of teatime – leaving the fields with a promise, we would be back again in the morning.

*

Finally, evidence of medieval life begins to present itself in the plough. We've ventured deeper into the fields, curious to see what lies beyond the scrubland, discovering a sweeping slope leading into a small valley. The village is more prominent here, reduced to chunks of stone, sherds of green-glaze pottery, fragments of shelly ware, and wedges of tile – all churned into a sea of brown earth and leftover straw.

We are in our element. This has to be the heart of the settlement. Within an hour Ellie's run out of pockets in her jazzy patterned, green, grey and orange 1990s shorts, weighted down by too many pottery sherds – although, let's be honest, can you ever have too many?

'ELLIE!' Lucie suddenly shouts, gasping like she's stumbled across a hoard of Anglo-Saxon gold.

'WHAT?! WHAT?!' Ellie replies running over, trying not to lose any of her carefully collected sherds in the process.

'Don't kill me,' Lucie holds up her hands in admission, 'but LOOK at that handle,' reaching down and pulling the largest chunk of medieval pottery Ellie's ever seen from the depths of the plough.

'That's a BEAST!' Ellie cries. And it is, it's an almost complete section of green-glaze jug handle, finely fluted with striations running

DEATH

the length of it, and covered in a myriad of earthy tones as a result of an uneven medieval firing. It's the pottery find of dreams. Ellie does her best not to hate Lucie for it.

We do try not to get too distracted by the wealth of pottery we've stumbled across – which is hard – the tactility of each sherd appealing irresistibly to us as makers. Used on a daily basis throughout history, pottery does tend to be a common field-walking find (it was brought to Britain millennia before metalworking) and despite bearing very little monetary value, the craftsmanship behind every piece bears a historical resonance that is difficult to ignore: this ancient craft is credited with being one of humanity's earliest inventions, and an important introduction to our isle around 4000 BCE which marked a shift from hunter-gatherer to settled farmer.

Unable to switch off this instinctive desire to search and hoard, we are often led astray by these easily found historical treasures accumulated on the surface, even though the hard-earned discoveries that lie under the ground have proven themselves to be the most rewarding. But you'll be pleased to hear some digging does get done. This new slope actually proves to be full of signals, the vast majority small offcuts of lead, another major sign of medieval activity, but the Middle Ages aren't the only occupiers of this land clamouring for their stories to be heard.

'Ellie! Dig this one!' Lucie calls out to Ellie who is busy pottery hunting further down the slope, a solid *16* on the Vanquish demanding to be found.

Sifting through the straw and rubble, the pinpointer, too, insists on discovery, shrieking its directions into the air.

'ROMAN!' A call the village will be familiar with by now.

But this Roman is unlike the others, materialising into the dwindling light is Rome's so-called 'greatest' Emperor – the one who reunited the empire under one ruler for the first time in nearly eighty years – Flavius Valerius Constantinus, better known as Constantine the Great.

First impressions are struck in the form of a strong, militaristic and stable ruler, Constantine's helmeted and cuirassed bust exuding confidence and power through the traces of dirt dusted across the surface of our coin. The reverse only further imbues this sense of stability and permanence to a reign we are clearly meant to deify, commemorating his vows for a prosperous twenty years on a votive altar underneath the celestial globe and stars – suggesting Constantine has secured the validation of God himself. It's one of the first in a series of more ambiguous, Christian-leaning reverses which would soon dominate Roman coinage, and an important reminder of Constantine's conversion to Christianity – becoming Rome's first Christian Emperor – a religious turning point that would reshape the future of the empire.

Large, bronze and silver-washed, this follis, originally minted in Trier around 321–323 CE, still carries the weight and message, *Beata Tranqvillitas*, or 'Blessed Tranquillity' – a blatant example of imperial propaganda designed to provoke respect and awe within every palm it was passed to – still working over 1,500 years later. Without a doubt, it's the best Roman coin we've found yet, and a rather unexpected find of the day. And one thing's become absolutely certain – this area needs further investigation.

*

By the third day of digging, we've come to the realisation that this might be one day too many. It's increasingly harder to heave our weary bodies out of bed in the morning. Our muscles cramp up from the endless traverse of an unrelenting environment and prolonged heat exposure. But here we are, tools in hand, succumbing to the elements once again. Determined to work the hell out of this small, productive slope.

Among the pottery sherds, small targets start to make themselves known, Lucie locking into some kind of detecting flow state as find after find fills our trusty tin.

BEEEEPPP – a floral Medieval belt mount. *BEEPPPBBEEEEEPPPP* – its more utilitarian, square counterpart. *BEEEP* – a fragment of lead. *BEEEPBEEEEEEPPPBEEEEP* – another lead fragment, this time bearing a strange incision, scratched into its surface.

DEATH

'Do you think we've uncovered a hotspot?' Lucie suggests optimistically.

If there was any time to unleash gridding, it is now. This is the secret weapon in the detectorist's arsenal – a tried and tested technique, consisting of walking regular straight lines from all angles, covering every inch of the target surface. Easy, methodical and a way of ensuring nothing is being missed, even if it's a boring way to spend your time.

'I'll grid the slope,' she announces, the hard glint of determination shining in her eyes.

Another signal rings up a few steps into her new line. It's consistent, loud, in the low teens on the VDI, not unlike the ones we've been digging all morning.

'Ellie!' She calls – it's time to dig.

'More lead!' Ellie reports, the excavation quick and efficient, the artefact only a few centimetres below the plough and readily sniffed out by the pinpointer.

'Anything interesting?' Lucie queries, her mind already on the next target, pacing out a few more steps down the line, swinging low and slow, only half listening to Ellie's reply, her full attention on the chirps and beeps coming through her headphones. She pauses to flick a piece of green-glaze from the soil, catching sight of Ellie over her shoulder diligently rearranging the finds tin to make space for the newly acquired fragment of lead.

'LUCIE!' Ellie shouts suddenly and with urgency, catching Lucie off-guard, who whirls back around in an instant.

'They match!' Ellie follows up, looking mildly frantic, still crouched in the dirt over the finds tin.

'What do?' Lucie calls tentatively, not wanting to move from her spot, and lose her line, unless absolutely necessary.

'The lead fragments! It's two halves!'

'Two halves of what?' So long for the line.

On the open lid of the finds tin, Ellie rearranges the two pieces of lead, the twisted, jagged ends meeting in the middle to form a complete, slightly crude, crucifix. The faint, incised, lines of decoration visible on both halves, distinctly made by the same lightness of hand, and meeting with a certainty far from coincidence.

'Are you impressed?' Ellie beams, looking down at the reunited pieces.

'I'm impressed I found them,' Lucie smirks.

Ellie rolls her eyes.

'Yes, I'm glad you keep every scrap of lead,' Lucie laughs, 'but what is it?'

1349, JUST NORTH OF OUR VILLAGE

The church lies still, carcasses of sheep rot alongside the wheat, and rain patters relentlessly onto the roofs of empty houses. In the short space of two years, Britain has lost somewhere between a third and a half of its population. But the plague has taken more than the lives of the occupants in this hamlet, it's infected the survivors too, embedding a blankness behind their eyes; the fear of death long-removed by the sheer repetitious volume of it experienced over the last few weeks.

Previously, death had been an important passage, and part of life. It was a public occasion, involving a priest, the family, and the swirling void of demons, dangling the powers of temptation over those teetering on the brink between this life and the next. Prayer and confession was the only way to ensure the safe journey of a soul, the deathbed providing the final chance for all sinners to lessen their time spent in purgatory, and the reassurance the family needed that they had done everything within their power. A 'good death' was longed for in the Middle Ages – a well-prepared ritual – but there were no 'good deaths' to be found within the plague, only the gnawing realisation that God had abandoned mankind.

Richard, the priest, is one of the few souls left there, his bumbling charm lost among the vacancy of the village, weighted down by the burden of the deathbeds he couldn't attend – the quantity and speed of deaths, long beyond the work of a single man, even a man of God. As soldiers on the frontline, the clergy have taken heavy losses; 60 per cent of all permanent clergy died in Lincoln, losing 40 per cent overall in the wider diocese, with many unaccounted for – losing their faith and abandoning their flocks. With this absence of priests, confession is ordered to be

DEATH

received by any layman or woman – the unattainable power of religion slipping.

Trying to ignore the damning silence which threatens to overwhelm him, Richard, dutifully, heads towards one of the remaining occupied houses. He's never heard the countryside so quiet before – with too much suffering to announce, they've long given up ringing the death bells. Raising his hand to knock resignedly on the rough, wooden door before him, he pauses, hearing its dwellers stirring within, and then the distinctive, condemning sound of the death rattle on the other side.

The fever that grips those fallen foul to the plague, is more violent and powerful than any experienced in living memory. Confession – even with the hard-to-come-by help of a priest – isn't often attained, the sufferer too delirious and unresponsive to form coherent thoughts, let alone sentences. It's impossible to imagine how desperate those times must have been for the families, losing their loved ones both physically and spiritually. Tormented by the thought of their soul suffering eternal damnation, you would have done everything humanely possible to grant them absolution. In this case, in the latest damned house in the hamlet, that meant hastily shearing a crude cross out of lead, pressing it within the hurriedly wrapped folds of the death shroud, and praying for their salvation from a God who you aren't certain exists anymore – their body another addition to the overcrowded graveyard, their neighbours, too, bearing small, crude, lead symbols – one final hope, sent down into the earth. In Richard's wearisome eyes, there have been far too many taken from this village who weren't afforded the chance to repent.

Born from the devastation was revolution – funny how a global pandemic can rewrite history and create new opportunities. The survivors – just shy of over 50 per cent of the population – emerging changed.

The peasants were starting to get ideas about which particular piece of land they wanted to farm, and how much money they should work for. This shift of economic power goes down badly with the ruling elite, who pass various ordinances to try and retain the order of pre-plague England. But faced with an abundance of land and a shortage of labour, the only way to reset the balance was to adapt; maybe even employ women to work in the fields, allow daughters to inherit tenancies and landholdings, and embrace new landowners wanting to climb the social ladder.

Religion doesn't emerge unscathed either. The majority of its senior clergy have perished and there was a distinct idea that the new members weren't cut from the same cloth as the old flock – so to speak. A horrific death toll such as this one was going to test people's faith, but it also drew people closer to God in a way that was different from before, more private and less institutionalised.

For our hamlet, already a smaller settlement than its neighbours, it was simply abandoned, not deemed worthy of renewal; what few survivors were absorbed by the surrounding villages, while the timber and stone was plundered. A settlement that has occupied this landscape for the best part of three-quarters of a millennia, suddenly reduced to rubble and ruin, ploughed out into the soil as if it had never been there – life, inevitably, moving on.

*

The week after our three-day-stint in the fields, we excitedly park up in the village for round two, revived from a long weekend of rest. Eagerness spills out of the car with all our gear, unable to talk about anything more than our frantic need to get digging.

'Should we search the opposite slope to where the lead cross came up?' Lucie ponders, packing her bag ready for the short hike ahead.

'We've got to search *everywhere!*' Ellie replies, handing Lucie the Vanquish and pulling her finds bag over her head.

Supplies secured to our backs, we make the familiar walk through the Buckle Field, grass lapping at our feet as we hike the worn-in farm track past the Field of Dreams. At the top of the rise, our field slowly comes into view …

'Shit …' Ellie says in disbelief. 'Stan's drilled it.' The field before us a new texture, seeded into uniformed straight rows harbouring the next cereal crop.

'I wanted to go sceat hunting!' Lucie cries.

'Looks like we're back on pasture,' Ellie mutters glumly.

DEATH

As soon as harvest had begun it was over, our plans shattered as if they, too, had been struck hard by the plough, the endless agricultural churn consuming the lost village once more into its earthy depths. Who knows which fragments it will choose to relinquish next year…

9.
SHEEP

NOVEMBER 2021, LINCOLNSHIRE, ENGLAND
We've made a breakthrough with one particular tenant farmer on the estate – Adrian – the owner of the sheep Lady H is so fond of. Maybe she's had a word, or maybe we've simply worn him down enough and he's realised we aren't going anywhere – all of a sudden daring to let us near his precious sheep flock, a feat he wouldn't have dreamed of last season.

'Christ, Adrian's given us the green light,' Ellie announces in disbelief, sliding her phone back into her pocket.

'To detect alongside his sheep? That's wonderful news!' Lucie delights.

'Well, what's left of them …' Ellie winces, uncertain how to break the unfortunate news to Lucie, conflicted over her feelings towards this new opportunity – the result of a 'great escape'. Adrian's cherished flock had broken free of their constraints, outmanoeuvred a wooden fence, swarmed the village, and regrettably ended up feasting on a hedgerow of toxic yew.

'He's had quite enough of his "useless ewes",' Ellie recites, reaching the dark end to this rather sad tale.

'Jesus,' Lucie mutters.

It might not have ended too well for the poor sheep – as little as one half, to two pounds of yew can be fatal to them – but we try not to think too deeply about the circumstances under which we suddenly find ourselves in, granted free reign over this vast pasture that has taunted us for months.

*

'This is where we're going to find gold,' Lucie announces into the biting wind and empty plain of our newly acquired pasture field. Behind her, Ellie's halfway over the metal farm gate, laden down with her spade and finds bag.

'Lucie! You really shouldn't say stuff like that out loud,' Ellie objects, tossing the spade into the short grass and making the final dismount with a small grunt, firmly believing it's best not to upset the metal-detecting gods when every outing hinges on chance – much like you know, to never count your money at the table.

'I know, but this is different, it's a given,' Lucie replies, feeling it in her bones.

'It's bad luck,' Ellie complains, taking in the long sweep of this truly daunting looking field. She's grown accustomed to Lucie's blurted declarations, but talks of gold are a dance too close with fate and she is reluctant to indulge in such fantasies any further for fear of disappointment – an assessment proved wise as we clamber, spent, back over the metal farm gate many hours later, forty holes dug, thirty-three of them shotgun shells, five nails and two ineligible eighteenth-century halfpennies. A whole lot of nothing to show for our troubles; maybe we'd be better off tackling a different section of pasture. The field is cursed. Lucie should have kept her mouth shut.

*

It's research and not feelings that determine our digging direction for the day. Ellie's still feeling jaded by the so-called 'gold field', offering up news of a promising-looking public footpath she's identified from old Ordnance Survey maps, running at the height of the new pasture instead.

Public footpaths have served us well so far, and this one begins at the nucleus of the village, cutting past the manor house and straight

SHEEP

up the hill towards the main road. For a village cut off by an escarpment there are only so many ways in and out – winding arteries connecting to the outside world.

Today, there's only one road to the village, but how do we know this is the original route of passage? Maybe the answer lies in the scars carved into the hillside, in the cut-aways and tracks now relegated as public footpaths. We've identified six interlocking fields, which make up the patchwork of possible entry points into the village; a long strip centred around one, small, tree-lined field that lies directly above the manor house and the church – surely the heart of trade and visitation to the settlement. We'd be foolish not to investigate.

Naturally, investigating doesn't prove to be that simple, the straggling survivors of Adrian's flock are grazing away in the main field we've earmarked for examination – out of respect and not wanting to damage our newfound farmer-detectorist relationship, we choose to bypass, hopping a leaning wooden stile in the adjacent field, and heading straight up. Ellie's trainers slipping occasionally on the mulchy leaf matter and damp grass.

'Blimey,' she murmurs as we approach the steep slope looming above us – more sheer and vertical than we could have ever comprehended from the village.

'See you at the top,' Lucie grimaces, brashly deciding to swing her way up.

Ellie groans and begins the arduous drag up the hill, trying not to look back at the beautifully flat land we've left behind us, and praying to God that Lucie doesn't find a signal on this extreme gradient – she does, leaving Ellie struggling to keep her footing and dig on the horizontal at the same time.

Admittedly it's not a particularly far distance to climb, but it does require a moment to sit down upon reaching the crest – the sheer hike testing our fitness more than we anticipated. We are above the treetops, looking down on a village drenched in an autumnal palette, the last of the leaves swaying in a biting breeze, magnified to a gale here on the edge of the precipice. A dusting of green has taken root across the foreground, spreading among the deserted medieval village and the Field of Dreams – all the arable within our grasp, out of bounds for the approaching winter. We can't help but wonder how far the permission stretches, nothing disrupts the expansive Lincolnshire horizon, fields we've never seen before appear like postage stamps beckoning in the far distance.

'The footpath's over here!' Ellie calls, struggling back to her feet, eager to get moving again before the cold invades our bones irreparably – both of us momentarily forgetting what had brought us up here in the first place.

Grudgingly pulling herself away from the view, Lucie follows suit, gaining a brief glimmer of motivation from the narrow search area provided by Ellie's footpath research – we won't be traipsing up and down the hill that's for certain.

As hours pass, the view begins to torment us. The cultivated arable in our periphery, a reminder of easier times, where finds were rarely more than a few centimetres below the surface, the earth broken down and easy to dig. Pasture, on the other hand, requires a sturdier mindset; finds are deeper, and signals are easier to miss, masked by centuries of undisturbed layers – the digging overall tougher, with no room for error. We are both required to be present in the task at hand, working seamlessly to pinpoint targets and dig with minimal disturbance to the turf, lest we upset both farmer and livestock.

'Well that's one pound profit so far,' Ellie quips, trying to keep the mood light as she adds it to the 1936 George V penny and military button in the finds tin – an abysmal exchange for our efforts.

Lucie doesn't conform to Ellie's boundless optimism, leaving only the swish of her waterproof trousers as she walks off, choosing to swing her frustrations out further down the footpath instead. Relentless disappointment pushing the limits of her patience.

Trudging behind, squashing a mushroom under her trainer, Ellie pulls her denim jacket closer against the wind, praying the next target pulls us out of this detecting slump.

'Ellie!' Lucie calls her over from a gulley cut into the hillside. Maybe this will be the one.

'Coming,' Ellie replies.

'Quick!' Lucie still swinging over the patch, seemingly injected by some burst of hope. 'It's in the twenties!'

Ellie whoops and drives the spade into the slope, flicking out a plug with the enthusiasm of someone who hasn't already been digging for several hours – the allure of a good signal always working wonders. Lucie's even propped herself up ready to film the occasion, so it must've sounded good.

Guided by the pinpointer's screams, Ellie carefully cuts into the sidewall with the edge digger, removing the compacted soil and applying just the right amount of pressure to prise out a large rectangular object with her fingertips. It tumbles into her palm.

'A buckle!' Lucie shouts, elated for the first time in hours.

Ellie brushes the soil from its surface, revealing elaborate swirling scrolls and a heart-shaped decoration across its trapezoidal form.

'Whoa,' Ellie exhales.

This could be the fanciest buckle we've discovered yet. An example of a new style dating from 1620–1680, which emerged from the changing attitudes and fashions following the Restoration of the monarchy after the English Civil War – where the monarchy and nobility claimed back their authority within society. Reflected here on a grassroots level, these simple fasteners become elaborate accessories to determine your social status. Utilitarian, purist values were out, and cultural expression, individualism and indulgences were back in – and yes people really could read you in a glance by the buckle fastening your girdle.

'I'm happy with that!' Lucie chuffs, thankful that at last our luck seems to be turning.

*

Ellie's drenched to the bone, kneeling on grass that has been collecting water for hours; it puddles around her knees as she leans further into the latest hole. Lucie watches solemnly a few paces away, shrunken into her soggy puffer jacket, hood pulled tight over her headphones, an inefficient barrier against the sideways onslaught of the unrelenting wind and drizzle. Both of us are utterly exposed, bearing the brunt of the weather on this blasted headland, like mountain goats caught in a storm.

'What?' Lucie shouts, Ellie's call whipped away by the wind. Pulling a headphone away from her ear, instantly missing what little warmth it provided, she listens intently, still not catching Ellie's reply.

'Say again!' She calls, moving closer, her head yanked abruptly to the side by the headphones' ratty cable, forgetting she's still connected to the Vanquish abandoned forlornly on the side of the hill – its all-weather screen protector being given a run for its money, Lucie long past any attempt to protect the exposed ports from saturation.

'Shotgun shell!' Ellie screams, waving it into the wind, her denim jacket flapping solidly, weighed down significantly by the water it's soaked up like a sponge.

'Fuck this,' Lucie replies, 'I'm done. I need to get off this hill.'

To be fair to Lucie, it has been two hours since we'd found the buckle.

'What about down there?' Ellie shouts, pointing down into the field that Lucie cursed a few weeks ago with her false declarations of gold.

Questionably, we decide to continue the dig despite the cold and the water which has penetrated every feeble layer on our bodies. Less deranged people would have given up, gone home, had a hot shower, and buried the trauma experienced on this hill over a glass of wine. We agree to endure, we've already succumbed to the elements, how could it get any worse? Gripped by a blend of stubbornness, perseverance and stupidity we drag ourselves to the bottom corner of the field and heave our weary bodies over the slippery metal gate – we could really do with acquiring a set of keys for these farmer padlocks.

Slapping onto the muddy slurry accumulated on the other side, Ellie bends to pick up her spade from where she unceremoniously tossed it, pausing to roll the hem of her trousers higher, and resisting the urge to wring them out.

Lucie's flailing on top of the gate, her boots unable to find purchase on the bars, Vanquish held aloft in one hand, if it wasn't still attached to her headphones she would've lobbed it by now – no concern for the consequences.

'Jump!' Ellie encourages.

Lucie half jumps, half tumbles from her perch, wiping a splash of mud from her puffer in disgust, closing her eyes and trying to push lingering thoughts of the day from her mind. As if someone is out there listening, the deluge pauses, slows and almost stops entirely.

'It's a miracle,' Ellie laughs.

'Thank God,' Lucie joins in, striding out into the new field with a renewed sense of direction. 'Let's swing our way home!'

Bullet casings join Ellie's new collection of spent ammunition accumulating in her finds bag. 'Swinging our way home' proving to be an indirect amble across the field, with various pit stops for every sound in Lucie's ears. The rain starts up again, but we barely notice it. The setting sun tinting our surroundings with a warm yellow glow. Ellie's crouched over a hole, flicking out yet another shotgun shell from the dirt clod, strangely content considering this is hour six, there isn't an inch of dry clothing on her and all we've really found of substance is a buckle. Chuckling to herself at how utterly crackers this hobby is, she sweeps all the loose soil back into the hole and flips the clod back over, her, her digging ritual abruptly interrupted as Lucie shouts out of nowhere.

'Oh my God!' Lucie's looking back towards the hill we'd spent all day searching, pointing frantically. 'Ellie. Look. A rainbow!'

Materialising through a shower of hazy droplets, ushered in on the rays of sunshine, a double rainbow arches itself across the whole width of the field, one end landing on the boundary line, the other inside the field.

'Is that where we're going to find gold?' jokes Lucie, 'Can you imagine?'

'Shall we follow it?' Ellie's already picked up the spade.

'Fuck it, why not.'

It's a different pair of detectorists who prance and swing under the rainbow, the hours spent swearing into the tempests on the side of the hill forgotten, replaced with a childlike excitement in the magic of this natural phenomenon. There isn't a soul around for miles, just us and the rainbow, but maybe someone is out there looking down on us, blessing us for our tortured perseverance. Ellie's got her phone out, recording and photographing every moment, both of us completely enchanted at the surreal nature of our surroundings. This is what metal detecting is all about, Ellie thinks, it's the unpredictable magic of the outdoors, the finds are just a bonus.

'You're not going to believe this Ellie, I've got a signal!' Lucie shouts from a few paces ahead.

'You don't,' Ellie replies astounded.

'I do. A twenty-one, sounds good you know.'

We both share a glance, too afraid to voice our treacherously hopeful thoughts – could this be the gold?

*

Gold has had humanity captivated in a trance since it was first smelted in Ancient Egypt over 5,000 years ago. An inert, alluringly buttery material with a low melting point, it might not be the most chemically interesting of all the elements, but that's entirely the point. It's dense, malleable and virtually indestructible. An ounce can be beaten into a sheet covering 100 square feet, a cubic foot of the stuff weighs half a ton, it doesn't corrode, tarnish or oxidise, and it's relatively rare – all of the gold ever gathered in human history only amounts to a cube roughly twenty-five metres on each side.

It's no wonder, then, that gold has become heavily intertwined with the divine, inspiring myths and legends, battles and genocide. Generally it's used for either money or adornment – but its true appeal far transcends any literal application; bestowed with the power to grant great political and commercial prestige. It's been a dangerous temptation for kings, emperors, explorers, prospectors and average people alike.

They say the search for gold has inspired humanity's greatest achievements and caused its gravest mistakes. It's pushed man to the furthest corners of the world, yet left destruction in his wake. Just look at the Age of Discovery from the fifteenth to the seventeenth centuries, where a small gold market and rising gold prices in Europe provided a dangerous opportunity to tip the scales in the favour of those explorers intrepid enough to go and find it. And so they did. Tempted overseas by reports like the writings of Marco Polo's travels to the Silk Road in the thirteenth century – bearing tales of palaces roofed in gold – and whispered legends of mythical cities of gold to be found in the 'New World', explorers such as Christopher Columbus and Sir Walter Raleigh delved deep into an obsession. In the short space of three months Columbus mentions gold more than sixty-five times in his diary, and Raleigh becomes so consumed with his search for El Dorado he commits treason, which inevitably leads to his own execution.

Between 1492–1525 the European 'known world' more than tripled, and more gold flooded into Europe than ever before – far dwarfing the pitiful efforts of the Roman's gold mines in Africa, Portugal, Spain and Dolaucothi in Wales (Britain's only known Roman goldmine). This wasn't the first instance of gold fever – if myths are to be believed, gold's first victim is probably Jason, led astray by one golden fleece – but to the South Americans, it was a colonial-grabbing episode of looting, exploitation and enslavement which wasn't humanity's finest hour.

Yet it wouldn't really be until the nineteenth century that we saw the true bewitching power of this golden material, where a growing gold shortage sparked a global infatuation. This time, however, instead of adventurers backed by their nations, it would be regular people descending into the frenzied search for gold – grasping at any opportunity to hit the 'mother lode' and make their fortunes.

The United States, Australia, Canada, South Africa and New Zealand all found themselves the subject of the gold rush; a feverish descent onto prospective goldfields that saw San Francisco emptied out in a mere matter of weeks after word broke of gold discovered at Sutter's Mill, California in 1848. The influx of Forty-Niners, as they became known – with over 100,000 arriving by 1853 – panned and mined out America's biggest gold rush. This mass migration would be characteristic of gold rushes across the globe, and where the gold-seekers went, the businessmen followed – introducing drills and dredges – marring landscapes and overtaking native communities.

The search for gold has left its mark worldwide, an all too familiar sight for Lucie, whose childhood growing up in New Zealand's South Island was shaped by the wild and often lawless gold rushes of the 1860s. Previously, the South Island was a place of dense forest, occupied only by the Māori, native bird song, and a great variety of streams and rivers that would turn into raging torrents in the fraction of a second. The Otago gold rush of 1862–1864 changed all of that, prompting an influx of gold-seekers who carved out settlements, hacked out infrastructure and grimly started communities – enduring harsh conditions only for the promise of riches.

Golden Bay, Canvastown, and Digger's Creek, locations Lucie knows well, were shaped entirely under the influence of gold fever. It's a powerful thing, the search for gold, ensnaring people in a lust that seems to survive the centuries. Even today – a period where our money has transcended the need to physically bear value or even be linked to a gold-standard backing – gold reserves remain an imperative form of maintaining economic stability. Humanity and gold are intrinsically interlinked – it's no wonder that we are still out there actively looking for it.

*

As if we'd actually find gold at the end of the rainbow, holding out our hope till the last signal – that was a cruel delusion if there ever was one – the bullet casing sat coldly in Ellie's hand, erasing all remaining warmth from her body.

'Let's call it a day,' she sighs, ready to toss her spade in the Panda and kick off her sodden trainers, all the magic of the outdoors thoroughly shattered by another arduous find.

'It's going to get dark soon anyway,' Lucie replies, 'I'll detect my way to the gate.' You have to hand it to Lucie, to continue swinging till the bitter end – much to Ellie's silent disapproval that she might have to dig one more hole.

Ellie marches ahead, leaving Lucie to slowly follow behind, the coil gathering water with every brush against the ground – whatever futile hope or resolute stubbornness lingering within her, slowly diminishing with every step, closing the distance between us and our escape route. On the final stretch to salvation, mid-stride, a clear tone rings out through her headphones making her heart jump. Taking a step back, swinging again, a *19* flashes across the screen confirming what she heard. Another swing, then a *20*, the digits dancing between themselves chanting: *19-20-21*.

'Ellie, stop! Come back!' she calls, narrowing down the target with each move of the coil. It's an almost identical signal to the last, but she can't let it go ignored, one final desperate attempt to make the last few hours worth it.

'It's probably another bullet casing,' Ellie grumbles, thoroughly unamused, we are so close to reaching the final gate, the only thing separating her from misery and a hot shower back home.

'Last hole, I promise – we have to dig it,' Lucie pleads.

Ellie reluctantly retraces her solemn trail of footsteps flattened into the damp grass. As much as every bone in her body is screaming at her to leave, she knows deep down there isn't an option, she can't leave such a cracking signal undug – and be forever haunted by the unknown.

'You'll hear it with the pinpointer, one second …' Lucie lies down propping her phone up against a tuft. 'I'll film you digging.' This new signal is awakening energy and inspiration she thought she'd left up on the hill, and she's filled with an unshakeable desire to capture the ASMR-esque crunch of the spade for our adventure vlog of the day.

She was right, the pinpointer located it immediately – whatever was hiding below the surface was waiting to be found. With Lucie watching through the screen, Ellie cuts a small plug with her spade, dropping to the floor and pulling back the clod, grass clutched in one hand, eyes trained onto the emerging dark void below.

Ellie chokes, as if all the air had been suddenly sucked from her lungs, straining each syllable into existence.

'What?' Lucie focuses hard on keeping her phone steady, adrenaline threatening to overwhelm her, Ellie's reaction unheard of.

'YOU! Ohhhhh …' Ellie, her words falling all over themselves, is stupefied by whatever is lying in the dirt, visible only to her eyes. She slams the clod back over in panic, and meets Lucie's gaze over the top of the phone. For a beat Lucie is silent – she knows in her bones what this means.

'Is it gold?' she asks fevered.

Ellie is sat wide-eyed in response.

'You're fucking joking me?' The remaining calm in Lucie's voice evaporates in an instant, nervous tremors starting to make themselves apparent on the phone's steady footage.

'I'm not fucking joking you! I'M NOT FUCKING JOKING YOU! I'm really not joking you!' Words finally spill out of Ellie's mouth in hysteria. 'You need to look in the hole right now, you need to see what I saw,' she rambles. She needs Lucie to experience this moment, too – from the digger's perspective – it's once-in-a-lifetime.

Slowly lifting the clod back up under Ellie's encouragement, Lucie lets her eyes rest on what's buried, gasping involuntarily – it seems that losing the ability to speak is infectious. In the bottom of this very shallow hole, resting among the topsoil which had come loose and is crawling with ants, a large hammered coin glares back. Its bright, buttery hue shines unmistakably against the cold damp earth.

'Oh, my God,' Lucie breathes. It might be the most beautiful thing she's ever seen.

The starboard bow of a golden ship breaks through the soil as if riding the crest of a muddy wave during a storm surge. Nestled safely among the rigging, a shield bearing three lions commands the seas and our heed.

'Holy fuck …' Lucie whispers under her breath, 'What do we do?'

✱

SHEEP

Fifteenth-century England was riddled with diseases. Plague was still hanging on – rearing its ugly head in a series of epidemics – smallpox and pneumonia were rife, too, and Henry VII's invading army are claimed to have thrown a brand-new disease into the contagious broiling pot in 1485 – the English sweating sickness, a fatal affliction that saw victims sweating to death in as little as twenty-four hours. All in all, it was a dire time to fall ill. Britain in particular had virtually no town physicians and no health boards prior to 1600 – true medical science was only beginning to emerge alongside herbal remedies, humoral theory and astrology.

It was a sickly environment that provided ample opportunity for the monarchs to assert their divine right over their subjects. Beginning with Edward the Confessor (1042–1066), we see the emergence of 'touching', which became regular practice after the reign of Henry II (1154–1189). This was a cure brought in for the disease known simply as 'the king's evil' or 'scrofula' – a form of tuberculosis, characterised by large swellings in the lymph nodes of the neck, forming masses. Supposedly the king's touch would alleviate the suffering, a treatment furthered by the giving of a coin to the sufferer to bear on their person. It's a miracle only possible through the powers granted by God – and helped by the fact that scrofula wasn't always fatal and could go into remission of its own accord. Edward I touched up to 2,000 diseased individuals a year, but it was a practice that seemed to end with Edward III, and succumbed to a century of neglect, revived only in 1485 with the emergence of a new dynasty – the Tudors.

According to history, this latter half of the fifteenth century was occupied solely by dynastic disputes (although we are certain normal life trudged on as always); especially as following Edward III's death, the weak and unstable rule of Henry VI had thrown up questions over the rightful heir to the throne. Two rival Plantagenet houses – York and Lancaster – rose up in protest, both claiming a rightful descent and sparking the series of civil wars known as the Wars of the Roses. Ironically, the conclusion to this struggle at the Battle of Bosworth saw Henry VII crowned – a man with possibly one of the weakest and most slender claims to the throne in the conflict, and he knew it.

THINGS WE FOUND IN THE GROUND

But rather than give in to the weakness and instability threatened by his tenuous claim to the House of Lancaster, Henry devoted his reign (1485–1509) to consolidating the security of the English Crown – his success, building the foundation for his son and granddaughter, Henry VIII and Elizabeth I, two of the most famous monarchs in history.

There were several methods through which he strengthened the throne; he married Princess Elizabeth, Edward IV's youngest daughter, uniting the warring houses and ensuring his descendants inherited both strands of the dynasty; he filled the royal coffers with gold, much to the disgruntlement of the nobles he crippled; and finally he revived the practice of touching, introducing a full ceremonial service, and intertwined it with the Angel – a gold coin first introduced under Edward IV and dripping with religious iconography, depicting the ship of state sailing under the Royal coat of arms, surmounted by Christ's cross on one side and on the other, the archangel St Michael spearing a dragon.

What better way to prove he was the rightful king – as intended by God himself – than through performing miracles and simultaneously imbuing the Angel as a symbol and physical reminder of his royal power. The use of a gold coin for this purpose, too, was quite ingenious. Gold coinage had only been a permanent feature of English coinage since Edward III, and ordinary working people likely wouldn't have come across one in their average lives, their high values circulating largely among merchants, traders and the nobility. A labourer would have only earned around 4d (pence) a day, and an Angel was worth 6s (shillings), 8d – that's almost three weeks' worth of wages. Passing an Angel onto a sufferer therefore symbolised not only the divinity of Henry VII, but also the economic strength, stability and power he brought to all of his subjects.

Henry might not have invented the gold Angel, but in many ways he is the monarch who *made* them. He started a tradition of Angel touch pieces, which continued far beyond their disappearance from circulation during the reign of Charles I, their iconography living on

SHEEP

in the gold touch pieces produced right up until the final touching under Queen Anne, 1702–1714.

*

'I need a moment, I don't think I can film.' Lucie's phone is trembling with both excitement and fear of ruining what could be *the* footage of our lifetimes.

To find a gold coin is enough to remove the air from your lungs, but to find an Angel, and especially one of Henry VII – the man who cemented their hallowed place in society – is dumbfounding to say the least.

Ellie reaches her hand towards the coin and cautiously brushes off some loose soil, hesitantly flipping it over to reveal the other side – terrified of damaging it.

We lose the ability to speak again.

The archangel Michael stands frozen in time, his angel wings stretch abreast the flan, a scaled armour coating his forearms and legs, a feather-like skirt and shoulder plumes accentuating his breastplate, poised over the dying form of a dragon. His cross spear, which looks to have been gifted from the heavens itself, disappears into a wide slack-jawed muzzle and serpent-like tongue, a tail curling off into the background, its lower body and legs entangled underneath Michael's stance – the whole divine look completed by the halo encircling his head, fronted by Christ's cross. A beaded circle surrounds them, ringed by Latin letters bearing the inscription:

'HENRIC' DI' GRA' REX ANGL' Z FRA' – Henry by the Grace of God King of England and France.

As the coin emerges from its 500-year resting place, the ebbing rays of sunlight glance across its hammered surface, Ellie turns it over slowly in her fingers, light bouncing off the holy scene for the first time in half a millennia – if anything could make you believe in God (or erase the sodden socks, bitter chill and gruelling finds of a bad day's detecting), it is this coin.

Passing it between us, we begin to understand the longing that gripped Christopher Columbus, Sir Walter Raleigh and the fortune

THINGS WE FOUND IN THE GROUND

seekers of the gold rush. You can read about finding gold, and you can hold gold down at the jewellers, but to truly understand gold fever, you've got to find it in the depths of the earth.

We barely speak on the journey home, unable to put words to what happened out there in the field. It turns out Lucie was right all those weeks ago; we just had to earn our right to find it first.

10.
WINTER

DECEMBER 2021, LINCOLNSHIRE, ENGLAND
'Let's walk from here.'

We both agree. The potholes have become far too unbearable to risk travelling any further in the Panda. Time to ditch. Unloading all our gear from our marooned vehicle, the final approach will have to be made on foot.

*

Our last few visits to the village have seen us become frequent flyers of the manor house, and the gold field that we've hammered relentlessly – to no further avail. We've been so frequent in fact that Lady H has started to keep a steady supply of Lincolnshire plum bread (best served with a wedge of Cheddar or – even better – Lincolnshire Poacher cheese) in the pantry – ready to while away the hours gossiping over a hot brew and lavishly buttered slice (the family have learned not to expect us home anytime early on a digging Wednesday). Considerably more civilised than the sad remains of a Tesco meal deal consumed in the 'comfort' of the Panda, or the damp edge of a field margin.

Lady H is becoming as familiar as an old friend, and we like to think she's growing rather fond of us, too – maybe almost as much as we are of her. With all formalities dropped, conversation takes place huddled over the PVC gingham tablecloth in the kitchen (more finds friendly), sat in our muddy digging clothes among her British Museum gift-shop cushions, and sharing the space with an elephant tea cosy, an iPad and a pile of heavily annotated newspaper clippings. Digressing over our leftover crumbs and empty teacups, snippets of Lady H's life are revealed to us, stories piling up alongside the slices of toasted plum bread, carefully fished out with slightly scorched bamboo tongs, from a conveniently placed, dark green Bakelite toaster behind her.

Each tale is more remarkable than the last, pulled from her memory with only a brief closing of her eyes. There's travelling around India as a young couple with her late husband; an unorthodox visit to an ancestral grave in the depths of Ireland – one located in the private garden of an unsuspecting, middle-aged couple's church renovation (the pulpit of which had been transformed into a bar, much to Lady H's utter wonderment); and even the personal boat tour to a recently discovered Roman city in the Middle East, after she just so happened to be seated at a formal dinner next to the lead archaeologist the night before.

Mid-debrief over the latest episode of *Digging for Britain*, and amid a brief tangent into the 'marvellous shades' (to quote Lady H) of Professor Alice Roberts's hair, discussion inevitably turns back to our metal-detecting exploits (mainly the gold), and, more importantly, Lady H's estate managers.

Upon hearing about the back-and-forth dance Ellie has been performing to wrangle specific field rights out of said estate managers – circling fields, ringing tenants, sending emails and of course religiously updating Kieran, all without ever being privy to a map of the estates entirety – Lady H appears downright miffed by the charade, offering a fresh round of tea in solidarity, and plots to resolve the situation over another steaming cup.

The next day, Lady H has personally moved Heaven and Earth as we receive a prompt and overly apologetic email containing a map and full permission rights to the whole breadth of the estate; and it's a damn sight bigger than we ever dreamed – we've got a lot more digging to do.

*

THINGS WE FOUND IN THE GROUND

This new part of the permission is isolated compared to our usual haunts, the excitement of the new map and a lack of arable land this time of year seeing us venture further afield, so to speak. We are essentially in the hinterlands of the estate, trekking to the bottom of a poorly maintained farm lane, to be precise, and, according to farmer Stan, exactly where we should find a couple of fields left to seed.

The gaze of the village was far, far away in the distance, obscured by a wooded copse and a thick curtain of early-morning mist. Gingerly, we follow Stan's instructions; duck below a padlocked barrier, cross a small concrete bridge, and make a left turn into the misty void. There should be a couple of fields there, he said …

For the next mile we walk along the raised bank of a small dyke; built up over centuries of dredging the murky water below.

'Do you think there's anything down there?' Lucie ponders.

'You can't be serious,' Ellie replies, looking sceptically into the uncertain depths of the still water.

'Only if we get desperate …' Lucie laughs. She's being serious.

*

Following the path along the waterway, bare tree branches are the only entities to breach the veil, damp air clinging to our hair and clothing as we disappear further away from civilisation – the copse to our left throwing out the occasional squawk and tortured scream.

'That's where they breed the pheasants,' Ellie offers as a tentative explanation for the frankly horror-film-esque noises piercing through the gloom.

We continue in an uneasy silence, both searching furtively for the field to appear.

'Can you feel that, Ellie?' Lucie murmurs.

There is something powerful, almost primordial conjured by the stillness in the air.

'This is the kind of place we'll find a hoard,' she whispers, breathing life to the thoughts filling her head.

WINTER

'It does feel ancient,' Ellie echoes in agreement, now having decided to humour Lucie's premonitions.

Fields slowly pass us by, until our presumed destination finally comes into view.

'This looks like the one, don't you think?' Ellie prods at the ground with her spade, as if testing the waters. It looks unkept, with old stubble and weeds sprouting out from all directions. It isn't a particularly large field, by any means, nicely contained by two dykes and hedgerows on either side, but big enough to keep us occupied for the next few weeks.

'I'd say so,' Lucie confirms, 'This is where Stan said it would be.'

'Where should we start?'

✳

You'll probably be aware by now, how metal detecting and mud tend to go hand in hand. You can't expect to go out without acquiring a fine layer of soil on your clothing, your hands, under your nails, and in Ellie's case, your face – unless, of course, you happen to be Lucie, who has Ellie for that. We thought we were pretty well acquainted with mud – until we step foot into this field.

Down here, between these dykes, the mud is like glue – thick, gelatinous glue that has us moving like bugs across fly tape. And unsurprisingly, we've discovered metal detecting doesn't have quite the same appeal when the ground has the resistance of Velcro. It's one hell of a baptism for Ellie's new hiking boots (a gift from Lucie, who never wanted to see her white trainers again), but the mud is bonding itself not only to our boots – both of us growing several inches taller with every step – but also to our equipment. This might as well be some hellish military bootcamp.

'ELLIE, I can't lift the coil!' Lucie cries out.

Ellie grimaces, using the edge of her spade to shave the mud clinging limpet-like to the bottom of the Vanquish coil, deafening Lucie in the process. All she succeeds in doing, however, is transferring the mud from coil to spade, then from spade to edge digger, clawing it off the edge digger with her hands, and then subsequently transferring it to her trousers; merely a case of moving the mud around and not actually getting rid of it.

And all that is accumulated during the swinging part of metal detecting, the part that doesn't even require getting up close and personal with the mud. The digging is a whole different story – it's a nightmare.

By the third hole (the first two finds were shotgun shells), Ellie is plastered head to toe; it's smeared across her face, it's in her hair, it's ruined her *Time Team* beanie, and you can't even see the new hiking boots – now indistinguishable from their surroundings. Lucie winces at the wet slap of Ellie's knees as they hit the filth, and shudders at the fact she's abandoned any pretence of using her gloves, needing to *feel* through the gloop to ascertain the metal objects from the muck.

An hour in and with nothing more than a featureless, battered eighteenth-century halfpenny, a decorative bird brooch (probably Victorian), and several pounds of mud clinging to every fibre of our being – we are seriously thinking about throwing in the towel.

'This is pointless. It's more mud wrestling than metal detecting.' Ellie is cold and wet, regret is sinking in and she's using every ounce of her remaining will to stave off the utter horror of just how incredibly caked she is.

'Let's just try this one,' Lucie offers up another signal, waving the Vanquish over a particularly promising target. One last attempt, and if it's another shotgun shell, we're gone. Ellie wearily plods over, dragging her feet heavily across the mud, kneeling down once again with a sickening slap, she doesn't even bother to use her spade to dig, the mud so viscous the pinpointer passes through easily, becoming one with the sludge, completely submerged. Yet, its haunting electronic screams still cut through the weary air of trepidation hanging over us – a glimmer of hope in our darkest hour.

'I've got it!' Ellie calls, signalling to Lucie who squats down, phone outstretched, ready to record. Just in case.

A small, imperfect disc emerges from the sludge, gripped tightly between Ellie's muddy fingers. 'ROMAN!' she shouts ecstatically – a coin this size, it's got to be.

'Are you sure?' Lucie hesitates, far too tired to be fooled by pipe dreams.

Ellie smears the mud congealed to its surface, revealing an unmistakable, but very worn bump – a Roman bust.

'ROMMMAAANNN!' We both scream in delirium. Two lunatics, cheering like pigs in muck.

'Quick, get it in the chat!' Ellie hands the Roman over to Lucie for further inspection.

Sharing our adventures as Roman Found has unearthed a sense of belonging with the other, equally enthusiastic, dirt-addled individuals digging around on the internet, so we've started a group chat dedicated to our mutual obsession: helping each other identify finds, and share in all the woes, tales and detecting humour that comes with the territory.

'I wonder what the guys will think?' Lucie agrees.

This Roman is different to the ones we've found previously. It's thicker, heavier and covered in a strange, orange-tinged crust, blurring the details on its surface. Lucie flicks a picture into the chat.

The responses come flooding in.

'Now that's promising.'

'I'd zap that girls,' advises one of our digging peers, who is always overeager with electrolysis (a cleaning method we won't be trying), where coins are submerged in an acidic bath and tortured by an electric current until the crust comes off.

'Hundred per cent a crusty denarius, nice work!'

Followed by a row of fire emojis.

218 BCE, PARTWAY DOWN THE ALPS

Hannibal is cold and weary, worn down after a five-month march from New Carthage. He's crossed the Pyrenees, rafted thirty-seven African elephants across the Rhône River, almost passed over the Alps and it hasn't felt half as heroic as the history books have made out.

He's suffered boulder attacks from rogue Gauls, a treacherous snowstorm that saw unwitting soldiers slip and freefall into nothingness, lost around half of his men in a series of tragic and violent ways over the entire course of this journey, and contracted an eye infection that will soon take half his vision. Yet somehow, 12,000 Libyans, 8,000 Iberians, 6,000 cavalry and an unknown number of elephants (perhaps only one), have survived the gruelling, impossible journey; trudging along a self-constructed road to outmanoeuvre the impending snowdrifts, driven only by his own long-standing hatred of Rome.

Italy lies stretched out before them, and from far above the coniferous treetops they can almost taste the triumph. Never mind the defeat of the First Punic War. Time for round two. Victory, it seemed, was within their grasp; first at the Battle of the Trebia (218 BCE), then the Battle of Lake Trasimene (217 BCE), and most famously the Battle of Cannae (216 BCE) reaping vast casualties on Rome's forces. Not too bad a start for the young Carthaginian general.

But as the persistent thorn in Rome's side, Hannibal caused a much larger impact during the Second Punic War than the entire decade of warfare he'd waged, before being disappointingly recalled to Carthage – who were facing greater dangers at home from the Roman General Africanus' invading army. Rome was teetering on the verge of bankruptcy. War was expensive. Armies had to be fed, maintained and weapons had to be manufactured, the public treasury was positively empty.

Gold reserves were having to be coined, patriotic (and wealthy) members of the public called upon to pay towards the war effort, and bronze found itself relegated as second-rate coinage, suffering a sharp decline in weight (needed elsewhere as an important war material) – shocking for a metal which was the foundation of the entire Roman monetary system.

So perhaps Hannibal's legacy on Rome isn't one of an adversary, the guy who almost took Rome, it's the denarius; a silver coin introduced in 211 BCE as part of a fundamental change to Rome's monetary system, now relying on silver for weight value (instead of bronze), a necessity in light of the economic challenges caused by the Second Punic War. The denarius carried the Roman economy for almost five centuries, struck until the reign of Gordian III in 238 CE, and surviving even longer as a unit of account (we all remember pounds, shilling and pence, right? Aka £, s and

WINTER

d) – *a coin so deeply embedded into the history of Rome, that we have to pinch ourselves that we've actually found one.*

*

'Shall we livestream this afternoon?' Lucie propositions, clearly feeling a shift in optimism. We've been livestreaming these digging sessions as part of our creative urge to document and share our adventures, and perhaps it would provide a welcome distraction from the mud.

'Yeah, why not! We're on the DENARIUS!' Ellie replies, seemingly revitalised, given a new lease of life.

This giddy high proves itself to be temporary. Ellie's been chatting nonstop about our denarius find to the handful of viewers on Live, but even her unwavering optimism is starting to become tainted by the mud-filled horrors threatening to creep back in.

Sore muscles that have never been used before are protesting strongly against their gruelling grind to sucker our boots from the gloop – you can't even tell anymore that Ellie's pinpointer used to be orange – and to top it all off, for the entire time we've been on Live, we've found nothing but shotgun shells. It's proving hard to keep a smile on our faces.

'Maybe this is where they hunt the pheasants,' Ellie mutters dejectedly to herself, as shotgun shell number 50 gets tossed unceremoniously into her bag, heaving herself up from the sticky muck with a tired groan. It's getting dark now, too, the inky fingers of dusk creeping across the ground – sundown by 3.30 p.m. – a depressing marker of the English winter that Lucie still isn't used to.

'Okay!' Lucie announces to the Live, tired of our run of bad luck, aware we are running out of daylight and growing desperate to prove herself and our detecting skills to our twelve watchers. 'Does anybody have any suggestion of where we should look next?'

'Ooh!' Ellie perks up, experiencing a jolt of camaraderie at the challenge thrown out to our backseat, sofa-detectorists. 'Pick a spot, any spot,' she performs, grinning through the fine crust of mud coating her cheeks.

The responses come flooding in.

'Go left.'

'Look under the tree.'

But there's one message in particular that stands out and it's not the usual words of encouragement ...

'I'm a medium. I've just been approached by a Roman legionnaire called Nigel, he's got a message for you ... *Walk towards the hedge.*'

'Can't argue with the spirits,' Lucie decides, striding towards the hedgeline, swinging away.

'I can't say Nigel is a very Roman sounding name,' Ellie grumbles, diligently following a few steps behind with the phone (and it's not, it actually originates from the Gaelic-Irish name 'Niall' – poking a large plot-hole into the medium's claims – the Romans never conquered Ireland).

'SIGNAL.' Lucie stops dead, a few feet from the hedge, a shrill sound almost blowing her ears off.

'No. Fucking. Way.' Ellie deadpans. Mind blown at the coincidence – or perhaps real-life spiritual encounter – that lies quite literally at our feet.

'C'mon then Nigel, what you got for us,' Lucie goads, taking the muddy phone back from Ellie, our anticipation tense and excited in the cool, crisp dusk. Visibility is dropping rapidly, we should probably have left the field by now – it's going to be a long, long walk home in the dark.

Feeling the pressure, watched over by an expectant Lucie, our spiritual guide Nigel, and the twelve faithful livestream viewers, the digging is quiet, no one daring to breathe for fear of scaring away the phantom treasure.

'There's something here!' Ellie's voice shakes into the twilight, uncharacteristically high, in a fever pitch.

'WHAT IS IT?' Lucie blurts, the livestream messages going wild.

Ellie is frenzied – stuttering, floundering around in the mud, 'We ... we need a torch ... Lucie ... I think it's another denarius.'

'You're fucking kidding me.' Lucie fumbles with the torch on Ellie's urgently offered phone, her hands shaking, and it's nothing to do with the bitter emergence of the early night.

WINTER

The piercing white torchlight cuts through the dark, landing on the relief of a strong side-profile, a heavy brow, a well-groomed beard and that distinctive laurel wreath tied tight with a ribbon. A heartstopping image rising from the clay-smeared surface of the small, grey coin held in Ellie's fingertips. Publius Aelius Hadrianus, otherwise known as Emperor Hadrian, a man who made quite the mark on Britain – one seventy-three miles (eighty Roman miles) long that took at least six years to complete: Hadrian's wall.

*

Gay. Traveller. Self-absorbed. Generous. Lonely. These are just a few of the words used to describe Emperor Hadrian, the man at the helm of Rome's greatest hour.

Ruling for nearly twenty-one years, between 117–138 CE, Hadrian led during the period the Roman Empire was at its height – but also at a turning point – teetering on the precipice of becoming too great and too mighty to stand the test of time. Luckily for Rome, Hadrian was an intellectual, a thinker and observer, recognising the fundamental flaws in the Empire he'd inherited and laying down the policies to enable its future longevity.

Under Trajan's militaristic reign, Rome had conquered and claimed new territories and was now suffering as a result; it simply couldn't keep on expanding, not with the trouble already brewing among the natives of its newly occupied regions. But Hadrian decided he didn't need to wage wars to solve his predecessor's problems – what he needed was boundaries.

So acting on decades of experience (Hadrian was forty-one when he succeeded to the throne, following a thorough military career) and the elusive pull of an inquisitive mind, Hadrian spent over half his reign travelling the Empire, visiting his most heavily garrisoned provinces and the remotest stretches of the 'known Roman world' – gaining first-hand experience of the places he had only read about.

He travelled more than any other Roman emperor, leading by example, without frills, luxury or indulgences. He demanded the highest standards from the men who accompanied him, exuding a discipline and fairness that made him both popular among his troops as well as cultivating one of the most professional, organised and effective armies in Rome's history.

But this wasn't the intended result of his travels. His aim was to consolidate Rome's borders and the empire within, constructing vast physical reminders in his most volatile provinces, such as the Upper Germanic-Rhaetian Limes – today the longest archaeological monument in Europe, a 550 kilometre-long fortified frontier stretching from the Rhine to the Danube – and Hadrian's Wall. He is known as Rome's greatest builder; after all, our world today is scattered with the impressive monuments of his legacy – Villa Adriana in Tivoli, The Pantheon in Rome, Hadrian's Library in Athens, just to name a few – his passion for the arts was spared no expenses, so why should his borders be? Why not start decades of construction in a troublesome region which the majority of the Roman Empire would never see?

These barriers, however, transcended the need for physical defence, standing as a deep psychological reminder of the separation between Romans and Barbarians – of the powers of the state, the dangers that lie outside it, and the need for the safety it harnesses within. They are architecture used as an intellectual weapon, Hadrian's greatest legacy and one hell of a way to make a political statement. They didn't need to be seen to have an impact, they simply needed to exist.

In many ways, his reign was dedicated to the stability of the Roman Empire; even in death he left it in safe hands, adopting heirs to secure future successions over two generations. But that doesn't mean his rule was entirely a period of peace. Hadrian's visits to these difficult provinces didn't come without significant Roman losses, and then there was the Second Jewish Revolt – the final violent struggle of the Jewish-Roman Wars which ended with a suppression of Jewish nationalism as Hadrian did his best to erase their ties to the province; renaming the area and banning them from Jerusalem. A harsh insight into the brutal and skilled military general who didn't have any qualms at the thought of crushing uprisings against him – maybe we should be adding 'ruthless' to the list of descriptions for Hadrian.

WINTER

Hadrian broke the mould of the Roman emperor in more ways than one. Physically he was the first to appear with a full beard for centuries, sparking a new trend. And his intellect – while not winning him any favours with the Roman Senate, who much preferred to possess the upper hand over their emperors – saw him turn his back on the ideas of what made the Roman Empire great; choosing to build on what he inherited rather than add new unstable territories to the already volatile mix.

You could call him a visionary, one of the greatest Roman emperors to ever rule, but are there really any 'good' Roman emperors? In the muddied records of history, it's hard to tell – the history books are irrevocably written by the victors. But no matter how people describe Hadrian, it's impossible to ignore the evidence of his achievements, which have left a mark so deep on the Roman Empire that it's still visible today. We can't tell you if he was good or bad by today's standards, but looking down on his proud likeness, you can understand how far his influence stretched, making it all the way to a remote field in an isle known to the Romans as the 'edge of the world'.

*

'I can't believe that just happened, it's going to make an INSANE video,' Lucie declares, riding on our second denarius high of the day, this latest one in a completely different league to the first – crisp and crust-free.

'It's a good thing it happened on Live or no one would believe us,' Ellie laughs, thinking of the flurry of messages that flooded the livestream chat, we almost couldn't end it, but we'd found our treasure and it was far too dark. Night creatures were starting to stir.

'I'm going to download the video now,' Lucie exclaims, stopping in her tracks, an obsessive need to save this moment overtaking any need to continue walking back along the dyke.

Video Not Available to Download.

'Are you fucking serious?!' Lucie's raging.

'What's happened?' Ellie questions, quite eager to get walking again and make it back to safety.

'The stream hasn't saved, it's glitched out,' Lucie's flabbergasted.

'What do you mean it hasn't saved?!'

'It must have been the spirits …'

The rest of the trek back to the car is undertaken in an uneasy silence. Our thoughts occupied. Maybe we start to believe it, even with the highly improbable nature of a native Irish Roman legionnaire, it certainly felt like someone – or something – was out there nudging us in the right direction.

*

But the tale's not quite over yet.

The group chat has been going off all night. One denarius is exciting, enough to get people talking, but two, in the same field, metres apart. That's all the signs of a hoard – a stash of coins, purposefully buried for safekeeping. Maybe even buried by Nigel.

The thought unlocks a fever – hoard fever. It's an infectious desperation, prompting rash decisions, such as returning immediately, the following day, before our boots have even had a chance to dry out. Who cares about the mud, it can't be worse than yesterday, right?

Wrong. Looking down onto the field – sorry, the bog – yesterday's traumas are embedded plainly across its surface. A sorry-looking mess of sunken footprints and claw marks that look more like they've been left by trapped wild animals than detectorists. Only yesterday's sins turn out to be nothing in comparison to the horrors facing us today. Add constant drizzle and the high probability of developing trench foot to the sombre forecast. The dig ahead couldn't look any bleaker. But if anything can motivate us to get back in the trenches, it is the prospect of a Roman hoard.

'Fucking hell,' Ellie groans, struggling to pull her hand free from the gloop's snare. A sad battle for the soul-destroying reward of another shotgun shell.

WINTER

'Jesus,' Lucie mutters, pushing the alarming sight to the back of her mind and wading further across the field – on a mission for denarii.

'Let's try near Nigel's hedge,' Ellie suggests, keen to get to the bottom of the denarii speculation quickly. The rain has made the already-bad ground conditions utterly abysmal. She only has to look at the mud and it's somehow found its way onto her. And, of course, the area around Nigel's hedge is the absolute muddiest part of the field. It seems to be thicker, stickier here than anywhere else. Maybe someone was looking out for us yesterday, but they certainly aren't present today. Ellie's drowning in it. It feels like a whole new low.

'Okay, we might be onto something,' Lucie calls, a suspiciously familiar-sounding signal ringing in her ears. 'Sounds veeeeerrrryyy similar to ol' Hadrian.'

'Let's do this.' Ellie grins.

'Fuck, yeeeeesssss,' Lucie sings as a coin emerges from the muck – well, half a coin, but we've got to start somewhere.

'Denarius,' Ellie smiles contentedly, spinning it carefully between her fingers, somehow forgetting the constant onslaught of rain as it sees the light of day for the first time in over 1,800 years. 'This is the SPOT.'

'Let's grid.'

*

Having an area to focus our efforts on certainly helps morale in these wet, cold and muddy times; driven by purpose and direction instead of blindly hoping to stumble across treasure. But it's also a harsh and bitter lesson in perseverance and determination.

In theory, gridding is the 'best' way to metal detect, but that's under normal ground conditions, here the more we walk over it, the worse it gets – the mud turning into slurry as it's churned over by every sinking footstep. Stan almost needn't bother ploughing this field after we're done with it.

Just as we start to think we've committed too deep, that maybe we should come back on a drier day, hoard fever starting to ebb; another signal has us halting our solemn march – slowly sinking the longer we stand.

'DENNAAARRRIIIUUUSSSS!' Ellie whoops triumphantly from her elbows, deep in the slop, attempting to clean off the mud from its surface, only to smear on even more in the process.

'Is it another Hadrian?' Lucie asks excitedly, not able to discern any features through the thick coating of mud.

'Not sure,' Ellie replies. We attempt to clean it further to no avail – an impossible task when you find yourself digging in a quagmire.

'It's got to be a hoard,' Lucie hushes. With three ½ denarii under our belt now – all in varying states of crustation – hoard fever has reached its height. We allow ourselves to devolve to a primeval nature, we don't even care about the mud, unlocking a mental safe-space deep within, a mind museum if you will, just waiting to be filled with denarii.

It takes all day. Another dusk till dawn shift. Requiring hundreds of painstakingly gridded lines. An unwelcome amount of shotgun shells. An array of mystery finds, unidentifiable until clean. An immeasurable amount of rain. An intolerable amount of mud. The solemn sacrifice of Ellie's hiking boots, which will simply never be the same again. The accidental consumption of an alarming amount of mud over lunch. The beginning of the end for the Panda's upholstery and suspension system. And a merciless survival lesson in the powers of dissociation to overcome utter diabolical conditions.

Shellshocked is the only word to describe the *trudge* back to the Panda, all this, for one more battered denarius and a fragment so small it could be described as a splinter – joining the speck in infamy. But we are satisfied at last that we have removed every trace of Roman coin that remains, for this season at least – four ½ denarii. And a splinter. That's one small hoard.

11.
WOMEN

JANUARY 2022, LINCOLNSHIRE, ENGLAND

It's taken a good few weeks to recover both physically and mentally from the Nigel 'hoard' experience – well, less of an experience, and more of a mud ritual, and not of the cleansing, spa variety. We've emerged changed, vowing to stay on pasture and close to the safety of the village for the foreseeable future – or at least until the weather's dried out.

But mud isn't the only thing we've left behind in that field, Lucie's said goodbye to her twenties, Ellie's white trainers are back on rotation (the hiking boots never did recover) and she's firmly in her committed-relationship era. Plus, after a year of dutiful service, we've decided to retire the Vanquish 340.

It's been a difficult decision, and one we haven't taken lightly. Its replacement has burdened us financially, but we're completely invested in the hobby now. Our weapon of choice: the Minelab Equinox 800, a fully submersible, top-of-the-range and arguably best-selling metal detector the world over – known fondly within the hobby as 'The Nox'. It's not a switch-on-and-go situation, it has customisable programmes, Bluetooth and software updates, which is all sounding, dare we say it … a bit nerdy. We've even lobbed a carbon-fibre shaft in there to spice things up a bit. If the Equinox 800 were a Ferrari, it makes the Vanquish 340 look like a Little Tikes Cozy Coupe – talk about taking off the training wheels.

WOMEN

It's hard to know how you'll take to a new machine. Some you click with more than others, and not to get sentimental over a piece of moulded plastic and tangled wires, but the Vanquish will always be the machine that found us gold – you never forget your first love, and the same goes for metal detectors, it seems. It takes around six months to become closely acquainted; you need to learn its sensitivities, its limits, and to trust your ears to the point where you can name the find before it comes out of the ground – although it will still find ways to keep you on your toes.

If we were to give you any piece of advice (this is still not a how-to guide, by the way), leave your old machine at home, and, yes, everyone should have a back-up machine in case of emergencies, but, during this initial break up phase, no contact is best – trust us – it's always too tempting to go back to what you know.

But we're ready to learn a new machine – at least, we think we are – and who knows, maybe we'll unlock a new level of detecting in the process?

*

To break in the Equinox we're treating it to some virgin land – the largest section of hillside pasture in our arsenal. Eagerly turning up at the crack of dawn, the winter frost crunching underfoot as we hop the leaning, wooden stile, the Equinox slung over Ellie's shoulder, nestled safely within a pristine carry bag emblazoned with the Minelab logo – the result of some overzealous purchasing – Lucie's surprised we didn't end up with matching Minelab outfits too.

Setting up basecamp at the foot of a small hawthorn tree, Ellie can't get the carry bag open quick enough, pulling out an immaculate machine, still bearing its protective screen sticker.

'Let's get going!' Lucie's raring to go.

'We've gotta set it up first,' Ellie says nervously, waving a small pamphlet.

Hunched over, carry bag discarded, our breath hanging in the air as we study the slim user manual, we've successfully adjusted the shaft length, plugged in the coil, and powered up the LCD display, but we cannot for the life of us get the bloody Bluetooth headphones to connect. Mobile-phone reception is questionable at the best of times in the village, yet here we are, excruciatingly downloading a YouTube video on Lucie's phone after frantically searching, 'How to pair Equinox 800 to headphones'. Why we didn't do this before we got to the field is anyone's guess.

'Get to the point, mate,' Lucie watches on restlessly, the video eating through her monthly data allowance and patience.

'Okay, that should do it,' Ellie says, pushing and holding what looks to be the same small button we've been helplessly prodding at for the last twenty minutes.

The headphones and Equinox chirp in tandem, followed by a more reassuring '*BOOOP*' – then a headphone symbol illuminates in the top right corner of the LCD screen – success.

'Why didn't it do that the first time?' Lucie frowns.

'God knows,' Ellie mutters, tossing her the headphones and mentally preparing herself for the next task – choosing our search settings.

One eye trained on the brief instructions, the other on the LCD screen, Ellie takes a deep breath before plugging through all seven settings, swearing profusely as she accidentally enters the advanced menu and deletes numbers off the search range.

Over her shoulder, Lucie watches with concern.

'What the fuck's "threshold"?' she asks, as Ellie purposely avoids making any adjustments to that particular menu.

'No fucking clue,' Ellie responds, finally figuring out which button to press to access the eight pre-programmed search modes – the Vanquish has four buttons you can press, this beast has twelve.

'Aha! Field one,' she announces triumphantly, locking in the factory programme she had read was best to start with.

'Do we want five tones?' Ellie turns to Lucie, who responds with a blank stare.

'We could have one, two, five or fifty?'

WOMEN

MARCH 2022, LINCOLNSHIRE, ENGLAND

Adrian's flock are rotational grazers. Every week they pop up in a different pasture field on the estate, bundled into his trailer and pulled by one, very battered, green Land Rover on a never-ending trip around the village.

The benefit for us – chasing the sheep – the living, breathing lawn-mowers, beautifully nibbling the pasture down, buzz-cut style. The optimum conditions for getting to grips with the Equinox, and even better yet, they've just trundled out of the manor-house field, which eluded us on our last visit to this section of pasture.

On top of all this, Lady H has very kindly offered us priority parking on the manor-house drive. It's like the stars have aligned.

*

The headphones connect instantly this time, remembering their partner.

'Little bastards,' Ellie mutters, still enraged at the trouble they caused last time – a dig full of trouble-shooting; bringing us a die-cast tractor, a pre-decimal Elizabeth II penny and a medieval buckle fragment, much to our tested patience.

Today is already looking more optimistic. The headphones are connected, we've made it into one of our most sought-after fields, and its tree-lined boundaries are offering much-needed shelter from the gusty, spring winds. Ellie's discarded our – no longer pristine – Minelab carry bag at the foot of the low, limestone wall which keeps the sheep from escaping into Lady H's treasured floral garden, and the complicated set-up goes much smoother this time, with less swearing.

At the furthest end of the field, fifty metres before the far metal gate, a grand walnut tree stands in solitude, just coming into leaf, pale green flowers adorning its branches. Lying directly across the old public footpath, which cuts diagonally across the field – before trailing up the hillside behind – its generous boughs must have offered a welcome shelter for lovers, walkers caught in the rain, and many a picnic beneath its shade.

THINGS WE FOUND IN THE GROUND

This footpath is what's captured our attention, a diagonal search area identified on the National Library of Scotland's side by side geo-referenced map viewer, marked by a double dashed line and 'F.P.' annotation. Comparing recent satellite imagery with antique Ordnance Survey maps, has become a favoured pastime of Ellie's recently, a way of understanding the use of the village over time and the footpaths lost over the centuries – aka the best opportunities to go 'coin shooting'.

Starting our search in the corner closest to the village, we follow the old footpath faithfully towards the walnut tree – well, to the best of our knowledge, its previous existence erased from the surface. Against our own advice, Ellie's forced to carry the Vanquish alongside Lucie, waiting for its moment to double-check any offered signals, a crutch that's more of a hindrance than a help.

'Ellie, let's check this one!' Lucie beckons, one hand grasping for the Vanquish, the other swinging the Equinox furtively over a loud *21*. Armed with one in each hand she performs a double-swing dance, the Vanquish volume on maximum, screaming into the idyllic quiet of the English countryside, the Equinox echoing its insistent call inside Lucie's headphones.

'Yep – that's a ringer,' she announces confidently.

Ellie struggles not to roll her eyes at the ridiculous scene we've created, crunching the spade through the damp grass, and reaching a gloved hand into the claggy soil below, the pinpointer shrieking persistently – deeper, deeper. Clawing through the sticky muck at the bottom of the hole – the recent rain unhelpfully raising the water table – a smooth, dark circle rises from the waterlogged depths.

'COIN!' Ellie shouts.

Rubbing it between her fingertips, Ellie attempts to remove the gluey sludge streaked across its dark, jade-green surface, peering into its worn features, just making out the date – 1863? – struck into the bottom. Turning it over, her suspicions are confirmed with the appearance of the smooth, almost featureless, yet still identifiable, bust of England's second longest reigning monarch, Queen Victoria, facing left.

'Good ol' Viccy,' Lucie remarks, 'this must be the footpath!'

'Viccy' slides into the foam security of the finds tin, Lucie confidently striding forward before hitting another deep target no less than five metres away.

'Vanquish!' she calls.

Ellie hands it over. When did she become Lucie's personal caddy?

Target affirmed by the screeching of the Vanquish, another dark-green coin springs from the side of the hole, tumbling with a velocity built up over decades of compression into the earth, leaving behind a hard, round, shell-like impression and an orange stain, which leeches into the water pooling at the bottom.

'Another one!' Ellie whoops. 'Eighteen-eighty-seven,' she reads, immensely satisfied both of the coins have emerged from the period – according to the maps – that the footpath was most popular, before being replaced by a new route in the early twentieth century. We've got to be right on top of it.

This new addition is also worn, but in much better condition than the last. Britannia, the female embodiment of the British Isles, rising from a deep green, mottled with patches of black. A small lighthouse and a ship out to sail flank either side of the seated goddess – an image first used by the Romans, presented here as an imperialist symbol of the British Empire at its peak during Victoria's reign.

'We're on a roll!'

By the arrival of the third signal, Ellie's reluctant to hand the Vanquish over, forcing Lucie to let go of her lingering attachment to our plastic beauty – it's time to move on.

She's right, too – it's another coin, and in even clearer detail than the other two already in the finds tin. Almost jet-black, speckled with flecks of green, Britannia isn't a featureless seated figure, she's wearing a gown, with delicate drapery crossing her body, and a Corinthian helmet perched atop her head, crested by a thick plumage. She's leaning on a shield, bearing the Union Jack and holding a trident with her left arm, its three prongs distinctive instead of rubbed away into obscurity; '1860' is marked below – a significant year – seated in the palm of Ellie's hand. It's one of the very first issues of this new bronze coinage.

THINGS WE FOUND IN THE GROUND

Previously, small change was struck out of copper, a heavier metal prone to corroding, which would stain fingers when damp and even gave off a 'bad eggs' smell. The switch to bronze – a lighter and more durable metal made from 95 per cent copper, 4 per cent tin and 1 per cent zinc – was welcomed by society, more suited to delicate Victorian tastes; it lightened pockets (both physically and literally as a result of rising copper prices), and set a precedent for decades to come.

On the other side, the reason for this early coinage's iconic name – the 'bun head penny' – is distinctly apparent through the mud smudged across its plane. Victoria's waves of hair are swept back, a laurel wreath – reminiscent of the Roman busts we've seen many times before – encircling her crown and tied beneath her plaited bun.

As the hat-trick is added to the tin, we both look at each other, silently acknowledging the confirmation that we've found the lost footpath. One's a fluke, two's a coincidence, but three – that's a pattern.

*

Queen Victoria was a hugely popular monarch during her rule, becoming somewhat of a symbol of stability and national pride. But arguably it wasn't her long reign of sixty-three years and seven months, the expansion of the British Empire, the booming industrial revolution, or even the waves of social change experienced under her rule that made her popular – it was her ability to connect with the public, to be relatable with them on every level.

You could term Victoria the UK's first influencer, sharing her and the royal family's lifestyle through newspapers, prints, postcards – virtually every piece of new ephemera created by the industrial age. She set trends, popularising the white wedding dress, the Christmas tree, tourism in Scotland, mourning – her presence on the throne even added fuel to the campaign for women's suffrage – but she was simply just being the 'ideal' woman, capitalising on the family values and moral code of the Victorian era.

WOMEN

At this time in the nineteenth century, due to the vast social changes created by the Industrial Revolution, society had become more divided than ever before: there were rigid divisions between social classes as new wealth widened the gap between owner and worker, but the most restrictive divisions of all were those placed upon gender. Beginning at birth, a girl was considered to be a disappointment, an extra mouth to feed, without any of the hopes of carrying on the family name. Any chance of a successful future centred solely around the aim they would attract a husband and birth him a son – sadly, it's shocking yet not surprising that until 1914, young girls had a higher death rate than favoured boys; who were fed better and sent away for a decent education.

This disadvantage didn't end with childhood for women; it continued throughout their entire lives. Shackled by ideas that becoming too educated could damage their ability to conceive children, and that work was something only acceptable for lower-class women out of utmost necessity, they were trapped in this society. There was a shortage of men, yet marriage was their only way to gain social position by relinquishing to their husbands all control of their bodies, property, earnings and children. They couldn't 'work' but they had to run the household, engage in expected 'feminine' activities such as charity work, needlecraft and other acceptable accomplishments, and offer any assistance possible to their husband, like balancing the accounts for his business – unpaid, of course.

For these middle-class ladies, the hardships of the lower classes – where women were employed in the factories, the coalmines, and domestic service – might have seemed like a liberation. If they dared to outlive their husbands or – God forbid – fail to attract one, the little acceptable occupations available to them, to earn any kind of living, were to become a teacher, dressmaker (an occupation threatened by the widespread introduction of the sewing machine in 1850) or, worse yet, the dreaded governess – which was only one step up from becoming a servant.

It must have been so significant for these women to see Queen Victoria emblazoned across their coinage. Especially this youthful, promising effigy we've discovered, which was issued for fifty-seven years, between 1838–1895, with only minimal changes – our variation designed by Leonard Charles Wyon. Victoria herself may not have, privately, been a supporter of women's suffrage – famously declaring it to be a 'mad, wicked folly' in words aired after her death – but, unwittingly or not, she found herself a compelling symbol of female power, at the helm of a period that saw significant social reform; with twelve universities and colleges admitting women into their degree courses, industrialisation expanding women's employment opportunities and an active campaign for women's rights by the end of her reign. She may have, in a way, 'just' been a wife, mother, and widow, performing to society's expectations, but simply by existing as a long-lasting monarch she indirectly inspired a nation of women to step out from the confines of the domestic sphere.

*

By late afternoon, we've abandoned the Vanquish back with the carry bag by the limestone wall – much to Ellie's delight, she's sick of lugging that thing around. Lucie's starting to trust the Equinox, it turns out they both speak the same language, albeit one more fluently than the other. The transition is certainly a learning curve, just not an unfamiliar one – we've already inadvertently laid the groundwork.

Emboldened by this new confidence, we leave the public footpath behind – it's well and truly trod now – covering an area between the walnut tree and a suspiciously moat-like ditch running in front of the wall. But as the most prominent feature in the field, it's hard to resist the walnut's lure, and we soon find ourselves being beckoned in by its branches waving gently in the wind.

'I've got a high twenties here, Ellie,' Lucie's swinging repetitively over a patch in the grass, sweeping from all angles, just catching the tone here and there.

'You sure it's not iron?' Ellie questions, put off by the flakiness of the signal – learning a new machine takes its toll on the poor digger, often meaning more bad signals are dug than good.

'I think we should dig it anyway.' Lucie chooses to listen to her gut over Ellie's suspicions. The walnut tree watching quietly behind us.

Ten minutes later, Ellie's cursing Lucie's gut. She's up to her elbows in damp, claggy soil, the hole seemingly bottomless, the pinpointer remaining the same persistent pitch with every scoop of earth – it's fever pitch, 'I'm on top of it!' scream tantalisingly out of reach.

'Do you think it's in the side?' Lucie offers some unwanted direction.

Ellie pretends not to hear, silently fuming as the next layer of earth is removed and the pinpointer indeed starts favouring the side – one thing Lucie hasn't got to grips with is the built-in pinpointing function on the Equinox, which seems to be sending Ellie consistently slightly off-target. It's a step up from the pivot and swing manual technique required for the Vanquish, but a delicate skill to master.

Lucie doesn't comment as Ellie gently pokes the sidewall with the edge digger, secretly pleased she was right. With a flick of the wrist, a clump of earth topples into the bottom of the hole, glinting a flash of silver up at us and erasing any leftover frustrations in an instant.

'What was that?' Lucie gasps.

'That was a something!' Ellie shouts, reaching for the cylindrical object, buried among the spoil. It's tinged with an orangey stain, mud obscuring its identity. A swipe of Ellie's thumb confirms the blinding silver colour.

'Wha—' Lucie's question gets cut off as Ellie removes more of the mud caking the object, revealing a distinctive, domed top, decorated by a concentric mesh of irregular annulets, and a smooth, defined base inscribed with two beaded cables.

'A THIMBLE!'

'It's not squished?' Lucie's shocked. We've never found one so pristine and unmarred before – still perfectly round despite its fragile walls.

'Do you think it's silver?' Ellie answers with another question.

'Could it be aluminium?' Our brains try to rationalise the probability of a find so perfect, picking at every opportunity to shatter the illusion.

THINGS WE FOUND IN THE GROUND

'I don't think so, it's heavy,' Ellie's struggling to comprehend what her eyes are witnessing – surely, it's a trick?

'Wait,' Lucie's suddenly serious, the penny dropping.

'Have we just found treasure?'

✱

A thimble might not seem like a great treasure, but, as an object over 300 years old and containing at least 10 per cent precious metal, this humble artefact marks our second addition to Lincolnshire's treasure tally – besides, who's to say it wasn't a great loss to the woman who dropped it?

Our thimble dates from Stuart England (1603–1714), a period of significant change and evolution gearing up to the first Industrial Revolution of 1760. Socially, Britain was emerging from the patriarchal society of the Middle Ages and heading towards the 'separate spheres' of the nineteenth century, when men and women were meant to exist in entirely different worlds – the public and the domestic, respectively. Now, don't get us wrong, medieval England was still a time of gender disproportion, with women possessing very few rights; but they were expected to participate in society, get involved in the harvest, trade in the markets and towns – and on rare occasions run their own businesses and pick up various types of irregular work to save up for marriage. Stuart England, on the other hand, saw a widening sexual division in labour, as agriculture was radically restructured, removing the farming practices women were previously responsible for. With women's 'work' becoming increasingly unpaid and confined to the home as a result, marriage was now one of the only ways to survive.

Defined by their sex, their marital status and the class level inherited through either their husband or father, women had very little they could call their own; they were more likely to live longer than men, yet there were very few possessions that they could keep hold of without the consent or support of a man. Except, that is, when it came to the household. Under English common law, wives could own no property or personal goods, however, domestic articles – your curtains, tablecloths, cutlery, crockery, books and sewing implements, for example – were entirely theirs and often left in wills. Suddenly, it's no longer 'just a thimble' we are holding, it's one of the few objects a woman had agency over in a world that was generally entirely out of her control.

Thimbles are one of those often overlooked objects, with a vague early history here in Britain – prior to the mass importation of brass thimbles from Nuremberg, Germany (the centre of the European thimble-making industry) in the fifteenth and sixteenth centuries. There's likely a number of reasons behind the thimble becoming a regular household object, its practical use for starters, and especially by the time of our thimble, in the seventeenth and eighteenth centuries, they had become an important symbol and regular gift of courtship. Ironically, as one of the few items a woman could own, they were also a potent symbol of all that trapped them – their domesticity. Of course, silver thimbles like this one wouldn't have been intended to mend the household linen, they would have been a rather nice, expensive gift, but the weight they carried wasn't just determined by their silver content, rather the expectations of an oppressive society.

As a double-edged sword, the silver thimble is tainted by imbalance, a small fragment of women's power, wrapped in an air of misogyny and confinement; a compelling artefact, steeped in women's history – only, should it belong on the shelves of rebellion or oppression?

*

14 DAYS LATER, LINCOLNSHIRE, ENGLAND

'When do you think we'll get the thimble back?' Lucie asks, halfway up the hillside behind the manor-house field, striking a lean on the Equinox as Ellie excavates a small hole against gravity.

'Um, I'm not sure,' Ellie replies, flicking a shotgun shell into her finds bag. 'Laura said not too long – so maybe a few months?' (Lucie doesn't get a proper answer for almost another year, when an email lands unexpectedly into Ellie's inbox announcing the thimble's safe release from the treasure process.)

The rest of the hike up the hill proves unfruitful, seldom for a nineteen-millimetre spanner likely dropped from a farmer's toolbag. We could claim the trek was slightly easier than our last visit, our leg muscles aching less, but Ellie was still out of breath at the top – pretending to soak in the view, which was admittingly still just as breathtaking as last time, and study the dig ahead to recover.

'The path should meet the road over there,' she points to a stile in the fence line, marking the end of the double-dashed line we began exploring last week, having just followed it up the hillside, with its junction to the long footpath running the height of the pasture – you might remember this one as the source of our traumatic rite-of-passage that (eventually) led us to gold. 'That would have been the main route of travel,' Ellie ponders. 'So maybe we should give it another go?' She's understandably keen to keep further exploration firmly on the flat plateau – if the gradient is enough to put her off surely travellers from yonder would have felt the same…

Turning right at the stile, it's easy to stay on track with the old footpath, the centuries' passage of feet trampling the earth into a sunken hollow bordered by the current walled boundary and a raised embankment on the right-hand side. Lucie takes it slow, with only the length of the field to cover before the footpath is cleaved by the wooden fence separating this portion of pasture from the next, she wants to make sure she's covering every inch. We weave slowly in a dance, from stone wall to embankment, the Equinox gathering the morning dew with each successive sweep of its coil.

It isn't long before a signal halts the procession.

'It's going, duh-duh-duh-duh,' Lucie announces, excited – she's never heard a tone like it.

'What do you think that means?' Ellie questions, leaning closer, almost ear to ear with Lucie to pick up the faint sound of the signal emanating from her headphones.

'Only one way to find out,' Lucie challenges, jamming down on the large, central 'pinpoint' button on the Equinox's control panel and sweeping back and forth in increasingly smaller passes as it screams a sci-fi-like sound somewhere between a car's reversing sensor and the wheezing and groaning of the Tardis materialising into reality – before emitting a solid tone as the coil sits directly on top of the target.

'There you go,' she indicates, wiggling the coil over the spot, before standing back and assuming her position as spectator – job done – Ellie taking over the excavation with an enthusiastic vigour that sees the three-sided plug flicked out in seconds.

'I see something!' she shouts a few minutes later, the urgency in her tone prompting Lucie to join her at the edge of the hole, the Equinox falling to the grass beside her, with no worries about getting her ears yanked off – thank the Lord for those Bluetooth headphones. Heads, and phone pressed together, we watch with bated breath as a small, silver disc comes into sight at the bottom of the hole. It's bent into the shape of an 'S' and rubbed smooth on both sides, but not by the passage of time – this wear is deliberate, intentionally made by hand.

'It's a love token!' Ellie grins – always happy by the discovery of a new artefact.

'A what?' Lucie quizzes.

'Love token!' Ellie replies. 'They used to bend them into this shape as a gift, or promise to their lover – it's symbolic,' she explains, referring to the long practice of the 'killing' of an object that dates back to pagan sacrifices and early worship as a symbol of personal sacrifice – only, by the sixteenth century, it was a symbol made to each other instead of to a saint or deity.

Lucie looks at it in awe. 'Do you think it was lost on purpose?' she muses, imagining a jilted lover and sordid affair.

'Maybe?' Ellie chuckles. It's funny how we're uncovering these personal objects intertwined with devotion and intimacy as she's starting to fulfil that portion of her life – finally – or perhaps she's only just beginning to notice them clearly.

Now 'official' with Katie, settling into a relationship has been wholly less daunting than Ellie feared. There was no awkward 'coming out' – her dad simply sent a screenshot of the two of them from the home-security camera into the family group chat, under the caption

'Ellie's new girlfriend' followed by a classic thumbs-up, and that was that. Meeting the parents went smoothly, a pub Sunday roast in idyllic Derbyshire, although Ellie has had to cultivate a liking for cauliflower cheese after clearing a plate of it out of politeness and in the act of making a good impression, so Katie's mum has taken it upon herself to make it from scratch whenever Ellie stays over. Katie's reassured Ellie they *never* had cauliflower cheese growing up. Plus, despite the Romans starting to become a banned topic, Katie's doing a good job of putting up with the metal detecting – we'll see how long that lasts after they move in together and Ellie brings half the field home each week.

Returning to our lazy weave, Lucie goes on the hunt for more of these 'duh-duh-duh-duhs' – rather grateful for the padded protection of the Minelab headphones as the wind whips up out of the valley. Listening carefully to every signal appearing, she mentally logs the target IDs and tones against the trash Ellie digs, getting to grips slowly with the Equinox's language.

Tiny lead bullet – a dull *10*. Ring-pull – a low and bouncy *14*. Shotgun shell – a solid *17*.

She pauses over a sketchy mid-*20s*, turning and swinging from different directions and not satisfied with the fluctuating signal she gets in response.

'Shall we dig?' Ellie questions, dusk approaching rapidly and leaving her eager to get back in the dirt before our time runs out.

'Hmm, I'm not sure, I don't like it,' Lucie walks away – not convinced – it's probably iron.

'I'll just dig it anyway!' Ellie calls after her, intrigued by the promise of a *20* – those don't appear that often.

'Knock yourself out!' Lucie shouts over her shoulder.

Ellie regrets choosing the flaky signal almost instantly, the spade glancing off rubble embedded into the soil – turns out the embankment might be the remains of an old walled boundary separating the footpath from the field. The pinpointer locks on immediately, however, screaming persistently into the depths of the hole. Spade abandoned, Ellie whittles down using her edge digger and fingers to prise out chunks of limestone. Fifteen minutes later, she's still digging. Lucie's waiting impatiently further down the footpath, checking the signal beneath her feet constantly, as if it might walk away the longer Ellie takes.

'Okay, I'm coming,' Ellie calls, resigned after a few more minutes, about to admit defeat to the rubble, flicking out the last stone with the edge digger.

'Lucie!' she shouts, the corner of the signal's source peeking out into daylight.

'What?' Lucie jogs over, Equinox abandoned, summoned instantly by the excitement in Ellie's voice, joining her over the hole and peering at the part-submerged artefact.

'The fuck's that?!'

In answer Ellie gently smooths the earth around the object, feeling for its edges and curling a fingertip under a corner to apply the right leverage to free it from the clutches of the soil. It slides free, a rectangular shape caked in mud, muted glimmers of gold glistening underneath. She swipes a thumb to remove the claggy dirt, and decorative reliefs reveal themselves – any tentative words about what it could possibly be are lost in the enchanted gasp from Lucie.

'It's stunning,' she breathes.

In Ellie's gloved grasp is a small, slim box, hinged on both ends and sealed by a highly decorative pair of lids. Both sides are engraved with scrolling fronds, the box's surface has been carved into a complex, leather hide shape, bordered by a twisting mass of tracery work. In the centre is a raised, decorative picture frame, mounting the tiny, yet incredibly intricate, lifelike portrait of a lady, with equally ornate writing crossing the width of the object and encircling the portrait.

'The Helen, needlecase. Patented, W. Avery & Son, Redditch,' Ellie reads out.

*

W. Avery & Son turns out to be a small, but highly renowned, Victorian needlecase manufacturer from a small village called Headless

Cross, on the south-west side of Redditch – the producer of the majority of the world's needles in the nineteenth century. They are best known for manufacturing figural needlecases, such as butterflies, elephants and even the Arc de Triomphe; but 'The Helen' has got to be the most socially significant design to come out of their short period of production between 1867–1890 (and a brief return in 1897 for the Diamond Jubilee).

'Helen' here on this needlecase is believed to be in recognition of Princess Helena, Queen Victoria's daughter, and one of the most active members of the royal family at the time, involved in extensive charity work, particularly in the exploits of women through nursing and needlework. Personally, it could be said that she conformed to society's expectations, marrying her third cousin, Prince Christian of Schleswig–Holstein, under the approval of her mother, bearing six children, and celebrating their golden wedding anniversary in 1916 – the only one of Victoria's children to do so. Yet, on the wave of social change which was building during the nineteenth century, Helena's extensive charity work – one of the feminine activities expected of a woman of her class – evolved into a revolutionary organisation that provided educated women with a rare opportunity for employment and independence.

This was the School of Art Needlework (known today as the Royal School of Needlework), founded in 1872 under the initiative of three women – Lady Victoria Welby, Lady Marion Alford and Princess Helena. They started in a small room above a bonnet shop, employing a group of twenty ladies, devoted to reviving the art of ornamental needlework which was threatened to fall into insignificance as a result of mass production. For fifty-one years Helena paved the way, becoming the organisation's first president and heading a campaign of fundraising which saw a purpose-built centre opened by 1903, and 150 women employed at the RSN's peak; she secured the work of Queen Victoria's funeral pall and intertwined the importance of hand embroidery with royal celebrations – starting a tradition stretching back to 1902 of RSN embroiderers working on the Coronation Regalia.

WOMEN

At a time where craft industries faced their biggest extinction as a result of the developing mass production industry, and women were just beginning their struggle for suffrage, Helena somehow managed to both save a decorative art and empower women with a livelihood; rescuing widows from poverty and educated women from diminishing under the shadow of their husbands. It's no wonder, then, or maybe a sign of the developing times, that in 1869, W. Avery & Son chose to place Helena at the forefront of their Demi-Quad needlecase (a flat-style case which could hold two packets of needles) – transforming a popular gift into a powerful symbol and lifeline of independence.

※

'That's really something special,' Lucie breathes, the needlecase still held between us in awe.

'I can't wait to clean it,' Ellie replies, knowing the details will come alive with a little attention.

'Do you think it still has needles inside?' Lucie asks, having hand-stitched many a hem through the years, her life before the pandemic cutting through her curiosity momentarily. But what would her previous life think of her now, having swapped her fabric shears and tailor's chalk for a metal detector? Talk about a change of direction. *You're supposed to have everything figured out by the time you turn thirty, and you couldn't be further from it,* her intrusive thoughts like to remind her.

With the needlecase nestled safely into the foam confines of the finds tin, we both blink back into our surroundings in a haze – easily getting lost to the act of searching. Dusk wraps around us, the evening drawing in like a cloak, the temperature dropping and the gentle murmur of birds settling in to roost in the trees below. Ellie checks her phone for the first time in hours and Lady H's contact fills her notification screen. One missed call, and one new voicemail, she taps onto it immediately – never one to keep the good Lady waiting.

'Um, Ellie. I know you're out there, do I put the kettle on?' Her voice crackles through the dirt-filled speakers of her phone.

Our new parking situation might be a good excuse to keep an eye on us.

'I'm taking that as our sign to call it a day.' Lucie chuckles.

12.

WARTIME

It has been several centuries since the county of Lincolnshire appeared as more than a solemn footnote in the history books, and thankfully the Industrial Revolution of 1760–1840 has done wonders for its self-esteem. New railway infrastructure created iron-working industries, which nurtured the growth of population, and engineering developments such as the first European-built combine harvester were rolling out of the city of Lincoln. Lincolnshire was starting to establish itself as a centre of engineering excellence, but the focus was still primarily agricultural – what other use was there for all the flat swathes of land dominating the county?

In 1914, everything changed. Archduke Franz Ferdinand was assassinated in Bosnia, and Britain pulled into a world conflict, the consequences of which no one could truly understand at the time. With over one million men volunteering to fight by December 1914, the home counties became completely devoted to the war effort, and the RAF set their sights firmly on the invitingly flat landscape of Lincolnshire. Airbases sprang up across the county, which was within spitting distance of Europe, reaching a total of thirty-seven by the end of the war. In response, Lincoln's industry pivoted direction: instead of combine harvesters and steam-driven threshing machines, Sopwith Camels, Royal Aircraft Factory B.E.2s, Bristol F2Bs, and Vickers F.B.5s flew out of Lincolnshire, carrying the mark of a winged imp.

WARTIME

Between 1915 and 1919, Lincoln was one of the largest centres for aircraft production in the world (manufacturing one in four British aircraft), the West Common Racecourse was repurposed into an Aircraft Acceptance Park (AAP) for aircraft testing, and this agricultural county became a frontline of defence against the oncoming German Zeppelins. But that wasn't enough for one industrial company of Lincoln, rising to the challenge set out by the Admiralty Landships Committee in 1915 and developing the innovative machine which would end the stalemate of trench warfare – the tank.

William Foster & Co had already been supplying the army with a caterpillar tracked tractor for the movement of heavy howitzer guns when they were chosen to work on a secret prototype machine that could tackle the mud, barbed wire, trenches and uneven terrain severely impeding the troops on the frontline. The first prototype, nicknamed 'Little Willie', emerged from the secret meetings held at the White Hart Hotel – between Foster's William Tritton, Royal Navy Armoured Car Sections' Walter Wilson and designer William Rigby – and was put through its paces on the South Common. Larger, operational tanks soon followed, arriving in Europe on 30 August 1916 and made by the hundreds of women, known as munitionettes working in Lincoln's factories.

Only, no one realised how much the tank would weave itself into the hearts of the public, becoming a symbol of Allied power and contributing to the war effort two-fold – both in the trenches and on the streets of Britain. Recognising the popularity of these new machines the Government capitalised on the tank to bring in much-needed funds for the war effort. The 'Tank Bank Campaign' it was called, seeing six tanks tour the country to raise money, with the most famous – the battle-scarred '141 Egbert' – auctioned off for permanent display in the town, which raised the most money – over £300 million – and an immeasurable amount of wartime spirit as people flocked from all over to catch a glimpse of these machines.

We were back on the map, unofficially as 'Tank Town' – a nickname carrying a legacy that goes far further than any footnote. During unexpected periods in its existence, Lincolnshire has found itself as one of the most important counties in the country, but perhaps the period it should be most proud of is the time it offered a beacon of hope to one of the worst conflicts Britain had experienced in its history – so far at least.

APRIL 2022, LINCOLNSHIRE, ENGLAND

Farmer Stan's given us a dangerous taste of the good life – drilled arable. With the entire estate firmly under crop, and little pasture we haven't already explored, he offered us a narrow window of opportunity before his beans grew five centimetres tall. It was a fever dream of a session over two weeks, torn between being wracked with nerves over disturbing Stan's crop, and delirious over the amount of finds produced out of the perfectly flat terrain.

And the finds tin was *overflowing*. We pulled out countless Roman grots, our earliest-ever hammered coin (a John I Short Cross), a beehive thimble, a turreted medieval annulet brooch, our first cut quarter (another Short Cross, this time a fragment snipped to make small change), a William III silver sixpence, rubbed smooth and bent into a love token, medieval belt mounts, strap ends, pot mends – the list just goes on. Lucie and the Equinox truly became one.

Sadly, that was last week. This week jolts us harshly back into reality – the beans growing faster than we can dig, leaving us staring wistfully back into the estate map. An outlier seems like one of the only options left – lest we fancy trekking up some mercilessly steep hillside pasture – a parcel of grass outside the confines and sanctity of the village, a leftover from the estate's heyday in the neighbouring hamlet. Following a short email chain with the estate manager, Ellie's uncovered which tenant farmer she needs to track down – Terry. Lucie prays desperately that his cows aren't in there already.

Thankfully, Terry gives us the go ahead, another limited opportunity to detect before his herd of cattle settle down for some spring grazing.

'Fuck, the grass looks long,' Lucie swears, peering over the metal gate as Ellie retrieves our equipment from the boot of the Panda she's precariously abandoned on the verge, tucked tight to the wall of an old gatehouse.

WARTIME

'Well, we could wait until the cows arrive ...' Ellie offers, knowing full well Lucie's distrust of these gentle grazers.

'Nah, I'm good,' Lucie replies instantly.

'Come and get your machine then,' Ellie laughs, rolling her eyes.

Only, Lucie was right to be concerned, the grass is indeed *long*. Practising a few sweeps, she can't see the coil for the grass blades, the weather gathering heavy clouds above in a silent threat. Admittedly it's not the best conditions for a day's detecting, but we can't deny our curiosity in this field – piqued by the long avenue of trees running down its centre, and the air of seclusion afforded by the high hedges, and wood copses enclosing it.

'I bet people dropped things down this old road,' Lucie remarks, making a beeline for the avenue – it does lead directly to the grandest house in the hamlet, after all, and offers the shortest grass available.

'Jesus,' Ellie groans as the spade refuses to pierce more than two centimetres into the compacted earth at its centre, the shock ricocheting through her spine.

'Fuck,' Lucie echoes. 'Change of plan, then.'

'Yeah, that's gonna break the spade,' Ellie flatlines glumly.

'That'll be where the gold is ...' Lucie mutters solemnly, voicing our shared discontent, turning off the avenue and disappearing into the sea of grass.

*

This field isn't kind to us. The terrain is inhospitable, every sweep of the coil a battle, the menacing clouds offering an unpredictable bombardment at any given opportunity. The finds have been nothing to write home about, either – a couple of old pennies. Ellie's clutching a finds tin which is looking considerably drier than we are, and Lucie's wielding the Equinox at maximum sensitivity in a futile attempt to pick up any signals tangled up in the grass – swinging through it with a technique she can only describe as 'bushwhacking'.

'Ellie, walk ahead, trample a path for me,' Lucie begs, struggling to pull the Equinox free from a particularly thick clump.

By some deluded miracle it works.

'ELLIE!' Lucie shouts, stamping down a wider patch of grass in a furious frenzy attempting to get the coil as close to the ground as possible, 'A SIGNAL!'

'Thank God!' Ellie calls, a few metres ahead.

She runs back and eagerly drives the spade into the ground, pulling back on the handle sharply in anticipation.

CRACK – she tumbles backwards with a cry of alarm, falling helplessly into a deep thicket of grass.

'Bloody hell, are you okay?!' Lucie shouts, alarmed by the dangerously jagged metal edge protruding from the ground and Ellie lying lifeless beside it.

'I'm okay, but I've snapped the spade,' she sits up sheepishly brandishing the handle.

Ellie's spade, our first digging casualty, not retired sympathetically like the Vanquish – but fallen in action.

'Do we have a backup one?' Lucie questions worriedly, not ready to give up yet.

'I think I've got one in the car.'

Ellie returns holding a black foldable camping spade. It doesn't last long, its flimsy frame bowing with the slightest of pressure. The signal still undug.

'Shit.'

'I can't dig with this!' Ellie snaps, frustrated by the predicament.

Before Lucie has time to speak, the heavens open and another deluge hits – and this time it's torrential. Quickly grabbing our sorry-looking tools, unable to dig, it seems we have no other choice but to make a dash for the Panda.

Heavy raindrops pelt the windscreen as we sit coldly in our sodden clothes, weighing up our very limited options – go home defeated or find another spade.

'Let's just buy another one,' Lucie pipes up. 'It won't take us long.' She's already found the closest hardware store on Google maps, 'We'll be back within the hour.'

It's a reasonable proposition that cuts short Ellie's catastrophising. She's stewing in the driver's seat, wishing she hadn't snapped the spade and cursing herself for not having a better backup on hand.

'All right – let's do it,' she agrees, roaring the Panda to life, her black mood beginning to lift at the offer of a sensible solution.

We shouldn't really be out in public in our current state – bedraggled, soaked to the bone, and Ellie looking like she's had an unfortunate run in with a ditch. But despite being absolutely drenched and down a vital team member, we firmly refuse to call it a day. Instead, we violate the local hardware store with our presence, effecting a short and efficient raid – from store entrance, to gardening aisle, checkout and exit – the spade replacement secured, a disgruntled janitor mopping the sodden trail of mud and water left behind in our wake.

Making it back to the field, the signal that started this whole fiasco is nothing more than a shotgun shell.

'Fuck's sake,' Lucie laughs – at least the downpours have stopped.

Ellie resumes her grass-flattening duties doggedly.

*

'This has gotta be something,' Lucie pleads, 'It's a twenties.' So far, our janitor-based crimes in the hardware store have been for shotgun shells and buttons.

'At least a penny,' Ellie agrees, grabbing the clod by the thick tuft of grass pluming out of the top. But the pinpointer has different ideas, screaming at a large object buried into the soil – much bigger than a penny.

'Whoa,' she gasps, as it comes free suddenly, springing into her palm.

'Is that a tiger?' Lucie exclaims as Ellie turns it over.

A tiger does indeed stand proudly in the centre of Ellie's hand, it's muddy, striped coat unmistakeable, poised below a curving banner – mid-stride – right paw outstretched as if offering a handshake, his tail curling towards his hind legs. Situated atop a mound

THINGS WE FOUND IN THE GROUND

of grass, a ribbon banner curls below, the word 'Leicestershire' just discernible in the dirt coating its surface.

'Do you think it's a cap badge?' Ellie questions.

*

The immense pressure of the First World War saw the British Army change from a small, professional army built out of close-knit units to a massive, conscripted force. It could have been a development that led to disaster on the battlefield, harbouring disconnection and confusion, if it wasn't for the pre-existing identities of the well-established regiments adopting the new recruits into a rich sense of national pride and belonging.

With regiments based around a location since the eighteenth century – generally a specific county or region – the identity of that regiment became rooted into the local communities, fostering a strong fighting spirit and camaraderie. Even the military regalia used by the regiments instils this sense of kinship, utilising military heraldry to channel heritage through symbols important to the regiment's own history. The humble cap badge becomes both a means of identification and an acceptance into a family, carrying the inspiration for a greater sense of belonging.

The tiger is a symbol of Lincolnshire's neighbours, the Royal Leicestershire Regiment – who were known as the 'Tigers' during the First World War. It refers back to their time in India, from 1804–1823, where they upheld an arduous eighteen-year stint laying down the foundations for the British Empire (an exploitative and devastating instance of colonialism today, but during the First World War, a proud example of service to their country). Awarded in 1825, and making an appearance on the cap badges thereafter under the word 'Hindoostan' (historically, the northern Indian subcontinent); the tiger stands as a reminder of the courage and determination of those who served before them – a strength to draw from in difficult times.

Nineteen Royal Leicester Regiment battalions fought in the First World War – from the trenches in France to the desert in Mesopotamia

WARTIME

– earning three Victoria Crosses and thirty-seven Battle Honours. They proved themselves over and over; at the Battle of Neuve Chapelle, breaking into the German position during the first planned British offensive of the war in 1915; and again in the stubborn defence of Épehy in 1918, despite constant attacks by three German divisions – just to name a couple. They battled through the war with bravery and dedication, losing approximately 9,000 Royal Leicester Regiment boys to foreign soil, and earning a significant honour from the crown in 1946 in recognition – the entire regiment lifted to 'Royal' status.

For the Leicestershire soldiers and fresh recruits sent to the frontline during the First World War, the legacy held within this tiger must have seemed like a formidable reputation to uphold – but uphold it they did.

*

As quickly as the tanks rolled off the factory floor, Lincolnshire disappeared from history (once again) with the end of the Great War – those thirty-seven wartime airfields reduced to just four by 1925.

It was a harsh time, the interwar period, felt solemnly by the entire country – which emerged in the grips of an economic depression – so at least Lincoln's newfound engineering prowess saw the city experience a chance for employment and residential development. And Lincolnshire wouldn't have to wait long – only the space of a generation – for the history books to come knocking once more. The arrival of the Second World War, in 1939, saw the county adopting a new identity – shifting from 'Tank Town' to 'Bomber County'.

Facing the growing threat from Germany, the RAF was tempted back onto Lincolnshire's flat landscape and close proximity to Europe in 1935. Over the following years and the course of the subsequent war, a whole chain of new bomber airfields were planned and commenced, disused airfields were repurposed and reopened, radar and wireless stations were planted along the coast, and major supply facilities were integrated into the infrastructure – opening a fuel depot along the River Trent at Torksey, and a huge munitions dump at Market Stainton. By the end of the war, in 1945, Lincolnshire had forty-nine airfields – more than any other county in England – and had become the home of 80,000 RAF personnel including those from the Commonwealth such as, Australia, Canada, and New Zealand, and two major groups of Bomber Command (5 Group and 1 Group).

The very first bombing operations of the war left the airfields of Lincolnshire, and an uncountable number followed – including the infamous 'Dambusters' raid carried out by Bomber Command's 617 Squadron in 1943. This vast military presence was undoubtedly life-changing for the county; the thrumming of aviation in the skies above, constant – day and night. The new airfields bringing road diversions and closures – even affecting routes which had been present for over a millennia, such as Ermine Street. The RAF created much-needed work and service, but it was mixed deeply with danger – after all, Bomber Command units suffered the highest casualty rate of any other branch of Second World War forces.

For six long years, Lincolnshire's big skies were filled with Avro Lancasters, Battle of Britain fighters, the United States Army Air Force (who took over five airfields), retaliating German bombers and Lincoln Cathedral, which had watched over this largely agricultural county for over eight centuries. The cathedral's central spire had been a beacon throughout its lifetime, guiding pilgrims and devotees to its sanctuary, but between 1939 and 1945 it was the turn of the returning airmen to look towards its spire for salvation.

*

As quickly as the digging opportunities appear, they soon fade – spring-time detecting confirming the unpredictable nature of the hobby. As the weeks pass, Terry's herd settles into the cap badge field, the grass munched elusively short, our bitter struggles among its jungle long forgotten. All that's left for us, in terms of fields, is the steep pasture we've been avoiding – a stretch of hillside cleaved by the entrance road to the village. It's vast and difficult to manage, relentlessly open to the elements, and a whole lot of effort to get up there.

'I've left the finds tin behind,' Ellie mutters quietly, looking dejectedly down to the car, which has become a mere dot below.

'I'm not walking back down,' Lucie responds flatly – it's not like Ellie to forget such a crucial piece of equipment. 'Hang on.' Rummaging around in her bag, she pulls out lunch, emptying her snack-sized Pringles tube into a sandwich bag and offering it to Ellie, who squats down, pulls a clump of grass and moss from the ground, and stuffs it inside to act as natural packing to protect any finds.

'Sorted,' she announces with a grin.

Several hours later, it becomes clear that Lucie needn't have sacrificed her Pringles – a battered Tombac button all that resides among the mossy bed. Munching her (now crushed) Pringles, lunch break is rather glum, the sparseness of signals adding a thick layer of frustration that even Ellie's trademark optimism struggles to clear. The sad meal deal we consume doesn't help either – offering no warmth against the bitter wind scything off the hillside.

'What about venturing into the middle next?' Ellie asks, turning to see her suggestion fall on deaf ears – Lucie lost to a furious scroll on her phone.

'There's another one!' she blurts enraged, trapped in the comments of our latest video.

Ellie sighs. 'Just ignore it …' She's beginning to wish we'd never shared the discovery of our gold Angel.

'Fake'; 'Planted'; 'Too clean'; 'Planted for clout'; 'Staged'; 'FAKE'.

At over one million views and counting, the comment section has spiralled far out of our control.

'I don't get it,' Lucie exasperates – it's taking every ounce of her willpower not to reply to the trolls. 'How can people think it's fake?'

'It doesn't matter,' Ellie huffs. 'We lived it, we know it happened.' But with the comments overpowering both of our notifications, making it impossible to glance at our phone screens for weeks without being reminded of the latest accusations, it's hard not to take it personally. Going viral is not all it's cracked up to be.

THINGS WE FOUND IN THE GROUND

'I *need* to find something,' Lucie sighs, standing up in a furious determination and stuffing her phone into her pocket – the comments out of sight, but far from out of mind.

Ellie follows solemnly, knowing we won't be leaving this field until we do. We aren't really sure what we are searching for – most detectorists approach the hobby seasonally, not venturing out during these torturous months where the crops are tall and only the difficult land is left to dig. In all honesty, we are probably seeking to prove ourselves in some way, and to show the comment section they are wrong, but above all we need to find a distraction.

'Oh, my God,' Lucie breathes.

'At last!' Ellie echoes.

A dainty artefact emerges between Ellie's grip. After a beat, she lightly brushes away the remaining soil to reveal a bright, navy-blue anchor – the fouled anchor – a symbol we first became acquainted with in Papa Rob's garden. This time it's surrounded by plant fronds and topped with a small regal crown, an enamel banner emblazoned with the words 'ROYAL NAVY' hanging below. But this doesn't look like a button, it's an intricately crafted shape, with a suspension loop perching on top of the crown – it must be a badge.

'Is there something else in the clod?' Lucie questions, the empty suspension loop raising suspicion.

Ellie drives the pinpointer back into the soil in answer, it chirping back happily with a positive affirmation. Grasping the identified handful of soil in her hand, the loamy mix falls away easily with the help of the pinpointer, sifting until only a tiny blue metal ribbon, tied into a perfectly formed bow, sits in her palm. Its enamel is degraded and patchy, yet strikingly colourful after all these years – the distinctive naval blue uniting the two halves.

'The suspension ring must have broken,' Lucie notes.

'Glad we found both parts,' Ellie nods, pleased, holding the two pieces close for a moment, before placing them delicately inside the Pringles tube with the Tombac button – it has been a *long* day but suddenly that doesn't matter.

'What do they say? Always check your holes twice …' Lucie smiles.

WARTIME

19 JANUARY, 1886, LONDON, ENGLAND

It's the wedding day of David Ogilvy, the 11th Earl of Arlie, and Lady Mabell Gore at St George's, Hanover Square. Ten years Mabell's senior, David is a respected soldier, having served in Afghanistan and Sudan as part of the 10th Hussars – the highly esteemed cavalry regiment. To mark the occasion, he's had a bespoke wedding gift made for his new wife; a gold, diamond and enamel brooch crafted into a miniature version of his own 10th Hussars insignia. It goes down incredibly well, Mabell is the first woman to wear a regimental badge, attracting much admiration and prompting her to claim herself as the start of a new fashion trend.

And she isn't wrong.

By the beginning of the First World War, and during the Second World War, these miniature brooches were made for all sections of the armed forces. They become a popular gift, dubbed 'Sweetheart Brooches', both handmade and mass-produced and widely available across the country, left behind with loved ones as a symbol of their boy on the frontline. It is said that every woman seemed to wear one; wives, girlfriends, and mothers.

With the majority of men drafted to the frontline, class and gender became blurred as society devoted itself to the national war effort. In 1941 all unmarried women between twenty and thirty years of age were called for national conscription and given the choice between; women's military service, of which Lincolnshire's Women's Auxiliary Air Force held the largest branch; industry work, at factories such as Ruston's and Hornsby's in Lincoln; or to move to the countryside and join the agricultural labour of the Women's Land Army.

The men were sent to the front and the women were sent to the fields and factories – both subject to different forms of displacement. So it seems to make sense that this form of jewellery became so prolific. The Sweetheart Brooches were an important connection to a person their loved ones thought of as home, a precious talisman worn to bring them safety, and being miniature versions of the force that had taken them away, enveloped the women in the same sense of belonging and pride invoked by the military symbols and badges as the men on the frontline.

This strong, emotional link between the frontline and the home front was capitalised on by the Government and turned into a form of commercial trench art; a valuable propagandic tool to increase the pressures of conscription and service as a visible symbol of the sacrifices made by men 'doing their bit' – and sacrifice is sadly the perfect word for it as these artefacts became intrinsically connected with loss, as over a million British soldiers were killed in action during the First and Second World Wars.

At that time, you might have seen a woman in the street wearing a Sweetheart Brooch – a blue and silver fouled anchor, hung beneath a ribbon bow – but is her brooch worn in patriotic pride, desperate hope, treasured memory, or in justification of the great loss they have suffered? Alternatively, is their breast empty? The brooch buried deep in a drawer, the reminder of the grief too overwhelming to bear. Sadly the latter leads to these emotional pieces of jewellery slipping – or being buried – deep from the public consciousness, their stories hidden from families, tucked into a shoe box on the top shelf as part of an archive of mourning which is too painful to open.

As a harsh reminder of loss, hope and national pride, we can't blame them for seeking to bury these artefacts in places they hoped would never be found.

*

The trek back down to the village is heavier than usual. Carrying our tools with weary bodies, the gloom of dusk dragging at our heels, the Pringles tin is weighed down by our unexpected find – and one solitary Tombac button.

'Let's get home,' Ellie says, shrugging her finds bag into the boot and tossing the spade unceremoniously after it.

Lucie responds only with a silent nod, struggling to pull her wellies off and dumping them into a plastic bag before slumping into the passenger seat.

Trundling up the hill, we pass the field, it looks much tamer from the car seat – almost picturesque – giving little clues to its wild unrelenting nature. Our bodies tell us differently, wind-worn and drained from hours of being overexposed to the elements. You'd think this would put someone off, being pushed to the limits by the minimal signals and little respite, but it's all forgotten when that find appears in the ground.

With the village disappearing in the rear-view mirror, Lucie sits quietly, watching the hedgerows warp into a blur of green through the passenger window; knowing all that's waiting for her in the attic bedroom is the turbulent emotions of loneliness, frustration and her own intrusive thoughts. Cautiously navigating dating again has come with its own set of afflictions, exacerbating her isolation from loved ones back home and bringing to the surface new fears of vulnerability after the abrupt end of her previous long-term relationship contributed to her swift international exit. The relentless barrage of criticism online – dubious opinions, with undertones of misogyny from the depths of the internet – is only adding to this feeling of being misunderstood, which the fields and the finds have helped distract her from – allowing her to escape for a moment into somebody else's story.

AUGUST 2022, LINCOLNSHIRE, ENGLAND

'When will I next see you girls?' Lady H asks, keeping the conversation to familiar territory after the weight of the last few hours. We are halfway between Arthur's house and the manor house, making slow progress down the village lane – Lady H careful to avoid the potholes with her walking stick.

'We'll be back next week,' Ellie replies with a smile, her hands shoved deep into the silk-lined pockets of her dark green and black blazer, Lucie a few steps ahead in a black dress and the darkest trainers she owns.

'Lady H!' A voice calls from behind.

'Peter, what a lovely service that was.' Lady H turns to greet a tall, clean-shaven gentleman who's caught up to us. 'You know Ellie and Lucie – my archaeologists.'

'Oh, yes, I've seen you two around,' he shoots us a warm smile, recognition dawning, not used to seeing us mud-free and in civvies. 'The village won't be the same without Adele,' he acknowledges. Paying his respects to the village's biggest advocate, jam-maker, soul of Sunday service, and gentle host of a much-welcomed winter digging refuge whenever Lady H visited her London home – Adele's husband, Arthur, always taking a keen interest in our discoveries over a steaming beverage and a homemade pudding.

'Oh, she will be missed,' Lady H agrees glumly, thinking of their small congregation at church – now dwindled to three.

'Did you get a chance to speak with Arthur after the service?'

'Yes, I thought he seemed to be handling it all rather well,' she replies, familiar with the difficulties of widowhood.

Peter walks with us to the drooping willow tree, marking the entrance to the manor-house drive, before disappearing down the lane at Lady H's insistence – refusing to hold him up any longer than necessary. Our procession ends at the side door, stepping off the gravel and onto the flagstone patio.

'Where's the next dig?' Lady H smiles, ready to retire for the evening.

'We're not too sure,' Lucie responds, 'there's not many fields available.'

'Hmm, have you tried the fete field?' Lady H suggests with this twinkle in her eye, hinting it's more of a demand than a suggestion. She's become accustomed to our presence in the village, wanting to give us as many reasons as possible to drop in for a treasured cup of tea.

Ellie's eyes immediately light up. 'The one by the old school building?'

'That's the one. Why don't you ring Kieran? I don't see why you couldn't.'

*

'Give me a second, I'll whip round it in the mower for you girls,' Kieran's hearty voice booms through the speakers on Ellie's phone, leaping into action at Lady H's suggestion.

Lucie cheers silently from her position next to the speaker – short, flat, pasture, sounds like the perfect day.

'You're a legend, Kieran.' Ellie grins, ecstatic at this reprieve from the brutal conditions on the hilltop.

WARTIME

The village fete field is only a short walk from the manor house, tucked behind a stone cottage and a bank of grey Edwardian houses next to the old school. It's a tiny pocket of pasture, more reminiscent of a garden than a field, bordered by leafy trees and a wooden fence which is occasionally visited by the odd cow nuzzling over.

Kieran's done an excellent job on the mower. The sweet scent of freshly cut grass still hanging in the air as we set up our gear in the far corner, mixed with an earthy undertone of nettles and cow parsley. After the vast expanses of open pasture we've been traversing, this field is invitingly small – there's nothing on the surface to get overwhelmed with here.

'Fucking hell, there's so many signals in here!' Lucie shouts, her first tentative sweeps of the Equinox exploding a cacophony of different sounds in her ears.

'Good,' Ellie replies, after weeks of hard-earned searching, she's liking the sound of easy targets and quick digging.

It takes Lucie a minute to adjust to our new terrain – going from searching for the slightest chirp to plucking out the most promising targets amid the noise. And it's impossible to ignore any in the screaming high-*20s*.

'Ellie. Dig this one!' Lucie calls, locking onto her first signal.

It's a rolled gold pocket-watch case, bent, and missing its movement – our first ever.

'Have you two found something?' Engrossed in the discovery, we don't notice the arrival of a visitor into the field. We look up in tandem, startled to see a lady on a large horse looking down at us.

'Um ... yes!' Ellie replies, put on the spot, offering up the pocket watch for inspection.

'Oh!' She's delighted. 'I turned up at the right time!' Her horse shuffles beneath her restlessly.

'We've only just started,' Lucie adds, wishing we had more to share.

'Well, best of luck to you then, girls, I'll see you around!' And with that, she gives her horse a light squeeze with her calves and trots away.

'That was odd,' Ellie turns to Lucie, watching our unexpected visitor bob down the hedgerow.

'I thought she was going to tell us off,' Lucie agrees, already swinging again with a chuckle.

'What kind of signals do you think we should look for?' With over a century of celebrations taking place here, the most likely objects lost would be coinage – the busy atmosphere creating easy chances for coins to tumble out of people's pockets unnoticed.

'How about a mid-teens – fifteen to sixteen?' Lucie proposes.

'Yeah, why not.' Ellie shrugs. After the success of our first signal she's happy to dig anything. Her job is fairly easy in here, the soil soft and pliable, with little resistance to her excavations. As soon as the grassy clod is flipped over, the pinpointer screams into action. Her fingers grasping onto something hard at the bottom of the hole, gently pulling, she teases and wiggles the artefact free until she can seize the main bulk of it, drawing it into the light.

We instantly know it's a toy. A horse frozen mid-gallop, its hind legs missing below the knee, reins curving down from its muzzle, a rider grasping onto them with one arm next to its mane, the other amputated at the shoulder, his head decapitated.

'That's so funny,' Lucie remarks. 'A horse and rider!'

'That lady must have brought us some luck.' Ellie chuckles in disbelief.

But rather than a lady out for a casual ride, our headless rider is a soldier mounted for battle.

*

Pre-First World War, Britain was gripped in a 'toy soldier craze' with around eleven million figures estimated to be produced in Britain – per year – before 1914.

And there was one British manufacturer at the forefront of this obsession: William Britain, the London toy maker – originally a brass-clock maker – who invented a technique for hollow casting in 1893, which revolutionised manufacture. Previously, toy soldiers had been of solid construction, imported from toy manufacturers in Germany and France, and accessible largely by wealthy families, but now, thanks to Britain, these lead figurines (the use of this poisonous metal wasn't banned in toy manufacturing until 1966) were widely available for the masses. And they loved them. The 1890s sparked the beginning of the toy soldier craze, with figurines exported across the world in pre-painted sets, William Britain's company shipping over 200,000 figurines a week in over 100 different varieties.

For Britain, this was the heyday of its empire, marking the height of its expansion, and fostering a strong sense of militarism with the public. Ideas of national pride, service and duty, were prolific, and a good war was in many ways something to be proud of. It's no surprise, then, that real-life wars directly influenced the toy soldiers, with sets produced for wars such as the Second Boer War of 1899–1902 as a form of propaganda.

It was a dangerously romantic ideal of war, young children waging warfare, and, without a doubt, it influenced many of the 2.5 million young men who volunteered for the Army at the start of the First World War – swept up in a patriotic fervour and national duty which had been fostered from a young age playing with tiny soldiers mounted on horseback.

*

The fete field lives up to all expectations. There's no chance for boredom. Ellie's constantly digging hole after hole, moving at a rapid pace through the signals Lucie provides. The finds tin can barely cope let alone close – no thanks to the oversized lead cavalry soldier and pocket watch taking up all available space. It's a good thing we've expanded our arsenal recently, the new coins pod (a small plastic, screw-top container filled with foam, and bearing pre-cut slots ready to protect any coins slid into its depths) proving its worth, as the multitude of coins we imagined would be here, start to materialise.

The coins come alone, in pairs, threes, and even quadruplets. It's essential to check every hole multiple times, as a whole pocket's worth of pre-decimal pennies and silver change is frequently scattered densely into the earth. A common loss, clearly aided by the collection of champagne toppers gathering in Ellie's bag, and, if the 1937 Coronation Medal for George VI and Queen Elizabeth is anything to go on, stark evidence of the entire village coming together in celebration. Perhaps for the last time.

But the evidence doesn't just point towards the small community centred here in the village, it also indicates the wider economic repercussions of two world wars; where Britain entered as a world power and left crippled by a substantial war debt – the global balance of power shifting indefinitely.

For over two millennia, Britain had relied upon a precious metal coinage system – with value based around gold or silver content. Sticking out of the earth in our latest target, however, is a large 'silver' coin which only contains 50 per cent sterling – the result of a level of debasement in 1920 that was unheard of since the times of Henry VIII – the immeasurable pressure on the supply of metals during the First World War driving silver prices out of control and ending the circulation of gold coinage forever.

'1942' is all that's visible on the edge protruding from the side of the hole, the latter end of the Second World War. By this point, Britain would have spent close to £7 billion on the war effort – and it couldn't continue. War Loans from America provided one of the only solutions to Britain's debt, a choice that would ultimately undermine Britain's world standing and cause eighty-eight million ounces of silver to be taken directly from the nation's pockets in 1947 – a total debasement necessary to repay the war debt. This was the end of precious metal coinage in Britain, silver replaced entirely by cupronickel, and the emergence of a new world order, with heavy lender, the USA, taking the global stage as a world superpower alongside the USSR.

*

'Shall we try a little number next?' Lucie throws out there. 'Eleven to twelve – sounds consistent.' With so many finds coming up, she's reluctant to ignore any good-sounding signals, regardless of their high reading on the Equinox or not – she's dreaming of an earring torn off mid-twirl, a ring flinging from a hand mid-gesture, or a cuff link ripped from a sleeve.

Only it turns out to be none of the above …

Ellie is scraping gently around the exposed gleam of grey metal, trying to establish its shape. Once it's suitably loose she prises it out between thumb and forefinger, its emerging form drawing out sounds of our immediate delight into the late afternoon.

'IT'S A SEAL.' And not the medieval Latin variety. A gentle, flippered sea creature basks on Ellie's open palm, nose raised to the air.

'OH MY GOD.'

'I LOVE HIM.'

There's nothing like a quirky and unexpected find to bring out your inner child.

*

William Britain's Toy Company had been out of the toy industry since 1917 – when it focused entirely on making lead shrapnel balls for munitions – and restarted in a world that had substantially changed. The British appetite for warfare had all but vanished, 880,000 soldiers had been lost on the frontline and families wanted no reminders of the conflict that had taken their beloved boys.

This was a social shift that had a profound effect on the toy industry. In response, Britain's invested heavily in new moulds – new figurines – recycling the lead munitions no longer needed for the war effort into civilian toy ranges and moving forward to promote a peaceful and optimistic approach to life. In 1923 the company introduced its 'Home Farm' series, building on its success with a Zoo, Horse Racing, Gardening, Circus and Mail Van range by 1940.

The coming of the Second World War, reignited a small appetite for military figures as the spirit of national pride and 'doing your bit' re-entered public consciousness and new weapons and vehicles used in the war were produced by Britain's in miniature for their children. But once again the toy industry was crippled as factories switched entirely to munitions production in 1941, and the market for warfare was damaged by a public weariness and national loss created by six years of world war.

Post-war Britain threw itself into a new era, one of looking ahead to the future, working towards full employment and technological development that would leave the austerity and pain of the war years far behind. And this included the military toys, which simply never recovered back to their pre-First World War consumer fever, instead it was the zoos, the farms, and, by the 1950s and 1960s, the space age which would occupy the imaginary worlds of Britain's children.

*

'Oh. Hello Arthur!' Ellie greets warmly as our second visitor of the day shuffles into the field, laden down by a tripod and camera.

'Oh! Ellie and Lucie!' he responds, surprised to see us digging up his birdwatching spot. 'Anything interesting lately?' He's a bit more reserved than usual, quiet and contemplative, but pleased to see us.

We show off our overflowing finds tin, Arthur particularly excited by the lead toys; and that's the thing with this hobby, it's never about the age of the finds, their value or even the rarity, the more artefacts we pull from the earth, it's their stories pulling us in.

Ellie puts the finds tin safely back into her bag as Arthur shares what brought him to the field, pulling a computer printout from his pocket – a grainy snapshot. 'It's a black-tailed godwit, Lady H spotted it on the village pond, she's very excited by it,' he explains. It seems Lady H has sent him on a wild goose chase of sorts – probably a well-intended distraction to keep him busy.

As he sets up his tripod among the trees, looking out towards the neighbouring field. We take that as our cue to leave. The fete field becoming a small haven once more – it's given us our reprieve, now it's Arthur's turn.

13.

RIDGE AND FURROW

MAY 2022, LINCOLNSHIRE, ENGLAND

We've exhausted Kieran's generosity with the mower; the last few weeks in the fete field have brought us a small sanctuary of enjoyment amid what has been a relatively tough off-season for us diggers. Admittedly, nothing you would deem 'Ancient' has emerged from our grassy sanctum, but a number of quirky artefacts have – sometimes all you want to do is dig holes knowing you'll find something interesting, regardless of its age.

Now, however, we're ready for a change of scenery – harvest really can't come soon enough. The fete field is essentially a small square no bigger than a tennis court to search, you barely have time to think in between signals, but there comes a time when you start itching for a challenge – to head out on a limb, into the furthest fields you've been putting off. For us that's a narrow, steep and skinny hillside pasture strip, looking down on our Roman field, and covered in an undulating swathe of ridge and furrow. We've always wondered what could be up there, but getting up there is half the problem.

'Jesus, watch out!' Lucie closes her eyes as the leaning stile crumbles under Ellie's weight, pitching her alarmingly onto the barbed-wire fence.

'Fuck.' Ellie tumbles ungracefully back into the Roman field, almost bringing the fence down with her and somehow emerging unscathed and ready for a second attempt. Tentatively testing the water with a foot back on the stile, the entire length of the fence wobbles back and forth, the stile completely detached from the ground, held up only by the tension of the barbed wire.

'I don't think this is a good idea,' Lucie says, envisioning Ellie ripping an artery open on the barbs, the air ambulance landing in the Roman field behind her as she attempts to stem the flow with her Patagonia fleece. 'We're gonna have to go the long way round,' she concludes resolutely, giving Ellie no choice in the matter – she's never been good with the sight of blood.

'Maybe there's another stile we can try,' Ellie offers, not willing to give in just yet.

There wasn't. A good forty-five minutes later, we are squeezed onto the verge of the village road as a tractor rumbles past at breakneck speed down the hill, this lane barely having enough space for two cars to pass. Gravity really isn't on our side, either, as these cars whizz off the main road above and around a blind corner, facing us with a treacherous game of chicken – are we going to see the car or will the car see us first?

'The gate's just up there,' Ellie puffs, pointing to a gap in the hedgerow.

Between the cars, we make a dash for it, the metal gate clunking open into a small, wooden sheep corral. At the second gate, Ellie struggles with the stiff spring-loaded bolt, it stubbornly refusing to leave the old horseshoe that has been re-used as its keep – some farmer-recycling at its finest. With a grunt she yanks it, the gate swinging out into the field. We've made it, at last.

'I'll detect to the top!'

After an arduous journey here, Lucie's raring to get going, striding straight up an almost vertical incline. Unlike the other pasture fields along this ridgeline, there's very few flat areas to detect here; the broad plateau found at the summit dwindled away to a lingering strip as if the hillside had simply slipped away. There's also not much shelter offered by the row of crooked, deformed trees arranged solemnly at the bottom of the field; the winds whipping harshly off the plains, crashing against the first obstacle they've encountered for miles, and shaping the growth of anything daring to vegetate here. But the hillside isn't as hostile as it first appears; several springs bloom across its sheer slope, cultivating pockets of thriving rushes, boggy pools and clusters of molehills. And then there's the rippling fluctuation of ridge and furrow – the peaks and troughs carved out by oxen dragging a single-sided plough, creating drainage and dividing the land into strips – revealing an abundant presence of farming activity from the thirteenth and fourteenth centuries. This medieval open-field system, one of the few features offering us some assurance in an otherwise uninviting and seemingly desolate landscape. Content with the knowledge that we – and Adrian's flock of sheep – aren't the only ones to tackle the escarpment, this land experiencing a multitude of lifecycles before being converted into pasture.

'It feels ancient up here, Ellie,' Lucie voices, coming to a stop at the top of the ascent and soaking in the atmosphere. Ellie agrees with a hum and a nod, both of us feeling like we are on the edge of the world; looking out onto our Roman field below. The landscape stretches almost endlessly, a patchwork of bright green and yellow, we can see the crops growing nicely (to Stan's delight, no less), the dog walkers setting off down the footpath we dug up in desperation, and in the distance, the bumbling figures of sheep nibbling away in a small pasture field.

'Let's dig some holes.'

*

By lunchtime, Ellie's had enough of digging holes. Any concerns we have about suffering from a lack of signals up here dissipated with the appearance of shotgun shell, after lead bullet, after airgun pellet – goddamn the pheasant hunters. The problem with all of this shooting detritus is that, made of brass, copper and lead, they give off great signals, and if there's one thing we've learned from metal detecting, it's never to ignore a good signal – an important lesson reinforced by the appearance of a Henry VIII half groat at an identical target to the shotgun shell next to it a few weeks ago.

'There you go, there's another.' Lucie is teetering on the brink of despair, another low thudding tone entering her ears – exactly the same as the last lead pellet. 'Seven-eight,' she mutters, stubbornly pointing Ellie to the spot and uttering the words, 'dig it,' before pottering on. She's thoroughly disheartened by this day of shot, and not prepared to stick around for more disappointment.

Ellie knows it's probably pointless as she trudges down and cuts out a clod of soil. We've almost traversed the entire cliff edge, left with only the final triangle of flat land before we'll have to succumb to the slopes; the wooden fence line ahead a formal reminder we are running out of land, scrabbling on the very edge of our permission.

On autopilot, she presses the button of the pinpointer, waiting for it to chirp into life before running it around the edges of the hole. With no success, she turns to the clod, scraping it over until a loud trill stops her movements. Peering closer, she scrats through the loose soil, freezing at the sight of the pinpointer's attention, her mind going blank in shock.

'LUCIE!' she shouts towards the figure diligently swinging a few metres away, raising her voice to be heard over the wind. 'I think you'll want to come back for this one!'

'What is it?!' Lucie questions, coming over to kneel beside Ellie.

'I'm not a hundred per cent sure,' Ellie admits, 'but if it's what I think it is …' She trails off, leaning nose first into the dirt clod, trying to confirm her suspicions.

'What?!' Lucie presses impatiently.

'I don't want to say it, but I think it's a Celtic coin,' Ellie stretches her finger shakily towards the object, sweeping away the loose soil covering its distinguishable features and cutting off any shocked response from Lucie who waits with bated breath. The distinctive and unmistakable form of a horse emerges from underneath Ellie's fingertip, both of us staring in shocked silence as she lifts it delicately from the soil. The coin is crumbly, oddly tinged purple, and worn so thin that daylight appears between the long galloping legs of the steed pictured upon it. It's certainly seen better times, but its dilapidated appearance doesn't diminish the hold it has over us; faced with our oldest found object, and a period of human existence which, until now, has eluded us – prehistory.

*

A period of around 900,000 years – since the first known human, homo antecessor walked the land bridge from Europe to Britain – spans the era before the Roman invasion and the start of written records for Britain. That's almost a million years of undocumented human history.

Our understanding of this gap begins in 55–54 BCE with the accounts of Julius Caesar and his attempted invasions. He describes a triangular island, filled with wood of every type, cattle, and a series of tribal kingdoms; whose inhabitants shave every part of their body, wear their hair long and dye themselves blue with woad. The most civilised inhabitants he claims are those in Kent, a migration of Celts from Gaul, Rome's long-standing enemy.

It's easy to view Britain's prehistory from this Roman viewpoint and overlook the centuries – millennia – of developing societies and migrations that transformed the island – bringing new technologies, beliefs and trade – before the sweeping transformation by the Roman Empire. But if Britain's prehistoric inhabitants were so uncivilised, then there wouldn't have been a Romano-British society emerging in the years after the invasion (the blending of two vibrant cultures, the Romans and the Iron Age Britons, whose gods, artistic styles and beliefs were adopted into Roman society). Neither would there have been the necessity for the largest garrison of all the Roman provinces for such a collection of 'disorganised' native tribes.

The truth behind Britain's prehistory is trapped within our landscapes – in the hillforts, barrows, burials, artefacts and coins left behind – offering the only unbiased view of a time we know very little about. It's a story of people, families, migration and settlement, craft and trade, and a diverse, unique community living and growing together on the periphery of the rapidly developing world on the continent.

*

RIDGE AND FURROW

'Is it all right if I borrow your callipers again?' Ellie asks Margaret quietly across the conference table – not wanting to disturb the silent focus of the other occupants diligently at work.

'Of course, dear.' Margaret slides them over between the thick reference books.

It's mid-afternoon on a Friday, the Lincolnshire County Council Office's taken over for the next few hours by a small group of retirees and Ellie – who, if you ask her parents, is apparently 'never at work'. Their task – plugging the latest archaeological finds into the database – a slow and methodical process that involves describing each item in such precise detail, any person reading the description could draw exactly what it looked like without seeing it; a level of detail that makes it only possible to enter around three to four items per Friday session. The tools of the trade are digital callipers and weighing scales (both of which Ellie still needs to acquire) and the cooperation of a laptop – progress significantly hampered during one particular session when no one could connect to the internet.

'Twenty-seven millimetres,' Ellie mutters, entering the diameter of our Roman umbonate brooch, and sliding the callipers back over to Margaret, who is waiting patiently, her next poly-bagged treasure lined up, ready for recording. Laura (the Finds Liaison Officer in charge of the session) has been flitting in and out, keeping an eye on her workers and meeting with finders dropping off their new finds to add to the never-ending pile for recording. She seems quite relieved towards the end of the session when she joins the group with her laptop – reaching the end of what seems like a busy week.

'Ellie, how have you been getting on?' she asks, inquiring both about the recording and the digging – always keen for the latest gossip.

'Oh, really good!' Ellie replies 'I've brought something to show you!' She's eager to get Laura's opinion on our crumbly Celtic, gingerly producing a small protective case from her laptop bag, offering it up for inspection.

Laura hums thoughtfully, turning it between her fingertips '*Corieltauvi*,' she murmurs 'probably silver ... heavily debased,' rattling off information almost scientifically out of habit.

THINGS WE FOUND IN THE GROUND

'This is the first Iron Age coin we've had.' Ellie interrupts Laura's musings.

'Very interesting,' Laura responds slowly, her eyes still trained on the horse, her brain slowly decoding and classifying the coin. 'Where did you find it?'

Ellie – as always – brings the map up, the other recorders slowly packing away in the background, and filing out with a parting wave, as Ellie and Laura dig deep into speculation.

'You know,' Laura says, studying the hillside and the surrounding areas intently, 'with Iron Age coins, where there's one, there will always be more.' She turns to Ellie with this trademark look of knowing more than she's letting on. 'If I were you, I'd get back out there.'

*

In Britain, the transition from the Bronze to Iron Age took centuries, developing slowly alongside the gradual waves of migration of Celtic tribes from Gaul on the continent.

Britain had already been in contact with the continent, supplying Cornish tin to support the Bronze Age in the Mediterranean; an international trade which went both ways with new ideas and materials passing between the land masses, such as the secret of smelting iron from iron ore which spread rapidly from the collapse of the Hittite Empire around 1200 BCE (the Hittites having discovered the technique centuries before), and was being practised in Britain by 800 BCE. The Iron Age forged on, Celtic tribes settling into southern Britain and local industry thriving among the explosion of trade and resources, until it got to the point where a further evolution needed to be added into this bubbling development pot of Iron Age Britain – the introduction of coinage.

These convex, gold discs flowed through the trade between Britain and the continent around 150 BCE – Gaulish coins, copied from the gold staters of Philip II of Macedon, to enable them to interact with the Greek world – until Britain decided to produce their own version, minting bronze potins and gold staters out of Kent. By this time, distinct tribal groups had emerged within the communities of Britain, and the establishment of Celtic dynasties and warring between the groups had facilitated the need for the accumulation of wealth and power through the gold bullion offered by the gold stater. The settling Celtic tribes kept their Gaulish names, carving out portions of Britain for themselves – the eastern region largely containing Lincolnshire, Leicestershire and Nottinghamshire, occupied by the *Corieltauvi*: a tribe noted in the history books simply for their lack of resistance to Roman invasion.

Settlement here consisted of open villages – instead of fortified hillforts – focused around the salt-making industry on the coast and the trade links offered by the Humber estuary, and supposedly dwarfed in significance by the dominant and warring southern tribes. But they were one of the earliest tribes to mint their own coinage, so there must have been an important need for a monetary economy, and as indicated by the existence of a lower value silver coinage – much like our silver unit known as a 'South Ferriby' boar type – a need for smaller denominations suggesting their use in everyday exchange.

With no written records, it's only the physical archaeology that can begin to construct the picture of our local tribes. Coins were struck sporadically and only upon demand, a range of gold staters, quarter staters, silver units and bronze potins, providing glimpses into a developing economy, and also a visual insight into the beliefs and mythology that governed these kingdoms. The horse and the boar expressive symbols of their gods and values, representing power, wealth and strength. Each new addition, a fragment of their story told through their own creations and not the exaggerated fiction created by a tyrannical empire looking to add Britain to its collection.

AUGUST 2022, LINCOLNSHIRE, ENGLAND

Harvest has *finally* begun. The earthy smell of freshly cut wheat lies thickly through the air, the tell-tale dust plumes wisping into the evening, marking the presence of a combine harvester fresh out of slumber, and the distant sound of tractors rumbling down the country lanes pulling trailers full of freshly gathered grain. But the farmers aren't the only ones making the most of the long daylight hours, we, too, are venturing out for an evening session.

With the arable fields opening up, the time for pasture is coming to a close, the once lush grass, now baked dry and browned after a long summer. Harvest hasn't quite reached our permission yet, but when it does, we know we'll be overwhelmingly busy, faced with the bombardment of all of our prime arable simultaneously and the digging cycle beginning once again – so we thought it best to make the most of the few moments left of this quiet interlude.

But it's not the only change in the air this August. New Zealand has emerged cautiously from its COVID-19 bubble for the first time since March 2020, with the full reopening of its borders. While the rest of us have all but slowly moved on, Lucie can't help but notice the fear still gripping her family and friends back home, cut off from the outside world and sheltered from the collective trauma of the pandemic. She's missed the arrival of her niece, her nephew starting school, her best friend's wedding, one sister's engagement and the other's separation; significant moments the remainder of her twenties has been sacrificed for, ostracised by her own country for the 'greater good'. The upcoming harvest provides a welcome distraction from her mixed emotions at the prospect that for the first time in two years, she could go home – if she wanted to.

*

'Whereabouts are you feeling in here?' Lucie turns, looking back to Ellie, who's making sure the gate is latched securely. This isn't the first time we've visited this field, a small trapezoidal patch of pasture, sandwiched between our Roman field and a row of village cottages. We found a trade token here last summer – an 1811 Newark penny, which emerged out of the economic and subsequent small-change crisis caused by the pressures of the Napoleonic War. It's a sheltered and peaceful spot to visit, offering only the occasional interruption by the local dog walkers and resident pair of Irish wolfhounds who like to knock the unsuspecting detectorist into their own holes with their enthusiasm.

'Shall we follow the footpath up?' Ellie replies, walking over, with our shadows already drawing long she's keen to start somewhere promising, the winding flattened track marking the continuation of the Roman field footpath demanding attention.

'Why not?' Lucie swings off. 'I wanna look near that tree, too,' she calls over her shoulder, a wizened oak tree overhanging the fence line in the far corner. This section of field appears separate from the rest, secluded by topography. It's higher in elevation to the low-lying ridge and furrow hugging the village, and situated on top of a natural earth bank running into the adjacent wood copse and suspiciously into the swamp Ellie's had runs in with before, almost as if it's an old waterway now run dry.

The short walk up there proves uneventful – apart from a battered and featureless eighteenth-century halfpenny – the footpath left behind, our search veering onto the grassy platform above the earth bank. As the signals pass by, a golden tinge settles over us; a warm haze of dying sunlight and harvest dust, interrupted by the lazy hover of midges and gnats, the gentle chirping of crickets in the dry grass and the occasional bleat from the sheep flock now scattered across our Celtic hillside.

'Crikey!' Lucie calls out, swinging quickly over a patch of wispy grasses, surprised by the large and loud signal announcing itself through her headphones.

'What have you got?' Ellie jogs over eager to dig before we lose the light, and alerted by the shock in Lucie's shout.

'Something big,' Lucie responds, still surprised we haven't come across this target before, the tone sweet and promising to her ears.

Ellie wastes no time in cutting a plug from the dry ground, the soil crumbly but aerated, the source of the signal coming from deep inside the sidewall, prompting some gentle excavation with the edge digger.

'Fuck.' She stops suddenly, paralysed at the sight of a large round silver object.

'What have you got?' Lucie asks, snapping Ellie from her stupor.

'You're going to scream,' Ellie warns, turning back to Lucie with a cheeky grin.

'Wait, wait,' Lucie scrabbles to the ground, peering over as Ellie removes a huge coin from the indentation into the sidewall.

Lucie gasps. It is the biggest silver hammered she has ever seen.

'Elizabeth I, 1569,' Ellie reads, her face still plastered with a wide grin. 'Got to be a sixpence – look at the size of it!'

'We need to grid,' Lucie responds firmly, determination setting in fast, like the dropping sunset about to disappear behind the treeline. There's nothing like the taste of a good find to send us into an adrenaline fuelled digging frenzy – Lucie unlocking an elevated hyperfocus she likes to call 'flow state' plucking out signal after signal, stopped only by darkness, the inevitable crash and Ellie needing to get home.

Two buttons and another hammered – a medieval long cross penny – follows. The sky drenched in a deep burnt orange as daylight diminishes, time slows and every inch of grass is relentlessly gridded.

'Ellie, signal,' Lucie calls, Ellie plodding over wearily having dug about twenty signals in the last thirty minutes.

'Little one, sounds good.' Lucie offers words of encouragement before swinging doggedly on – lining up the next target.

Combing through the clod, clumps of dry soil roll into the grass as Ellie scrapes around the patch identified by the pinpointer. What looks like a small rusty button appears under the latest scrape, Ellie peering closer and poking suspiciously, alerted by its unusual thickness.

'Lucie!' she shouts, interrupting her flow. 'Get over here, what do you make of this?'

'Okay …' she announces as Lucie kneels down next to her. 'Don't get too excited, but I think it might be another Celtic.' This prompts a wide-eyed stare from Lucie as Ellie pulls the 'coin' from the clutches of the clod, the grass rustling beneath us. Holding it between her fingers and flicking off a little bit of soil clinging to its concaved side, the distinctive wave of a horse hits the waning light.

'Oh, my God … It is,' Lucie says, instantly recognising the circular ring of dots as Ellie turns it over, the spiky arched back of a boar coming into focus, consolidating its identity. Holding our second Iron Age coin within a few months, it seems like we've finally earned the right to connect with the oldest occupants of our permission, the land choosing to impart its ancient knowledge only after we ventured onto its toughest pastures, withstanding at least six months of a hard-earned initiation.

'Do you think it's silver?' Ellie asks, the coin resembling the appearance of a crusty Roman denarius, encrusted with a rusty concretion.

'It's got to be, the condition's beautiful,' Lucie responds, no holes present between the horses knees of this Iron Age beauty. 'Oh, my God Ellie,' she adds, the shock setting in.

It seems Laura wasn't wrong – where there's one, there's more.

14.

RALLY SEASON

SEPTEMBER 2022, OXFORDSHIRE, ENGLAND
'What are you doing?' Lucie asks, watching Ellie fish about in the back seat before pulling out the Minelab carry bag with a considerable amount of force and half the camping gear with it, clattering rudely onto the tarmac of a Waitrose carpark.

'Never leave valuables in the car,' Ellie states – refusing to stray from gospel teachings deeply instilled into her from a young age – ramming a sleeping bag back into any available gap and attracting a curious stare from a well-dressed Waitrose shopper. The good people of Henley-on-Thames thoroughly disturbed by our chaotic arrival into their quaint riverside town – our chosen stop-off in our four-and-half-hour journey down to Marlborough in Wiltshire.

'Right …' Lucie stares back blankly, knowing full well any thieves unfortunate enough to rob the Panda would have a hard time retrieving any valuables with how tightly we'd packed it. 'We don't even lock our doors half the time back home,' she adds before walking off. Seriously, what's the likelihood of a theft in one of Britain's most desirable towns?

Ellie repacks the car diligently, unwavered by Lucie's Kiwi nonchalance, stubbornly slinging the carry bag over her shoulder, grasping the Vanquish with the other hand, and weaving between the parked cars to catch up with her – her progress hindered by the burden of no less than three metal detectors.

THINGS WE FOUND IN THE GROUND

'The bookshop's this way.' Lucie turns to her with a roll of her eyes, Google Maps already fired up and waiting on her phone. Leading the way through Henley's picture-perfect streets, we've got a lunch date with a man called Tom Ayling, whom we met through social media – one who has a penchant for rare books. A visit that now, thanks to Ellie, has to be in the company of a suspiciously large bag bearing a striking resemblance to a shotgun case.

We wouldn't normally advise going out of your way to meet strange men off the internet, even ones with a considerable online following – although we often turn up to undisclosed fields after being given nothing but a postcode, shared in secrecy the day before – but in this case Tom has tempted us through the door with a very old copy of Livy's *History of Rome*. And after all, what would a road trip be without a small detour?

*

'Tom, is it all right if we leave our detectors in your office?' Ellie asks, already resembling a bull in a china shop with the unwieldy length to her bag – or should we say a detectorist in a rare-books store – and not prepared to risk gracing the gastro pub with their presence.

Tom chuckles, taking the bag from Ellie with the air of a perfect gentleman, or perhaps he simply recognised the threat to his books the longer they stayed on her back – especially that slightly faded, well-read, green, clothbound first edition of Tolkien's *The Hobbit* (printed 21 September 1937, one of only 1,500 copies). But don't get us wrong, he is the perfect gentleman. Dressed smart-casual in a brown glen-checked blazer and pale blue, button-up shirt – the top button undone for a bit of character – he opens the door for us with a warm smile, ushering us out of the bookshop and across the way to his favourite lunch spot with the wry chuckle of a gentle and well-mannered soul.

'So, tell me about this weekend?' Tom asks in his soft-spoken lilting manner, the conversation ebbing away from our shared presence curating object history on social media with the appearance of food;

his curiosity thoroughly piqued by the peculiar nature of our arrival into his neck of the woods, and the ongoing hunt for history we are all involved in – although Tom finds his nestled into the shelves of forgotten libraries and auction houses, and not in the ground.

'Honestly, we've got no idea what to expect,' Lucie replies, tucking firmly into her Caesar salad with the vigour of someone facing their last supper – as she very well could be.

'It's two nights camping in a field. Apparently, there's going to be, like, twelve-hundred detectorists and fourteen-hundred acres of land,' Ellie adds, both of us feeling slightly apprehensive about partaking in one of the biggest events in the metal-detecting calendar – our first ever rally – not to mention doing it all again the following weekend in Cambridgeshire.

'Extraordinary,' Tom says, with his trademark little smile, speaking vibrantly with his hands over his pork belly and mash. 'And what kind of things do you think you'll find on such a weekend? I just love this idea of finding a story within these artefacts.' He would know, his ability to craft a tale from between the lightly stained, aged pages of his rare books turning him into somewhat of a connoisseur of storytelling online.

'Oh, we'd die to find a gold Celtic stater,' Lucie replies.

'We've found a couple of silver ones on our permission,' Ellie elaborates. 'It's just magical, holding something that comes from a time we know so little about.'

Tom's soaking it all in, the conversation flowing with the ease of lifelong friends – not fresh acquaintances – none of us afraid to speak freely about our shared passion. He's listening to our tales with a look in his eye that screams 'metal detecting's next victim' – and little does he know, he is. For he'll be joining us on such a weekend next rally season.

WILTSHIRE, ENGLAND
'Crikey,' Lucie whistles as suddenly our ramble through Wiltshire's country lanes, hits a standstill at the back of a queue of camper vans and cars, coming to a halt behind a black SUV tagged with a bumper sticker proclaiming, 'I'd rather be metal detecting'.

'We must be close,' Ellie replies, happily switching off the unreliable and frankly ancient satnav. Trundling through the queue, we turn off the hedge-flanked lane, through a farm gate and into a massive expanse of rolling, cultivated fields – quite the contrast to Lincolnshire's flat plains.

'Keep on following the road, girls,' a middle-aged man clad in high-vis directs, sending us on a winding farm track up and over, glimpses of the campsite nestled into a vast valley below flashing through the trees.

'Bloody hell,' Ellie says, as we crest the hill and a swarm of detectorists come into view alongside us, swinging away, the sun glinting off a humongous marquee in the valley, dozens of trader's tents encircling it, a sea of vans and camping tents as far as the eye can see – this is clearly the big leagues, this isn't just a Portaloo plonked in a field for the weekend, it's an institution.

'Yep, that's the last of the phone signal,' Lucie chimes, raising her phone high into the air as we descend deeper into the valley, her last message to Ash – our inside man and point of contact with the wider and commercial side of metal detecting – letting him know of our arrival, sent out into the ether. Our first rally season has come courtesy of our recent sponsorship by LP Metal Detecting (one of the largest metal-detecting retailers in the UK), welcoming us into their family of detecting ambassadors. So we're eager to make a good first impression in the field and not the digital realm – this is essentially our digging debut.

Now too late for farewells, we have no choice but to go all in. The family doesn't hear from us for the rest of the weekend, last known location, some field in Wiltshire, before all communication is severed and civilisation left behind.

'Hello, hello,' Ash greets us. He's your typical Welsh lad, with a cheeky sense of humour and sporting an LP Metal Detecting cap and matching T-shirt. Waiting for us with the marshalls at the campsite gates, Lucie's message has thankfully gotten through. 'Follow me, I've saved you two a prime spot!'

Taking us under his wing, we roll straight past general camping, up into the traders' sector, parking up directly behind the LP Metal

Detecting stand alongside Ash's own tent. 'This is where you want to be,' Ash winks, 'close to the action, get your tent up and I'll introduce you to Pete and the crew, find me in the LP tent.'

We pitch the pop-up devil – knowing all too well how painful it will be to pack down at the end of the weekend – lob the sleeping bags in, lock the car and squeeze down the side of the trade tents, straight into the arena. Ellie's wearing her jazziest 'Las Vegas' vintage shirt for the occasion, which screams 'come talk to me'.

There's only one word to describe the arena – buzzing – fuelled by the excitement and anticipation of the unknown waiting to be found out in the fields. In all directions, people are yarning about their latest finds over the sound system playing classic 80s anthems, others are inspecting the newest machines on offer adding beeps and chirps into the atmosphere, while even more peruse the stalls buying every metal-detecting accessory under the sun – some of which you'd never even dream you needed. A rich waft of cheese and tomato draws our attention to the stone-baked pizza oven in the corner, where we notice the bar – praise the heavens – there's more camouflage present than Ellie's ever seen outside of a militaria show and Lucie's already feeling a sensory meltdown brewing. We've walked into the metal-detecting mecca, and by God do we need a drink.

'One beer and a cider please,' Ellie requests over the high metal counter of the trailer bar – pulling her eyes away from the collection of personalised stickers featuring every metal-detecting YouTube channel, past and present, tagged on the side – and tapping contactless, she hands the cider straight to Lucie who clutches it like a lifeline.

'Time to mingle,' Ellie announces – giving the confidence of a *Searcher Magazine* cover girl (July's issue) – and armed with her beer, she leads Lucie straight over to the LP tent to break the ice. It isn't long before she's fully assimilated, meeting the boss, Pete, his partner, Helen; the rest of the LP crew and the *Searcher* boys in red now two beers deep into a conversation about contemporary Roman forgeries, Lucie still nursing her first cider.

Before we know it we are going to bed far too late for the early start in the morning; we've consumed a stone-baked pizza, four Jägerbombs, an uncountable number of beers, watched a comedy line-up in the big tent, chatted about Saxon sceats, Celtic staters, Roman siliquas, hammered groats, and, most importantly, which field to go to tomorrow. Ending up being tucked into our pop-up tent by our new bestie, *Searcher* Dan, who's kindly donated a blanket to stop us freezing to death overnight – we've overpacked, but not with any of the essentials as usual.

*

Dawn the next day, Saturday, brings a rude awakening from the campsite wildlife. Ellie rises early to fire up the Bunsen burner, boiling some water for instant porridge and coffee – an incentive to get Lucie out of her sleeping bag. There's a growing rumble in the arena, the dawn chorus of metal detectors turning on, detectorists slowly gathering in varying degrees of eagerness, and our signal to get a move on or we'll miss kick-off.

Lucie thought she was on the verge of a sensory meltdown last night, but there's nothing quite like waking to the sound of a thousand metal detectors to force you to leave the sanctity of the tent, disappear into a sea of camouflage and never be seen again – all before 9 a.m. There's T-shirts, tactical backpacks, tactical trousers, utility belts, hats, shorts, finds-pouches – people are geared-up. Yesterday was simply 'dress-down Friday'. Today, they mean business.

We stand near the safety of the LP tent, all 1,200 detectorists falling silent as a man clambers atop a box near the marquee clutching a microphone. He drones on for fifteen minutes, going through the rules, the regulations, the fields – and issuing various thank yous. Eventually, the moment everyone's been waiting for – raising an airhorn above his head giving a loud blast.

In an instant the arena is empty.

'Girls, don't run off, you're coming with us!' In the LP tent, Ash is nursing a hot coffee. 'Dan's letting us use his gator, we don't need to rush.'

*

RALLY SEASON

'God, I can't look anyone in the eyes …' Lucie groans.

We are holding on for dear life, in the back of a souped-up, off-road golf buggy, zipping past detectorists who left the arena in the first wave and are still hiking over the undulating terrain to reach the fields we've zoomed to in minutes. They must have watched us go past with pure vexation – whoops.

Ash has no qualms in veering off the farm track, right onto our chosen field, itself, lurching the gator to park part-way up an incline, all of us tumbling out onto cultivated earth, detectors in hand.

'See you at the top, guys,' Ash challenges, striding off with the air of a seasoned professional.

This field we've quite literally been dropped in couldn't be further from familiar ground – it's steep, stony, and arid, a triple threat for tricky detecting – physically tough in the digging department and too dry to ascertain any clear targets under the coil, the conditions resulting in poor conductivity. Part of a landscape of sweeping swathes of cultivation with barely a field boundary in sight.

'Guess we're going up, then,' Ellie turns to Lucie. With one of the highest points in the landscape above us, everyone is convinced it's an excellent vantage for ancient activity – or at least, that was the rumour circulating the bar last night.

Lucie dons her headphones in response, following Ash with a quiet determination.

A promising signal stops her in her tracks a short distance away – a *10–12* on the VDI.

Scrabbling around among the tendrils of straw, small white stones and loose dusty, earth, the pinpointer chirps happily; it doesn't take too long for Ellie to pinch a small, crude coin from the mix, placing it on her fingertip and gently brushing away the dust to reveal any details. The raised profile of a deity is barely visible on one side – but we know instantly that it's a Roman – it might be a grot, but it's our first rally find. A significant moment and, to our relief, a find in the tin.

At the top, you can almost imagine those who came before you, looking out at the same view below. The vast valley sheltering the campsite of a Roman marching army, perhaps even choosing the very same location where we've pitched our tents for their canvas barracks.

'Lucie, look! They're cordoning off part of the field ... Someone must have found a hoard!' Ellie beckons, encouraging Lucie to detect towards the red and white striped tape being hastily strung between a rectangular cordon of iron fencing-pins by a pair of high-vis-clad digging marshalls on gators – a detectorist loitering anxiously nearby.

Only it wasn't a hoard, it was an unexploded Second World War bomb – the field shut shortly after a flurry of walkie-talkie action, in preparation for the arrival of the bomb squad.

'Fuck, let's get out of here.'

*

Three more unexploded ordinances appear over the course of the afternoon. We choose not to hang around in one location long enough to chance one's unwelcome arrival, hooning around on the gator with Ash and exploring every field. In regards to our finds tally, we've managed to lose more things than we've found, Ellie's rather meek announcement of the loss of our edge digger – which is still somewhere in field 16 – landing us back at the LP tent to spend some of our beer money on a replacement.

'What on Earth is that noise?' Lucie startles as a haunting call breaks through the arena chatter.

Ash rolls his eyes. 'That'll be the French.'

And indeed, the French have emerged from their hillside camp and begun a slow procession towards the arena, their impending arrival announced by the enthusiastic playing of a replica Celtic war horn known as a Carnyx – a six-foot long, trumpet-like instrument, mouthpiece at one end, the stylised head of a boar at the other – played upright.

Our words over lunch with Tom, about not knowing what to expect, are coming true in so many different ways – the evening kicking off with a different kind of horn to this morning's send-off.

RALLY SEASON

'Ellie! Hog roast!' Lucie's attention is suddenly snapped by a passing detectorist clutching a polystyrene tray filled to the brim with an enormous white roll laden with lashings of pork and apple sauce. A quick scan of the arena confirms the source of this delicacy – a new arrival to the food court – a white gazebo harbouring an entire pig, spit roasted and cooked slow over a low fire.

'I think Lucie's decided tonight's dinner,' Ash chuckles.

Ellie, replying with a laugh, is already heading towards the long line forming around the gazebo.

Hog-roast rolls in hand, she returns to find Lucie deep in conversation with a bearded man clad in a khaki fishing vest.

'Ellie! Quick, James has got a stater!' Lucie calls insistently, beckoning her over, before turning back to the finder in question, with a smile. 'Can I hold it?'

'Absolutely,' he replies, placing the coin in the centre of Lucie's palm, 'Have a feel of that!' He's absolutely chuffed with his little gold gem.

It's between ten to fourteen millimetres, an Iron Age quarter stater, bright yellow-gold in colour, with an abstract horse (reminiscent of our own, albeit less valuable and more common denomination, silver units), made out of crescents and pellets, stamped across its flan. For its small size, it holds a considerable weight, a thick nugget of gold that enchants Lucie immediately, fascinated as she is by its somehow contemporary appearance, which is not unlike the abstract art of the early twentieth century.

'It's stunning,' she breathes, handing it back to James, who is shortly whisked off for photographs with one of the metal-detecting brands – the machine he found it with fresh off the production line – his discovery creating the perfect poster-boy moment.

'I'd love to find one of those,' Lucie whispers to Ellie wistfully, as she tucks into her hog-roast roll, which Ellie has been patiently holding for the last ten minutes (and, no, she didn't get to hold the stater).

Weary detectorists are starting to gather around us, returning from a long day out in the fields, and a long hike back to camp, brandishing finds and tall tales; whispers of gold in the furthest reaches of the estate, and a lost Iron Age settlement in the brand-new fields opening up in the morning. The arena is slowly refuelling – on hog roast and gossip – in preparation to do it all again the next day, but not before the hiking boots have been replaced with dancing shoes as the live band rocks up to the marquee.

*

There's no messing around on Sunday morning. Stater fever has engulfed the camp. We're already in the back of the gator – no time for coffee – racing to be the first in the new, freshly opened field.

'Ellie! Quick! We need to get moving,' Lucie calls, rapidly noise cancelling and setting up her machine. We've managed to arrive on the crest of the first tidal wave of detectorists to reach the field, and she's eager to maintain our position.

'Fucking hell,' Ellie mutters as she watches the first detectorists break the bank of stubble, descending across the field in an unstoppable swell, stragglers getting swept away as they crouch to dig some trash, with no respect paid for anyone's intended detecting line (a true faux pas in the community; there's nothing worse than someone cutting in front of you only to find gold). It isn't long before a shout echoes across the valley, followed shortly by the revving of a gator, which launches towards a small huddle gathered around a hole.

'He's found a stater,' a man reveals to us in a hushed, secretive tone as he passes by, geared up to the eyeballs in a Minelab pro-swing 45 harness, a CTX 3030 swinging determinedly from the end of the pendulum – news travels fast in the fields.

We share a glance, time to get moving, we desperately want to gain access into this exclusive stater club. With the initial rush ebbing, the field settles down, the detectorists thinning out, finding space several metres away from rival machines threatening signal interference. We've fallen into step with half a dozen fellow searchers, down the left-hand side of the field, lined by an avenue of trees, kept focused by the regular occurrence of a Roman nummus among our peers.

RALLY SEASON

'Signal – twelve to fourteen,' Lucie announces, settling into her new surroundings now the panic's over, and directing Ellie to a patch in the stubble.

'Roman!' Ellie calls in reply, almost instantly, the grot just below the surface; a spiky crown adorns its crude bust revealing it to be a barbarous radiate – a contemporary forgery likely produced during a time of economic crisis.

'Let's keep looking round here,' Lucie plots, locking onto the search area, spurred on by our first find of the day. We fan out into a lazy grid, heading towards the middle of the field, with the hope of more Romans – maybe even a brooch.

'Crikey.' Lucie stops dead, a loud *20s* almost deafening her. 'Ellie, dig that!'

'What is it?' Ellie replies, jogging over and lining up to dig.

'Something loud and crazy!' Lucie announces, stepping back to watch the excavation.

Ellie sifts through the soil with her hands, each sweep inching closer to the target.

'Oh, fuck—' Ellie sits back suddenly away from the hole.

'Be careful.' Lucie moves ten steps backwards, leaving Ellie and the hole to observe from a safe distance.

Protruding from the ground, fins up, is a two-inch mortar tail.

'What have you got girls?' an old boy has snuck up behind us, startling Lucie – who's already jittery.

'I think we've got a bomb,' Ellie responds, static from her position, not daring to move. 'Do we need to get a marshall?'

'Let's have a look.' He strides over and crouches down next to Ellie. 'A lot of fragments have come up in this area – take a look at this one!' He whips out a matching mortar tail from his bag, still with its charge attached, the shell thankfully missing. 'That's going on my mantlepiece,' he announces proudly. 'I reckon yours is just a tail,' he deduces. Squinting back into the hole, he turns to Ellie with a 'Do you mind?' With Ellie's nod of approval – placing our fates firmly in the hands of our detecting comrade – he reaches down and flicks the part-submerged tail with his edge digger. It tumbles into the hole, its explosive partner MIA – much to our relief.

'Awesome,' Lucie's voice suddenly comes from above, 'Roman Found's first bomb!' Deeming the situation neutralised, she's shuffled in for a better view.

Now it's out of the ground, Ellie's more than happy to show it off, the spectacle attracting a few more onlookers, as if we'd found a stater. It's the tail fin of a Second World War British round (an Ordnance SBML two-inch mortar, to give its official title), first produced in 1938, arriving just in time for the outbreak of war. An invaluable asset for close combat, it provided both smokescreen cover and high-explosive drops on enemies out of the reach of small arms fire; launched from a tubular barrel to guide it in flight (like a cannon), it could be operated by as little as two people – a 'loader' and a 'firer' – and is light enough to be carried by one. There were countless firing ranges and training grounds established across the country for practising combat tactics during the Second World War – this field apparently one of them.

Not the digging milestone we imagined ticking off this weekend, but rally season isn't over yet – we're about to do it all again next week at Detectival.

9 SEPTEMBER 2022, CAMBRIDGESHIRE, ENGLAND

Queen Elizabeth II, at various points in her reign, looks out earnestly at Ellie from the front pages of the newspapers spread across the petrol station's stand. Accompanied by messages of condolence such as, 'Our hearts are broken', 'We loved you ma'am' and the simple, 'Thank you', they mark a nation thrust into mourning and the end of the seemingly endless 'New Elizabethan Age' – and Britain's longest reigning monarch, at seventy years and 214 days. Ellie chooses one of the papers for her royal-souvenir collection, adding it to the petrol round, before continuing our journey down to Cambridgeshire.

*

'They're with LP! They don't need to join the line!'

We've caused a small commotion upon arrival, pulled between Ash's directions and the authority of the marshalls, as four different high-vis clad figures attempt to stop our passage. Normal traffic is being directed to park and join the line waiting to receive their entrance passes, but ours are being waved from Ash's hand – the golden ticket to freedom.

'Oh God,' Ellie mutters, wishing we weren't in such a distinctive vehicle (the yellow Panda not exactly the best camouflage) as Ash manages to usher us under some hazard tape, and through to camp – much to the disapproving glares of those diligently waiting in line.

'What a way to make an entrance, ladies,' Ash chuckles as we exit the Panda.

We've got more of the crew to meet this weekend, making camp alongside Pete the Sceat, Hammy Harris and Nath – Wales's best representatives in the sport – but first we've got to get our tent pitched. We've somehow accumulated more stuff than last time, the majority of which remains untouched inside the Panda, the pop-up tent refusing to pop after too many outings, caught awkwardly in the wind whipping across the campsite.

Securing it down with all the pegs we own – four – and a hope and a prayer, we slip through a gap in the fence and into the arena. It's similar to last weekend, but on a much bigger scale, a supersized marquee running its entire length, bordered by metal-detecting-brand stands, each trying to outdo the other; with huge inflatable arches, ten foot flags, and boasting elaborate test beds – pre-seeded with finds – to try the latest machines out in style, pushing them to their limits. But camouflage isn't the only uniform present among those passing between the stands, checking out the offerings, brightly coloured tunics stand out in the crowd – a tribe of Anglo-Saxons – mingling from their re-enactment camp erected next to the bank of food vans on the right-hand side.

'Ellie, a Mexican van!' Lucie shouts, a strong waft of cheese and spice alerting her to the presence of her favourite cuisine – nacho bowls and burritos, filled with your choice of bbq pulled pork, shredded chicken or chilli beans.

'That's dinner sorted!' Ellie shares Lucie's enthusiasm, commencing a beeline to the back of the queue – nacho bowls secured just in time for a savage weather system to blow through, driving us into the shelter of the marquee. The biblical rain that follows almost drowns out any chance for chit-chat, the canvas entrance-flaps whipping violently in the rising wind, as visibility reduces drastically, a dark drawing in, the blur of cascading water outside interrupted only by the frantic dash of a sodden detectorist making a break for cover.

It's a different vibe to last weekend – more solemn – all live music cancelled out of respect for the late queen's passing, a special request from the estate's landowner. The evening that unfolds focuses more on conversation and connection, chewing the fat with Detector Timmy and Pete the Sceat, beers sipped rather than chugged, people mindful not to reveal they were having 'too much' fun, entertainment arising from the shared experience of this defining moment in history, and, naturally, which field we should all visit tomorrow.

*

'You can't cook on that, girls.'

Pete the Sceat is appalled by Ellie's bedraggled appearance on Saturday morning, attempting to whip up some boiling water on the precarious arrangement that is our treasured Bunsen burner, disappearing immediately with a clatter back inside his own tent only to emerge with a proper portable camping stove – its single ring embedded into a rectangular hob-like system instead of screwing onto the top of a gas bottle.

'There you go, keep it for the weekend,' he says, a kind smile across his face. He's one of the old boys, a seasoned pro, taking pity and looking after us underprepared youngsters – breakfast porridge gets prepared in no time on his camping beauty.

If last weekend was the warm-up, this one is the main event, the biggest metal-detecting rally of the year, kicking off with the obligatory sound of an airhorn – which we hear from our arena-side seats as we tuck into our porridge. We've seen one kick off, we don't need to see another.

'We'd better get the gear,' Lucie rises from her seat reluctantly, still not adjusted to the early mornings of rally life.

RALLY SEASON

Slipping back through the gap in the fence, the scent of bacon, coffee and sweet woodsmoke from the Anglo-Saxon camp hits us instantly, the clattering of machines, spades and wellies squelching through the mud, adding to the cacophony of the revving of gators. The rush to get out in the fields awakening the entire campsite into a frenzy of activity.

'You two are next!' A shout comes from a passing gator filled to the brim with the boys in red, Ash at the wheel, running bus services, gesturing for us to wait where we are for the next ride.

'Let's take a look at the map,' Ellie suggests. 'Everyone was talking about Field Seven last night.' She's always an expert at gathering the Friday night intel.

We have to weave our way through a small crowd gathered around the map; a throng of faithful detectorists staring wistfully at an oversized printed canvas emblazoned with the satellite imagery of the area. Painted in a vibrant patchwork of purple and blue to denote all thirty-four fields on offer, and lashed onto scaffolding poles – the *mappa mundi* of the detecting world. Fragments of conversation flit between the group, fields talked about like lottery numbers, a mixture of red herrings and lucky draws.

'There's Field Seven,' Ellie whispers. It's an odd-shaped field to the far right of our designated detecting area, and if the rumours are to be believed, the heart of a Roman settlement.

Our conversation is interrupted by the screeching brakes of the gator pulling up behind us. Time to see if the gamble will pay off.

'One of yous is gonna have to go on the back!' Ash calls. The gator is only a two-seater, a sort of mini pickup truck, Ellie takes one for the team and clambers into the cargo box on the back, nestling among the crates of water and stray spades.

'Hang on!' The shout comes moments before we lurch off, Ellie holding on tight to her hat and the Equinox as Ash picks up speed through the fields.

By the time we arrive at the fabled Field Seven, the boys are already hunched over their holes, clearing the field of Roman coins, in an efficient and well-rehearsed sweep. It's an arable field, freshly ploughed and gently sloping towards a small farmhouse behind the hedgeline at the furthest end. Detectorists pockmark the landscape around it, searching the slopes to the right and the high pasture just out of sight – kick-off was only an hour ago, yet even the furthest fields are already occupied, we've got some catching up to do.

'Let's find some Romans.' And Lucie's off, swinging determinedly, leaving Ash to help Ellie out of the gator.

'Good luck,' Ash chuckles.

Any detecting progress is swiftly hindered mere minutes into the field, as detectorists succumb to the conditions. Sticky mud and foil drag people down in more ways than one, both physically and in spirit. We've gained several inches in height, mud clinging to our boots, spades, coils, gloves – anything it can attach itself to. The abundance of foil makes digging frequent but disappointing, the small, promising signals flooding all headphones, and filling finds pouches. It's not long before most have had enough, abandoning Field Seven for greener pastures – more work than they are prepared to suffer. Luckily (or unluckily) for us, we are used to sticking it out in tough times.

'We're gonna head to Field Eight.' The boys in red have come to give their farewells – they've found their Romans.

'Yeah, we'll catch up later,' Lucie replies, not ready to leave just yet.

'See you in a bit!' Ellie waves, knowing our fate was sealed in this field the moment a fellow digger showed us an enamelled, Roman bird brooch.

'People aren't digging the small numbers.' Lucie turns to her conspiratorially as the boys disappear past the hedgeline. 'We've just got to dig them all.'

Ellie agrees unwaveringly, clutching her spade a little firmer and dropping into step behind Lucie, ready for some relentless and muddy digging. We lock in.

*

'Another one,' Lucie calls, 'solid nine.'

Ellie drops into the mud with no reservations, her knees sinking into the clay. The soil is crumbly and claggy, sticking to her fingers in clumps and making it hard to discern the artefacts from the muck, relying heavily on the insistence of the pinpointer.

'There,' she suddenly calls, 'Lucie!'

'That looks like a Roman!' Lucie responds, kneeling closer into the action, the excavation painfully slow as Ellie does her best to pluck the coin from the mess.

'What is it?' Lucie presses, the coin grasped between Ellie's fingers at last.

'Gimme a sec,' Ellie says, ripping off a glove – which is too caked in mud to offer any help at this point – going bare-handed to remove the last of clay.

'Fuck – is that a denarius?!'

We look around to share the moment – the boys long gone in a distant field.

*

Well, it kind of is a denarius. It's a numismatic curio, a limes denarius, which was common under the Severan dynasty, in the second and third centuries, when, for a reason only speculated about, 'official' denarii were minted out of base-metal alloys, instead of the silver standard. Almost black in colour, the unorthodox mix of metals has produced a crisp, high-relief portrait of Septimius Severus – Rome's first African emperor, and father of infamous sibling rivals, brothers Caracalla and Geta. His laurel wreath is prominent amid tight curls of hair, a strong brow, sharp nose and pointed beard.

Technically, Septimius was never meant to be emperor, born in Libya and rising steadily through the military ranks to become the governor of the Roman province of *Pannonia Superior* – Eastern Europe. But a spate of murders, mutinies, and even an attempt to auction off the Roman throne to the highest bidder, saw the almost century-old Nerva-Antonine dynasty collapse and the Roman Empire descend into a turbulent civil war, the fate of the Roman throne so volatile that it became known as the 'Year of the Five Emperors' – one of whom only lasted eighty-seven days. At the command of a significant army, this was the perfect opportunity for Septimius, proclaimed emperor by his legions, to strike up an allegiance with one of his rivals – the Roman governor of Britain, Clodius Albinus – and march on Rome to take the throne. His military success commencing the dawn of a new dynasty – the Severans.

But Septimius was all too aware that the power behind his reign hinged on his military strength and relationship with the army – after all, he had just watched his short-lived predecessors fail. So he shaped it through significant military campaigns, strengthening the borders of the Roman Empire in the north, east and in Britain, committing between 35,000 and 50,000 soldiers to a campaign above Hadrian's Wall, which he personally managed, running the Roman Empire out of York for three years. Military reforms followed his campaigns, the army was enlarged and given a pay rise, which would have a significant consequence on the years to come as he drastically reduced the silver content of the denarius to around 50 per cent to foot the bill.

This debasement is what many believe could be linked to reasons behind the creation of the limes denarius, which could have emerged as a semi-official currency to pay soldiers on the unstable borders of Rome's frontiers – minted out of a metal alloy that wouldn't have been a damning loss for an empire already spreading its silver coffers incredibly thin.

*

'How did you two get on?' Nath's spotted us making our return back to the arena – he hasn't made it out yet, still nursing the consequences of the previous evening.

'Take a look at this, mate!' Ellie grins victoriously, caked in mud.

Lucie waves tiredly in greeting, her swinging arm spent, but there's a sense of accomplishment hidden in our dogged plod home, the Septimius Severus limes denarius burning a hole in our finds tin – and Ellie wastes no time in showing off our bounty.

RALLY SEASON

'Oh, that's lovely, that is,' Nath coos. 'Limes denarius, I've not seen many of them come up,' he hands it back with a proud nod. 'Where you off to – food?'

'Cheesy chips,' Lucie says, she's already selected the delicacy to revitalise her spirits. Nath escorts us to the burger van, the arena filled with the sounds of battle, the Anglo-Saxons clashing swords outside their camp.

'Number forty-two!' is shouted over a gaggle of tired detectorists clutching ticket stubs.

'That's us!' Ellie shouts back, eagerly receiving two cheesy-chip portions and loading them up with sauce before we drag our weary bodies over to stand near the LP tent.

'Girls, you look knackered, take a seat in my gator.' *Searcher* Dan's spotted us, still kitted out, standing awkwardly, attempting to scoff and balance our spade and detector.

'Dan, you're a legend,' Ellie replies, quickly taking up the offer and perching on the tailgate, Dan waving with a smile, before dropping back into animated conversation with the small gaggle around him.

'A few sceats have come up in field four,' Dan shares to his audience, the latest intel coming in via walkie-talkie.

'Sceats …' Lucie's got a dangerous look in her eye, sending Ellie a sideways glance.

'Oh God,' Ellie mutters, knowing that can only mean one thing – we're heading back out.

Mobilised by sceat fever, and catching a second wind, another three hours pass by in a small stubble field sandwiched between two woods and a high hedge – no gator ride involved to get here just the motion of our own weary feet. There's one other detectorist in here with us – a geezer who goes by the name of 'Three Axe Andy' – and all we've found is buttons.

'Shall we do some photography?' Lucie offers, the second wind starting to pass. 'The light's looking good.'

'Great idea,' Ellie responds. 'I'm done with digging.' She pulls out the DSLR camera she's faithfully carried around all day, just waiting for its moment, and passes it over.

'Oh, yeah – hold it higher – in that patch of light there.' Lucies getting into it, the Septimius Severus coming alive in the waning light, the long shadows accentuating its crisp details. Suddenly she's struck with inspiration. 'Oh, let's do some of you, too!' Ellie having to transition from digger to model, putting on her trademark smile and holding Septimius aloft, while Lucie performs a crouching, twisting dance before her – getting those angles.

'DIGGING'S OVER!' A loud shout interrupts our tranquil photography session.

'Is it six-thirty already?' Lucie looks out from behind the camera to spot a gator heading towards us at immense speed.

'Oh, we're just taking some photos!' Ellie calls over with a wave and a smile as the gator lurches to a halt alongside us, two high-vis clad marshalls at the wheel.

'Oh, lovely! Do you want a lift back?' one of them offers, sent on a mission to round up any stragglers.

'Absolutely,' Lucie replies, camera already switched off and clambering in.

Perched in the truck bed, there's no water bottles to nestle ourselves among – all of that consumed in the fields – our muddy boots resting against the tailgate as we bump down the farm track, back to base camp, the sun setting around us.

*

'Find any sceats?' Ash calls as we approach the bar.

'Only buttons!' Ellie laughs back.

'Detecting's shit, ain't it – here have a drink. It's Dan's birthday.'

The evening descends into a blur of bad karaoke, far-out dance moves from Helen and Detector Timmy, jiving Anglo-Saxons breaking character for the first time all weekend, and according to the bar lady – three bottles of Jägermeister – but there's one moment none of the attendees will ever forget: Ellie and Dan's iconic rendition of 'Barbie Girl'. It turns out we never needed to worry about our digging debut at rally season.

15.

BEETROOT AND FETA TART

AUGUST 2023, LINCOLNSHIRE, ENGLAND

Rally season is about to begin all over again. In less than two weeks' time we'll be back in the thick of it – overindulging in mud, beer and banter – and arriving in very different circumstances to the last.

First of all, we've finally managed to shake the pop-up tent, the entire boot of Ellie's car accommodating its upgrade, a Berghaus Nightfall Air 400 palace. And it turns out we were right, Tom Ayling was an easy convert to the dig life, already popping up in our DMs asking to borrow our backup machine – again – not put off by the washout that was Spring Detectival, and wanting to find his first Roman coin. But we do have some sad news to break to you: the Panda, our once reliable, yellow, dig-mobile became a death trap, collecting more problems than it was worth, and now resides as a small cube in a Lincolnshire scrapyard. Although we aren't sold on its replacement yet – a postbox-red 2010 VW Polo – after the glass fell out of its wing mirror on a road trip to North Wales visiting some Roman sites, and the troublesome loose ignition wires, that took over a month to diagnose, left us constantly stranded waiting for rescue. There's nothing like the minor teething problems of getting a new car.

It's been a busy year, our digging social life seems to have kicked itself into action; we've experienced field-side catering in Norfolk, courtesy of fellow LP advocate, Chris, whipping up delicacies in the boot of his car; we've been led onto the Thames foreshore for a mudlark by Si, London's biggest mud-lover; and we've taken unsuspecting friends on endurance tours of Roman ruins. And don't worry, we've made some great finds, too; we've found our biggest Roman yet – a Constantius I Follis – a rare Roman brooch, and we've even found treasure, pulling up a medieval, silver cruciform pendant on the final hour of Spring Detectival.

But we've got time for one more dig before we're back on the road, right?

*

'Do you know where we are going today?' Ellie asks, as Lucie climbs into the passenger seat, her finger hovering over the satnav waiting for instruction, nervous that Lucie's been left in charge of such crucial information as directions.

'Here, Sarah's messaged me the postcode,' Lucie shows Ellie the messenger chat in confidence. The safety net of the village isn't our destination this time. Lucie's been working the connections with her old family friends and secured an invite to their local farm – a couple of fields coming freshly available with harvest.

'It's one of the farms on this lane, I'm sure I'll recognise it,' Lucie – vaguely recalling visiting as a child – reassures, when the postcode ends in the middle of the Lincolnshire countryside. 'There, I think it's that one!'

Only, turning off the lane into the farm's drive, Lucie falls silent, looking around in confusion. 'Hmm ... This doesn't look right ...'

'I'll get out and check,' Ellie offers, flicking her seat belt off and stepping out into the small concrete yard we've found at the back of the farmhouse.

'Crikey, watch out!' Lucie calls, as a cockapoo vaults a garden gate, barrelling towards Ellie.

'Jesus, hello little one,' Ellie braces for impact as the curly, golden lass launches into her knees – begging for fuss. 'Aren't you a friendly doggy?' she tickles under her chin.

THINGS WE FOUND IN THE GROUND

'PEPPA!' A woman's head appears from behind the wooden garden gate. 'Oh, I'm so sorry!' she calls as she notices us, 'They're all very friendly!' And with that, she opens the gate latch and a whole flock descend upon us.

'I think we've got the wrong address!' Lucie shouts, thoroughly overstimulated by the enthusiastic cockapoos and the utter commotion we've caused, needing a hasty exit, and ringing Sarah immediately.

'We're at the wrong farm!' she announces as soon as the dialling tone connects.

'What's all that noise?' Sarah questions, barely hearing Lucie.

'The cockapoos!' Lucie shouts over all the excited barking, the woman we've disturbed attempting to round them up for a walk around the farm.

'Oh, we're just a bit further down the lane!'

'See you shortly!' Lucie hangs up, beckoning Ellie back into the car – she's busy furiously apologising and attempting to detach herself from an overzealous cockapoo.

'Oh yeah, this is the right place,' Lucie nods to herself as the second drive on the lane ignites a buried memory. 'I remember those trees. I knew it was a longer driveway.'

Ellie rolls her eyes.

'Welcome girls!' To our relief, Sarah appears behind the wooden gate leading into the farmhouse garden, three black flat-coated retrievers trotting round her feet.

'Why don't you come in for a coffee?' she asks, the dogs planting their paws on the top rail and leaning over, their long faces panting excitedly at the thought of visitors.

'That would be lovely,' Lucie replies, patting one gently.

'You're okay with dogs, right?' Sarah questions 'They're really friendly.'

Sarah takes us under her wing the moment we cross into her garden. She's an old friend of Lucie's parents from their Lincolnshire farming days and has plenty of questions to ask Lucie, wanting to know *everything* – the metal detecting, New Zealand, her sisters, how her parents are getting on and of course our upcoming 'Detectival' rally.

BEETROOT AND FETA TART

We easily get swept into her good-natured, bubbly charm, almost forgetting the reason for our visit in all the natter. Before we know it, our coffee has grown cold, and one of the retrievers has taken quite the shine to Ellie, pushing his way up to join her on her chair and pinning her for the afternoon – she has always had a way with dogs.

'I think your best bet would be to try the wheat field,' Sarah suddenly interjects, getting us back on track for the day and commencing action. 'I'll take you to it.' Standing up, she herds the dogs back into the farmhouse, re-emerging in a wide sun hat. 'It's only a short drive,' she reassures.

Not expecting extra passengers, Lucie and Sarah wait patiently as Ellie throws all our gear off the backseat, removes the parcel shelf and crams as much as possible into the boot – creating a small gap for Sarah to clamber in.

'Okay, where are we headed?' Ellie asks, mentally preparing herself to drive nicely in the presence of our new passenger, and not whip round the country lanes with no fear.

'Turn right out of the drive, then right again at the end of the road and follow the lane round until I say so.' Sarah's straight to the point – much clearer in her direction skills than Lucie – and so far unphased by the metal detector in her lap, settling into an easy conversation as the tall grasses and overhanging branches of the farm lane pass us by.

'There it is! Through that gap!' Sarah interjects mid-drive, directing us through an opening between the high hedges.

Parking up on the grain store, all three of us pile out, Sarah rambling away immediately, gesturing to the field behind us, which sways gently with tall grasses for hay, and promising she'll let us know when they get cut. Turning to the wheat field, she informs us that her and her husband have farmed it for decades, a freshly installed rewilding strip down the hedgerow to the left providing a gentle hum and a splash of colour as bees and dragonflies flit between the wildflowers. It's a hot one today – the beginnings of a heatwave for Britain – the freshly cut wheat stubble and open nature of the field taking on the appearance of a desert. The thick heat haze swimming in the middle of our vision interrupted only by a tall oak tree standing in solitude at the centre of the expanse, as if it's been outcast from the dense copse of trees shielding the field from the road.

'I'll leave you to it, then,' Sarah says. 'And good luck!' She starts heading out onto the lane. 'Oh, and head back around 1 p.m. – I'm making filo tart for lunch!' she adds, before disappearing out of view, embracing the walk back in the sunshine.

'Shall we start round the tree?' Lucie suggests, adjusting her machine cables, its lonely presence among the stubble the only shade offered on what is already a warm morning.

'That's got to be a good place to start,' Ellie agrees, thinking of our walnut tree back in the manor-house field and the lost artefacts cultivated under its canopy.

*

Lucie winces. 'That's a screamer.' She pulls a headphone away from her ear, as the signal threatens to deafen her on her second swing over, the oak tree looming in front of her. 'High twenties,' she notifies Ellie, who's hovering, ready to dig.

'That's got to be a something,' Ellie says, as she cuts through the dry soil, hoisting out a chunk, and thanking the gods this field isn't on clay like back at our village. The first signal is always one of the most exhilarating – the culmination of all your pre-dig anticipation – and a signal in the *20s* is not one to be sniffed at. 'Whoa,' she shouts, the pinpointer going nuts the minute it dips below surface level.

'What is it?' Lucie calls from above, peering over Ellie's head to try and get a glimpse of the target.

Ellie's chuckle cuts through the screams of the pinpointer, soil cascading as she lifts a crushed Diet Coke can from the earth. 'Trash!' she laughs.

'God, I hope there isn't any can slaw,' Lucie groans – the shredding of aluminium cans by the plough (aka 'can slaw'), a detectorist's worst nightmare.

*

Unfortunately, nightmares, much like dreams, can soon become reality.

'We've been out over an hour and all we've dug is aluminium,' Ellie huffs as she dumps the latest – a full-fat Coke can this time – into her finds bag, unimpressed at the large item taking up valuable space, yet bound by the laws of good detecting practice to leave no trace behind, and pausing to wipe a muddy smear of sweat from her brow.

'We've just gotta dig them,' Lucie sighs, feeling thoroughly plagued and jaded by every high *20s* that emerges on the Equinox's screen. There's no other choice, really. With such blatant signals as these, to walk away would only bring the blight of a different plague – the 'what if?' – in unknown territory like this, you simply have to succumb to its every want and need.

'I've literally got enough cans to have a barbecue,' Ellie deadpans, her exaggeration enough to draw a blurt of hysteria from us both, as yet another high *20s* blares through Lucie's headphones – more aluminium, just in the form of a lost dog tag this time.

'Let's try towards the wood,' Lucie announces, taking a moment to read the landscape. There's the slightest of inclines leading into the trees, a slim feature, but a feature nonetheless in an otherwise nondescript field, pulling her in. The copse's boughs seem to encourage this manoeuvre, whispering a lure towards their canopies. A small muntjac who must have received the same call, bounds past us at a rapid pace, before disappearing into the waiting trees, its white tail flashing a few times then vanishing into the shadows.

'Hmm, jumpy high twenties again.' Lucie's stopped a few metres from the treeline, Ellie ahead, trying to catch another glimpse of our fleeting visitor.

24-26-28-30 the Equinox sounds.

'That'll be another can,' Lucie groans.

'Urgh, should we dig it?' Ellie asks dejectedly.

'Probably should,' Lucie sighs.

Grumbling Ellie gets to work, her job becoming more of a chore at this point, with absolutely no reward for all this digging in the heat – not even a button.

THINGS WE FOUND IN THE GROUND

The pinpointer announces its readiness for action with a bright chirp, the only willing member left of our small team.

With the grudging motion of a vagrant on community service, the search commences, the screams of the pinpointer insisting on a little more dirt to be clawed from the bottom of the hole. Ellie freezing as a distinctive form slides into sight.

'Lucie!' she calls urgently, snapping Lucie's attention to the excavation.

'Oh shit—' Lucie's only words.

'Is that ...' Ellie stutters, 'is that a tiny Bronze Age axe?'

'Holy shit.' Again, Lucie's only words.

'Like a flat one?' Ellie presses frantically, needing a reaction from Lucie, a confirmation she's not delusional and hallucinating from heat stroke.

'Oh, my God. I think it is.'

For a moment we just sit – silent – next to the hole, the prehistoric axe head held between Ellie's hands. Both of us numb from the passage of this momentous digging milestone; discovering one of the oldest metal artefacts a detectorist can find in Britain.

*

Around 4,000 years ago 90 per cent of British DNA was replaced, as a new migration brought the Neolithic era to an end. Known simply for their distinctive bell-shaped pottery, the 'Beaker people' arrived from the Eurasian Steppe, bringing with them individual burial practices, barbed and tanged arrowheads, and metal tools.

Prehistoric Britain was a wild and untamed island, forested almost coast to coast with dense and varying woodlands of oak, lime and pine, and populated by waves of cultures migrating over from the continent. The last migration, of the Neolithic Britons in 4000 BCE, had started the gradual transition from the nomadic hunter gatherer to the more settled agricultural farmer, and the new technologies and beliefs introduced by the Beaker people would soon finish off the job; successfully domesticating the wilderness of Britain.

BEETROOT AND FETA TART

Over on the continent the Bronze Age had already begun around 1,000 years ago, so it's hard to imagine what the Beaker people arriving on Britain's shores around 2,400 BCE would have made of the Neolithic Britons, with their polished stone tools and basic pottery. But we do know they were quick to adopt their beliefs, with the impressive pre-existing stone monuments across the country, such as Stonehenge and Avebury, becoming a focus point for the rituals, ceremonies and communities of the new, emerging society.

This society didn't just emerge overnight, however, this was the beginning of a gradual shift brought in by the introduction of metal-working. Instead of knapping and grinding, people started smelting and casting, exploiting the rich wealth of naturally occurring British copper through vast mines, such as the Great Orme copper mine in North Wales – whose vertical shafts (dug painstakingly with bone and antler tools to a depth of at least seventy metres) produced an unbelievable 175–238 tons of copper throughout the Bronze Age. This copper was one of the main ingredients behind making Bronze – the material the age is named for – an alloy of roughly 90 per cent copper to 10 per cent tin, which was harder, more durable and anticorrosive compared to just copper itself, and made more effective tools than the polished stone axes Britain was used to.

Bronze transformed the landscape, the new technology speeding up development, with the faster exploitation of woodland resources seeing regions begin to take on distinct characteristics; trees were felled to create openings for farms, grazing pastures, arable land, and monuments; to create timbers for the construction of round houses and burials; and to fuel the fires on which to cook food, provide warmth and – with the introduction of metals – to smelt tools. Under the Neolithic era, settlements had been short-lived, communities moving with their herds along a network of tracks and causeways which crisscrossed the country, but as decades and then centuries of the Bronze Age passed and the landscape became increasingly tamed, the new field systems, cairn fields and grazing plains started to become the home of more settled and complex communities existing peacefully among a highly ritualised landscape.

And for the majority of the native Britons on the precipice of this new era, the flat axe – the earliest metal axe whose shape was inspired by its stone predecessors – would be their first contact with this new metal technology. But the flat axe wasn't just a tool. It's important to remember that for the Neolithic Britons, objects carried power and meaning; their worldview was intimately connected to nature, and the axe provided a means of survival and development through the felling of trees, construction of houses and creation of religious monuments – they are intertwined into the balance of life.

Stepping into the Bronze Age, this belief didn't just vanish, instead it became amplified by the advanced efficiency and prestige of these metal tools, and their significance crops up again and again in the archaeological record. Their earliest use in Britain is in 2049 BCE, where at least fifty-one individual bronze axes were used in the construction of 'Seahenge' – a circular timber monument discovered off the Norfolk coast – and they appear frequently in water sources where (mostly unused) axe heads are cast into the depths as offerings. But their most intriguing appearance has to be in stone carvings, found in the collection of stone burials at Kilmartin Glen in Scotland, Badbury Barrow in Dorset and predominantly on Stone 53 at Stonehenge – and strikingly, of the 115 axe carvings at Stonehenge, all are slightly different, individual, and blade pointing skywards.

It's impossible to assume the exact religious significance the Bronze Age flat axe held over the communities transitioning from the Neolithic to the Bronze Age – they could be linked to their ideas of individuality, ritual or even between life and death itself – but one thing is for certain, this object is far more than a simple metal tool; it's a rich glimpse into the very ethos of Bronze Age life.

*

'They're small, aren't they? Smaller than you'd think,' Ellie breaks the silence, her gaze unwavering from the axe held between her outstretched hands. It could be relatively easy to mistake this palm-sized object for a stone, if it weren't for the subtly flared body and the rounded blade edge, distinguishing it as the tool which tamed the British landscape; the blade hafted into a specially chosen branch and felling the native forests.

'Can I hold it?' Lucie asks, picking it gingerly from Ellie's palm and cradling it – mesmerised by its pitted and pockmarked surface which is reminiscent of a lunar landscape. Dark brown in colour and mottled with craters of orange and worn patches of pale copper green, it feels as ancient as it is – all 4,000 years.

'It's so incredible, and so perfect – and surprisingly heavy,' she comments, bobbing the axe carefully in her hand to gather its weight. It's not often you get to hold objects this old, feeling their tactility and gaining a better understanding of their *mana*, the power and prestige contained within, rather than the lifetime we spend peering through glass display cases.

Here in the west we used to have a deeper relationship with nature and the spirit world; much like the connection in the Bronze Age between their axes and the balance of life. It's one which became muddled through the motion of time, the rise and fall of civilisations (we're looking at you, Romans), and the increasing influence of new religions; but objects – especially those that have been lost – still retain their ability to communicate and hold the stories of the lives they've touched. We may not place such a great importance today on objects, but we still surround ourselves with personal items that hold deep emotional value, and inevitably, a connection to our own lives, self and belonging.

It's the passage of these lives that sees the ground become a great repository of history and memory, harbouring objects we can't even begin to conceive, that are often waiting for the perfect moment to reveal themselves. It's in these moments that we should listen to our ancestors – for us, our shared *whakapapa,* Māori descent – and remember this Earthly connection we've all but lost. In *te ao Māori,* the Māori worldview; *whenua,* land, *tāngata,* people, and *taonga,* treasure, are all connected – with *taonga* often choosing to find its own way home, through the people it believes are best to reconnect with its stories, and *wairua,* the living soul, guiding us through *tohu,* signs to the *taonga* below.

THINGS WE FOUND IN THE GROUND

'Thank God we dug that one,' Ellie laughs, shifting in her seat among the stubble, the aluminium in her bag clanking as a reminder of this morning's trial – we could have easily left for an early lunch, but something kept us out here persevering through the heat. Maybe it was the axe head, it too searching, waiting to be brought home?

*

'Okay, do you want to see the fun find, or the good find first?' Lucie calls, unable to contain the news, bursting through the farmhouse door and into the low-beamed kitchen to find Sarah bustling away, preparing what looks like a feast and not the 'simple lunch' she suggested.

'You're right on time, girls! Let's see the fun find!' she says, lifting a tray out of the oven and engulfing us in a rich buttery aroma, adding to the growing pile of fresh offerings sitting on the wooden kitchen island – lunch ready to be served. Turning to us immediately, she discards her floral oven gloves, the intrigue evident across her face.

'Do you need a hand with anything?' Ellie offers, hovering beside the island, aware we've interrupted a cook at work, and eyeing up the tray of golden filo pastry, scattered with molten feta and bright splashes of beetroot.

'It's all under control,' Sarah replies with a warm smile, the spread in front of her speaking for itself. 'What have you found?' She normally hears all about our exploits from Lucie's parents, and seems nervously hopeful that her farm will be proved a worthwhile visit.

Lucie motions to Ellie to pull out the finds tin.

'First, there's this lovely dog tag,' Ellie presents – keeping the finds tin close to her chest, obscuring its contents from Sarah's view – producing a bright blue bone dangling from between her fingers. 'Is it one of yours?' Ellie grins, her other hand occupied with tickling the chin of an over-exuberant retriever demanding attention.

'THE JUG,' Sarah reads out the letters stamped into its surface, 'What a character,' she chuckles.

'I know, it's quite a name,' Lucie agrees, 'I wonder who he belonged to?' she adds wistfully, picturing a black labrador bounding through the fields as Ellie places the dog tag back into the tin restlessly, shutting the lid quickly as if something else could leap out.

'So, what's the good find?' Sarah asks, curious to know, the quiet confidence on our faces and suspicious finds-tin activity hinting that we've got something special up our sleeves – we haven't interrupted lunch for nothing, after all.

'Are you ready?' Lucie grins from ear to ear, prompting Ellie to commence the big reveal. 'It's the oldest thing we've *ever* found,' she builds, enrapturing Sarah within the drama.

'You aren't ready ...' Ellie adds to the suspense, the lid of the finds tin lifting slowly, revealing a curious object sat amid the foam, our proud faces grinning above.

'What is it?' Sarah whispers, looking between us to the object held in such clear reverence.

'It's a Bronze Age flat axe!' Ellie blurts, knowing that in its uncleaned state and to the untrained eye, it doesn't look very remarkable, and desperate for Sarah to grasp its importance, 'It's over 4,000 years old.'

Sarah's stunned, processing the information and the unassuming artefact before her, jumping back to life after a beat with rambling questions 'And you found that here?! In the wheat field! ... Can I hold it?'

'Isn't it incredible?' Lucie says as Ellie passes it over.

Sarah holds it in wonder, turning it over carefully in her palm, feeling the weight of its undeniable presence. 'I was so worried you weren't going to find anything,' she replies, 'let alone something so old.' It's like she almost can't believe it, prehistoric Britain here in her farmhouse kitchen, 'I'm so pleased for you both.'

'It's made the day,' Ellie grins.

'Made the year!' Lucie corrects.

The dogs break the axe's spell over us, evacuating the kitchen in a frenzied flurry of wagging tails and barking, their sensitive hearing picking up a tractor pulling into the yard.

'That'll be Neil!' Sarah starts, passing the axe back over to Ellie with both hands and springing into action. 'Here, help me get lunch on the table.' She picks up a salad bowl and heads outside to the rustic wooden table on the patio. Before ducking under the doorway she pauses, turning back with a delighted smile. 'He's not going to believe this,' she gushes, 'A Bronze Age axe from *our* farm.'

Tools downed, we break bread in one of the most important rituals of the day for a farmer – lunch. The table laden with salads, dressings, beetroot and feta tart and one Bronze Age flat axe. The five of us gathered together by the same domestic routine that has existed on this farm since the first tree was felled and the land was cleared.

EPILOGUE

SEPTEMBER 2023, LINCOLNSHIRE, ENGLAND

Emboldened by the new suspension – and perhaps the reason for its necessity – Ellie drives the Polo off-road, straight into the field; lurching over the deep grassy ruts of the tractor tracks and pitching to a halt, part abandoned, in a high hedgerow of bramble and hawthorn.

We've been searching this field – this village – for over three years, almost every week, documenting and recording our finds and the adventures that follow. Only we've found a purpose in the dirt now, learning who we are among the grotty coins, broken pot sherds, personal artefacts, hammered silver and prehistoric tools. The objects of those who came before us, informing our own lives with each visit. It can be easy to get swept up in the fervour of the group digs, the rallies, and the overwhelming grind of modern life, but this quiet sanctuary in the Lincolnshire landscape is the much-needed escape – and a second home.

'Let's do this,' Ellie turns to Lucie with a grin, pulling the handbrake as high as possible to secure the precarious position. Harvest is well and truly underway and the familiar ground of our Roman field has just been cultivated for the first time this season, breaking down the new chunks of soil brought up by the plough in preparation for the planting of the awaiting winter crop, mixing the remnants of decaying wheat stubble into a blend of soil, stones and Roman pottery sherds – keeping us entertained between the signals.

EPILOGUE

'Ellie! Look at this!' Lucie's already been distracted from the swinging, crouched close to the earth, prising a large chunk of clay tile from its grasp – a piece of Roman *tegula,* a thick section of roof tile – in complete delight.

'What a beast!' Ellie caws, immediately jealous.

Are we even detecting at this point? The new wealth of pot sherds filling both our bags, traipsing across the field, part stooped, eyes glued to the floor, completely absorbed in the moment. Noticing Ellie's finding too much pottery for her liking – especially a particularly nice crosshatched body sherd – Lucie refocuses on finding some signals to keep her busy digging, and the potential surface finds for herself.

'Fourteen to fifteen, dig it,' she utters.

It's a barbarous radiate, the sight of a Roman coin reminding us why we've come back to our favourite field – detecting.

'Ellie! Another one – thirteen to fourteen,' Lucie's locked in, tuned into the low thuds of the little Romans.

'There!' Ellie calls, pointing excitedly to a small grey coin among the loose soil she's just turned over. 'Roman!' Brushing gently she plucks it delicately between her thumb and forefinger, grasping it there to examine the details struck into its surface. It's a type we haven't found before, a nummus of Empress Flavia Julia Helena – the mother of Constantine the Great, and the patron saint of archaeologists, credited with the discovery of Christ's true cross – commemorated alongside Pax, the Roman goddess of peace. The Roman Empire was a patriarchal society, women were expected to conform to a set amount of 'rules' and restrictions. So, it's not surprising their lives haven't been recorded in the history books written by men – mentioned as footnotes within a story they aren't in control of – coins such as this, one of the few ways we can gain glimpses into their existence; even if it's propaganda, an idealised image of the 'perfect' mother to a deified imperial family.

'Our first empress,' Lucie breathes. It might just be another Roman nummus – one of the hundreds of thousands left behind in Britain – but it's a significant milestone to us, and a chance to connect with an often overlooked part of Roman history.

THINGS WE FOUND IN THE GROUND

*

The afternoon passes in a pleasant ramble, imbued with the warm embrace of a place we've come to know well – the first dig back after a break is always one of the most cathartic. Enveloped by the gentle jabbering of thrushes flitting through the hedgerows, the clip-clop of horses hooves up the village lane, and snatches of the lively conversation between their lady riders drifting to us on the light, but persistent, wind. A lone pheasant ambles through the far end of the field, a hazy shape rustling through the blooms of wild carrot in the field margins, and our only companion as we search the churned earth, disturbing the rich earthy smell of the old stubble starting to decay. Pleased by the welcome sight of a *gloria exercitvs* nummus joining Helena in the coins pod – the fourth Roman addition and an old acquaintance – the Roman field never does let us down.

'Fourteen to fifteen!' Lucie calls, her shout interrupting the quiet foraging of the pheasant, which scatters in a flurry of feathers and frantic rattling. 'Sounds good!' she adds to hasten Ellie's pace.

Ellie arrives eagerly, her finds bag clinking with the weight of Roman pottery, digging a small hole at the directed spot with quick efficiency. The pinpointer leads her to a large clump of earth freshly broken from the ground – favouring its centre – which she breaks in half.

'Oh.' She stops with surprise. 'What is it?!'

A glimmering, triangular-shaped fragment, curved on its unbroken edge, is embedded in the tip of the clump resting in her hand – easily mistaken for foil, or a shredded shard of aluminium can.

'Is it silver?' Lucie questions, Ellie peeling it carefully from the clay, the tarnished scrap barely bigger than her gloved fingertip, and bringing it up to eye level for a good squint. 'Is that writing on it?' she adds as Ellie gently cleans the mud.

'That's definitely not English,' Ellie comments, puzzled by the small, looping and conjoined script following the curve – if she were to make an educated guess, it looks like a piece of foreign hammered coin. 'Is it Arabic?'

EPILOGUE

*

Do you often ponder how finds become lost, whether through accident or intention? Particularly ones that have become estranged thousands of miles from their home of origin. What sequence of events has led to its final resting place in a Lincolnshire field? The answer can sometimes be impossible to find; but for this fragment, its journey is quite extraordinary, beginning in the Middle East, before travelling along a trade route of furs, slaves and honey to Russia, where it fell into the hands of the Vikings.

The Viking society subsisted on a bullion-based economy, trading by the weight of silver instead of currency; to them, this Islamic Dirham was nothing more than a source of high-quality silver, an important fuel for their trade. Each subsequent transaction, and passage of hands, would have seen a new nick, cut or piece sheared from its body – testing the silver content and attaining the correct weight for purchase.

In 865 CE, as recorded by the *Anglo-Saxon Chronicle*, the 'Great Heathen Army' landed in England, claiming kingdoms from the Anglo-Saxons and carving out a portion of Britain for themselves, settling in an area known as the 'Danelaw' (a large area of northern and eastern England), bringing their extensive trade network and bullion economy to Britain. In Lincolnshire, the largest evidence for this is found along the River Trent at Torksey, where the Vikings' Great Army overwintered from 872–873 CE, leaving behind the largest concentration of Islamic Dirham finds in the British Isles – with over 120 Dirham fragments identifying the precise location of the camp (a discovery made by local detectorists).

As a one-off loss – sadly this isn't the start of a hoard, containing a wealth of ingots and other hack silver – this tiny fragment was likely lost in use, slipping from the scales of a Viking trader, probably making an everyday purchase necessary for their new life settled in Britain. An addition to the growing evidence of Scandinavian settlement here in the Danelaw, and a picture that becomes slightly clearer every time a local detectorist stumbles across one lost in a field.

THINGS WE FOUND IN THE GROUND

*

It never ceases to surprise us how the smallest, seemingly most insignificant of finds can hold the biggest stories – a turbulent tale of slaves, trade and settlement trapped within this miniscule shard of silver. What else is out there, hidden in these fields we thought we'd become so well acquainted with? It seems not all of their secrets have been relinquished.

Our huddle round the Dirham is interrupted by a voicemail from Lady H – the offer of plum bread and hot tea – bringing this afternoon's session to a close. Driving out of the field we first walked into with a bright-red metal detector and a £12 spade, with the knowledge there's a lot more out here, than what could occupy our finds bags.

So we keep digging.

SELECT BIBLIOGRAPHY

Books and publications are listed once, under the chapter where they are first used.

INTRODUCTION

Sills, D. "The Strange Story of the Fouled Anchor: An Inquiry into the History of a Naval Symbol." *National Maritime Historical Society's Sea History Magazine* 96, Spring 2001 (2018). https://issuu.com/seahistory/docs/sh_096_spring-2001/31.

Style, L. "The Rise of the Fouled Anchor: The Visual Codification of the Royal Navy During the 1700s." *The Trafalgar Chronicle* (2020), Journal of the 1805 Club, New Series 5, pp 87–92. https://www.1805club.org/resources/1805_www4/books/The-Trafalgar-Chronicle-New-Series-5/.

CHAPTER 1: EMPANDA

Allen, D., and M. Bryan. *Roman Britain and Where to Find It.* Gloucestershire: Amberley, 2020.

Bédoyère, G. *Roman Britain: A New History*, rev. ed. London: Thames & Hudson, 2013.

Bland, R., A. Chadwick, E. Ghey, C. Haselgrove, D. Mattingley, A. Rogers, J. Taylor, S. Bryant, N. Garland, S. Moorhead, and K. Robbins. *Crisis or Continuity? Iron Age and Roman Coin Hoards in Britain.* Oxford: Oxbow Books, 2020.

Budrovich, N. "From Ancient Scotland to Online Auctions: A Tale of Roman Nails." Getty, January 15, 2020. https://www.getty.edu/news/from-ancient-scotland-to-online-auctions-a-tale-of-roman-nails/.

Cottrell, L. *The Roman Forts of the Saxon Shore*. London: Her Majesty's Stationery Office, 1967.

Glasgow Steel Nail. n.d. "The Story of Inchtuthil." http://www.glasgowsteelnail.com/romans2.HTM.

Keppie, L. *Scotland's Roman Remains*. Edinburgh: John Donald Publishers, 1986.

Wilson, R. *A Guide to the Roman Remains in Britain*. London: Constable and Company, 1975.

CHAPTER 2: PERMISSION

Abdy, R. *Legion: Life in the Roman Army*. London: British Museum Press, 2024.

Bédoyère, G. *The Finds of Roman Britain*. London: Batsford, 1989.

Lee, A. "The Ninth Legion, the Boudican Revolt and the Founding of the Lincoln Fortress." Roman Lincolnshire Revealed, March 23, 2017. https://romanlincolnshire.wordpress.com/2017/03/23/ninth-legion-boudican-revolt/.

Lee, A. *Treasures of Roman Lincolnshire*. Gloucestershire: Amberley, 2016.

Lindsay, E. "The Disappearance of the Ninth Legion." Scottish History, April 23, 2020. https://www.scottishhistory.org/articles/disappearance-ninth-legion/.

Rogers, A. *A History of Lincolnshire*. Henley-on-Thames: Darwen Finlayson, 1970.

Whitwell, J. B. *Roman Lincolnshire. History of Lincolnshire Volume II*. Lincoln: History of Lincolnshire Committee. Lincolnshire Local History Society, 1970.

CHAPTER 3: LEAD

Jenkins, S. *A Short History of England*. London: Profile Books, 2018.

Kershaw, J., and S. Merkel. "International Trade in Outland Resources: The Mining and Export of Lead in Early Medieval England in Light of New Isotope Data From York." *Medieval Archaeology* (2023) 67:2, pp 249–282. https://www.tandfonline.com/doi/full/10.1080/00766097.2023.2262880.

Latham, R. E. *Revised Medieval Latin Word-List. From British and Irish Sources.* London: The British Academy, Oxford University Press, 2004.

Leahy, K., and M. Lewis. *Finds Identified: An Illustrated Guide to Metal Detecting and Archaeological Finds.* Essex: Greenlight Publishing, 2018.

Mortimer, I. *The Time Traveller's Guide to Medieval England.* London: Vintage, 2009.

Scott, B., and J. Mittleman. *A Brief Introduction to Medieval Bynames.* 1999. https://www.s-gabriel.org/names/arval/bynames/.

CHAPTER 4: TREASURE

Blair, P. H. *An Introduction to Anglo-Saxon England*, 2nd ed. Cambridge: Cambridge University Press, 1977.

Campbell, J., E. John, and P. Wormald. *The Anglo-Saxons.* London: Book Club Associates, 1982.

Stenton, F. *Anglo-Saxon England.* Oxford: Oxford University Press, 1971.

CHAPTER 5: LEMON DRIZZLE CAKE

Hodgett, G. A. J. *Tudor Lincolnshire.* Lincoln: History of Lincolnshire Committee, 1975.

Mortimer, I. *The Time Traveller's Guide to Elizabethan England.* London: Vintage, 2013.

Rogers, A. "Lincolnshire in English History." *History Today* (July 1970): 513–14.

Whitehead, R. *Buckles 1250–1800.* Essex: Greenlight Publishing, 1996.

CHAPTER 6: GROUP DIG

Carnell, P. "Medieval Jettons Discovered in Wiverton." *The Glavern Historian* 5 (2002): 3–16. https://www.bahs.uk/GH-Files/GH1-5/GH-5.2.pdf.

Fitz Nigel, R. *Dialogus de Scaccario: The Course of the Exchequer and Constitutio Domus Regis: The Establishment of the Royal Household*. Oxford: Oxford University Press, 1983. https://amesfoundation.law.harvard.edu/lhsemelh/materials/Exchequer.pdf.

Johnson, P. *Small Change: A History of Everyday Coinage*. Gloucestershire: Amberley, 2019.

CHAPTER 7: HAMMERED

Fleming, R. *The Material Fall of Roman Britain*. Philadelphia: University of Pennsylvania Press, 2021.

Guy, J. *Elizabeth: The Later Years*. New York: Penguin Books, 2016.

Irwin, D. "Edward I's Destruction of England's Jews." *History Today* 75, no. 2 (2025). https://www.historytoday.com/archive/feature/edward-destruction-englands-jews.

Johnson, W. "Textual Sources for the Study of Jewish Currency Crimes in Thirteenth-Century England." *British Numismatic Society* 66, no. 4 (1996). https://www.britnumsoc.org/publications/Digital%20BNJ/pdfs/1996_BNJ_66_4.pdf.

Morris, M. *A Great and Terrible King. Edward I and the Forging of Britain*. London: Windmill Books, 2009.

Wolfthal, D. *Medieval Money, Merchants and Morality*. New York: The Morgan Library and Museum in association with D Giles Limited, 2023.

CHAPTER 8: DEATH

Danziger, D., and N. Purcell. *Hadrian's Empire: When Rome Ruled the World*. London: Hodder & Stoughton, 2005.

Everitt, A. *Hadrian and the Triumph of Rome*. New York: Random House, 2009.

Melville Jones, J. *A Dictionary of Ancient Roman Coins*. London: B.A. Seaby, 1990.

Opper, T. *The Emperor Hadrian*. London: British Museum Press, 2008.

Polybius. *Histories*. Translated by E. Shuckburgh. New York: Bloomington, 1962. (Original work London: Macmillan, 1889).

SELECT BIBLIOGRAPHY

Perseus Digital Library. https://www.perseus.tufts.edu/hopper/text?doc=Perseus:text:1999.01.0234.

Sutherland, C. H. V. *Roman Coins*. London: Barrie & Jenkins, 1974.

CHAPTER 9: SHEEP

Hatcher, J. *The Black Death: The Intimate Story of a Village in Crisis, 1345–1350*. London: Phoenix, 2008.

Horrox, R. *The Black Death*. Manchester: Manchester University Press, 1994.

Kelly, J. *The Great Mortality: An Intimate History of the Black Death*. London: Harper Perennial, 2013.

Meents (née Felder), K. "Girdle-hangers in 5th and 6th Century England: A Key to Early Anglo Saxon Identities." PhD thesis, University of Cambridge, 2014. https://www.academia.edu/13237810/Girdle_hangers_in_5th_and_6th_century_England_A_Key_to_Early_Anglo_Saxon_Identities.

Meents (née Felder), K. "Networks of Meaning and the Social Dynamics of Identity: An Example from Early Anglo-Saxon England." *Papers from the Institute of Archaeology* 25, no. 1, art. 3 (2015). doi: https://doi.org/10.5334/pia.478.

Metcalf, M., and W. Op den Velde. *The Monetary Economy of the Netherlands, c. 690–c. 760 and the Trade with England: A Study of the 'Porcupine' Sceattas of Series E. Volume I*. Netherlands: Royal Dutch Society for Coins and Medals, 2010.

Platt, C. *Medieval England: A Social History and Archaeology from the Conquest to 1600 CE*. London: Routledge & Kegan Paul, 1978.

Williams, G. *Early Anglo-Saxon Coins*. Oxford: Shire Archaeology, 2008.

CHAPTER 10: WINTER

Bernard, J. "English Sweat: The Other Medieval Epidemic." *History Today*, May 15, 2014. https://www.historytoday.com/archive/english-sweat-other-medieval-epidemic.

Bernstein, P. *The Power of Gold: The History of an Obsession*. New York: John Wiley & Sons, 2000.

Flattun, J-W. "Angel and Sovereign: Henry VII's Royal Coins, Legitimation, and Relics of Power." *Royal Studies Journal* 8, no. 2 (2021): 76–101. https://rsj.winchester.ac.uk/articles/258/files/submission/proof/258-1-2475-1-10-20211210.pdf.

Levin, C. "'Would I Could Give You Help and Succour': Elizabeth I and the Politics of Touch." *Albion: A Quarterly Journal Concerned with British Studies* 21, no. 2 (1989): 191–205. https://digitalcommons.unl.edu/cgi/viewcontent.cgi?article=1067&context=historyfacpub#:~:text=In%201462%2C%20in%20defense%20of,but%20also%20a%20legitimate%20one.

Meyer, C. J. *The Tudors: Henry VII to Henry VIII*. Gloucestershire: Amberley, 2010.

Stone, P. "A Brief History of the Kings Evil." *The Ricardian: Journal of the Richard III Society* 6, no. 76 (1982): 14–16. https://richardiii.net/wp-content/uploads/2021/08/06-76-Title-page-and-contents.pdf.

Young, F. "The Gold Angel: Legendary Coin, Enduring Amulet." 2016. https://drfrancisyoung.com/2016/01/21/the-gold-angel-legendary-coin-enduring-amulet/.

CHAPTER 11: WOMEN

Laurence, A. *Women in England 1500–1760: A Social History*. London: Phoenix, 1996.

Perkin, J. *Victorian Women*. London: John Murray, 1993.

Steinbach, S. *Women in England 1760–1914: A Social History*. London: Phoenix, 2005.

CHAPTER 12: WARTIME

Blackah, L. *Your Towns and Cities in the Great War: Lincoln in the Great War*. Barnsley: Pen & Sword Military, 2016.

Laliberte, A. "'Of England's Soldiers of the Queen': Toy Soldiers and British Militarism in the Nineteenth and Twentieth Century." *The General* 9 (2024). https://journals.library.brocku.ca/index.php/bujh/article/download/4589/3343.

SELECT BIBLIOGRAPHY

Loarridge, E. "War Through the Eyes of the Toy Soldier: A Material Study of the Legacy and Impact of Conflict 1880–1945." *Critical Military Studies* 7, no. 4 (2019): 367–83. https://eprints.gla.ac.uk/193774/7/193774.pdf.

Otter, P. *Lincolnshire Airfields in the Second World War*. Berkshire: Countryside Books, 1996.

Roger, D., and P. Cooper. *Lincolnshire Women At War*. Lincolnshire: Heritage Lincolnshire, 1997.

Streeter, P. "Radical Object: Military Sweetheart Brooches of the First World War." History Workshop, November 21, 2018. https://www.historyworkshop.org.uk/war-military/radical-objects-military-sweetheart-brooches-of-the-first-world-war/#:~:text=These%20little%20brooches%20are%20miniature,female%20seemed%20to%20wear%20one.

Streeter, P. "Symbolic Jewels: The Military Sweetheart Brooch in Wartime Britain." PhD thesis, University of Sussex, 2018. https://sussex.figshare.com/articles/thesis/Symbolic_jewels_the_military_sweetheart_brooch_in_wartime_Britain/23301050?file=41074748.

CHAPTER 13: RIDGE AND FURROW

Caesar, J. *Caesar's Gallic War*. Translated by W. A. McDevitte and W. S. Bohn. New York: Harper & Brothers, 1869. https://www.perseus.tufts.edu/hopper/text?doc=Perseus%3Atext%3A1999.02.0001%3Abook%3D5%3Achapter%3D12.

Cunliffe, B. *Iron Age Communities in Britain: An Account of England, Scotland and Wales from the Seventh Century BC Until the Roman Conquest*. Great Britain: Book Club Associates by arrangement with Routledge & Kagan Paul, 1975.

May, J. *Prehistoric Lincolnshire*. History of Lincolnshire Volume I. Lincoln: History of Lincolnshire Committee, 1976.

Pryor, F. *Britain BC: Life in Britain and Ireland Before the Romans*. London: Harper Perennial, 2004.

Pudill, R., and C. Eyre. *The Tribes & Coins of Celtic Britain*. Essex: Greenlight Publishing, 2005.

Rudd, C. "Britain's First Coins." *Coins and Antiquities* (November 1998). https://www.celticcoins.com/wp-content/uploads/2015/01/Brit_First_Coins.pdf.

CHAPTER 14: RALLY SEASON

Butcher, K. "Debasement and the Decline of Rome." *In Studies in Ancient Coinage in Honor of Andrew Burnett*, edited by Roger Bland and Dario Calomino. London: SPINK, 2015. https://warwick.ac.uk/fac/arts/classics/intranets/staff/butcher/debasement_and_decline.pdf.

Markowitz, M. "193: The Year of Five Emperors." Coin Week, October 3, 2014. https://coinweek.com/193-year-five-emperors/.

CHAPTER 15: BEETROOT AND FETA TART

Johnston, R. *Bronze Age Worlds: A Social Prehistory of Britain and Ireland*. Oxon: Routledge, 2021.

Pryor, F. *Scenes from Prehistoric Life: From the Ice Age to the Coming of the Romans*. UK: Head of Zeus, 2021.

EPILOGUE

Beard, M. *SPQR: A History of Ancient Rome*. London: Profile Books, 2015.

Current Archaeology. "Viking Torksey: Inside the Great Army's Winter Camp." July 5, 2013. https://archaeology.co.uk/articles/viking-torksey-inside-the-great-armys-winter-camp.htm.

Green, C. "The Distribution of Islamic Dirhams in Anglo-Saxon England." Dr Caitlin R. Green, December 16, 2014. https://www.caitlingreen.org/2014/12/distribution-of-islamic-dirhams-in-england.html.

Naismith, R. "Islamic Coins from Early Medieval England." *The Numismatic Chronicle* 165 (2005): 193–222. https://www.researchgate.net/publication/265195344_Islamic_Coins_from_Early_Medieval_England.

Southon, E. *A History of the Roman Empire in 21 Women*. London: Oneworld Publications, 2023.

SELECT BIBLIOGRAPHY

WEBSITES

Ancestry: https://www.ancestry.com/
Anglo Saxon Coinage: https://www.anglo-saxon-coinage.co.uk/
Avery Needlecase Resource Centre: http://www.coulthart.com/avery/index.html
British Coins & Artefacts: https://www.rodblunt.com/
British Library: https://www.britishlibrary.cn/en/
British Museum: https://www.britishmuseum.org/
Colchester Treasure Hunting: https://www.colchestertreasurehunting.co.uk/
Dartmouth Toxic Metals: https://sites.dartmouth.edu/toxmetal/
Durham University: https://www.durham.ac.uk/
Egham Museum: https://eghammuseum.org/
English Heritage: https://www.english-heritage.org.uk/
Forum Ancient Coins: https://www.forumancientcoins.com/
Frameworks Network: https://researchframeworks.org/
Frome Museum: https://frome-museum.org/
Greyhound Derby: http://www.greyhoundderby.com/
Historic England: https://historicengland.org.uk/
Historic UK: https://www.historic-uk.com/
History Hit: https://www.historyhit.com/
Horncastle History & Heritage Society: http://www.horncastle-civic.org.uk/
Kirklees Cousins: https://kirkleescousins.co.uk/
Leeds Universities Libraries Blog: https://leedsunilibrary.wordpress.com/
London Museum: https://www.londonmuseum.org.uk/
Met Office: https://www.metoffice.gov.uk/
More About Thimbles: https://thimbles.host-ed.me/Early_English.html
Museum of New Zealand Te Papa Tongarewa: https://www.tepapa.govt.nz/
National Archives: https://www.nationalarchives.gov.uk/
National Geographic: https://www.nationalgeographic.com/

Natural History Museum: https://www.nhm.ac.uk/
Old English Teaching Arts: https://oldenglishteaching.arts.gla.ac.uk/
Pāua Industry Council Ltd: https://www.paua.org.nz/
Portable Antiquities Scheme: https://finds.org.uk/
Royal College of Physicians: https://history.rcp.ac.uk/
Royal Mint: https://www.royalmint.com/
Royal Museums Greenwich: https://www.rmg.co.uk/
Royal School of Needlework: https://royal-needlework.org.uk/
Shakespeare Birthplace Trust: https://www.shakespeare.org.uk/
Stonehenge Laser Scans: https://stonehenge.archaeoptics.co.uk/index.html
The British Academy: https://www.thebritishacademy.ac.uk/
The Collector: https://www.thecollector.com/
The Long Long Trail: https://www.longlongtrail.co.uk/
The Research Victoria and Albert Museum: https://www.vam.ac.uk/
The Royal Family: https://www.royal.uk/
The Royal Leicestershire Regiment: https://royalleicestershireregiment.org.uk/
UK Parliament: https://www.parliament.uk/
University of Cambridge: https://www.cam.ac.uk/
Viking Metal: http://vikingmetalwork.blogspot.com/
Visit Lincolnshire: https://business.visitlincolnshire.com/
YouGov: https://yougov.co.uk/

ACKNOWLEDGEMENTS

'What about metal detecting?' Four words from Ellie's Mum, Naomi, over 5 years ago now, which completely changed the course of both of our lives. Writing this book and reliving our journey into the dirt has been both a fever dream and a treasure we didn't know was out there waiting for us. So it's only right that our first thanks goes to her.

There are so many people without whom this book wouldn't have existed. For introducing us to the world of writing, we'd like to thank Tom Ayling for guiding us to Eve White Literary Agency, and the care of Eve, Ludo Cinelli and Steven Evans, who worked tirelessly, channelling our dirt-addled ideas into a proposal, and then supporting us every step of the way. Then there's the brilliant team at Harper North, especially Genevieve Pegg, Alice Murphy-Pyle, Jess Haycox, Millie Morton, Imogen Gordon Clark and Taslima Khatun, who loved 'Things We Found in the Ground' first, and made our dream a reality – a dream completed by our beautiful cover by Holly Ovenden.

Roman Found itself owes thanks to more people than we can list here, but these are the ones who have suffered the most. To our parents for their unwavering support and guidance, even when they were definitely tired of hearing about the Romans. To Uncle Tom, whose house has been our unofficial writing office and YouTube studio. To Aunty Zoe, who donated her soil sieve. To Ellie's grandparents, who have remained our biggest fans, and learnt new apps to keep up with our adventures. To Bruce Fine Papers, who have given Ellie far too many days off work and always been flexible with her working hours, even with less than 24 hours' notice. And to Katie, for still putting up with Ellie, the dirt, and the growing pile of Roman pottery and finds after all these years.

We'd like to thank Pete, Helen, Ash and the whole team at LP Metal Detecting for bringing us into the world of rallies and supporting Roman Found from the early days when we were still figuring ourselves out on YouTube. To Harry, Dan and the Searcher Team, we would have gotten nowhere without the gator rides, front-cover feature, and, of course, too many Jägermeisters. And to our Finds Liaison Officer, who helped nurture an obsession and always listens to Ellie's latest far-fetched research ideas.

There are all of our detecting friends, who've helped with the identification of finds, offered radios, coffee, spare blankets, fireside gossip, much-needed counsel, and a family we weren't looking for. Then there's this village we've grown to love – our second home – and Lady H and all of the people within it, in every way this book is very much a love letter to you and the many cups of tea, lemon drizzle cake, plum bread, kitchen chats and mower rides you've offered along the way. Of course, we wouldn't be able to do any of this without our landowners and farmers, so to you we offer our most humblest of thanks. And to the machines, including those no longer with us – the Panda, the Vanquish and all those broken spades – we thank you for your dutiful service.

But our biggest thanks of all has to go to the finds, whose stories have enchanted, humbled, and astounded us along the way. Thank you for entrusting us to tell them. And to you, the reader, the YouTube subscriber, the Facebook commenter, the Instagram follower, the Substack reader and the TikTok watcher. Your passion, enthusiasm and love of history are what keep Roman Found going. We can't wait to share our next adventure with you. So until then …

Ellie & Lucie xx

Harper North

Book Credits

would like to thank the following staff and contributors for their involvement in making this book a reality:

Fionnuala Barrett
Laura Braggs
Sarah Burke
Rhys Callaghan
Alan Cracknell
Jonathan de Peyer
Tom Dunstan
Kate Elton
Sarah Emsley
Simon Gerratt
Imogen Gordon Clark
Lydia Grainge
Monica Green
Natassa Hadjinicolaou
Jess Haycox
Jo Ireson
Megan Jones
Jean-Marie Kelly

Taslima Khatun
Holly Kyte
Rachel McCarron
Millie Morton
Alice Murphy-Pyle
Adam Murray
Genevieve Pegg
Amanda Percival
Dean Russell
Colleen Simpson
Eleanor Slater
Megan Smith
Hilary Stein
Emma Sullivan
Emily Thomas
Katrina Troy
Claire Ward

For more unmissable reads,
sign up to the HarperNorth newsletter at
www.harpernorth.co.uk

or find us on socials at
@HarperNorthUK